13th International Joint Conference on Natural Language Processing and the 3rd Conference of the Asia-Pacific Chapter of the Association for Computational Linguistics (IJCNLP-AACL 2023)

Student Research Workshop

Nusa Dua, Indonesia
1-4 November 2023

ISBN: 978-1-7138-8394-4

Printed from e-media with permission by:

Curran Associates, Inc.
57 Morehouse Lane
Red Hook, NY 12571

Some format issues inherent in the e-media version may also appear in this print version.

Printed with permission by Curran Associates, Inc. (2024)

For permission requests, please contact the Association for Computational Linguistics at the address below.

Association for Computational Linguistics
209 N. Eighth Street
Stroudsburg, Pennsylvania 18360

Phone: 1-570-476-8006
Fax: 1-570-476-0860

acl@aclweb.org

Additional copies of this publication are available from:

Curran Associates, Inc.
57 Morehouse Lane
Red Hook, NY 12571 USA
Phone: 845-758-0400
Fax: 845-758-2633
Email: curran@proceedings.com
Web: www.proceedings.com

IJCNLP-AACL 2023

The 13th International Joint Conference on Natural Language Processing and the 3rd Conference of the Asia-Pacific Chapter of the Association for Computational Linguistics

Proceedings of the Student Research Workshop

November 1 – 4, 2023

The IJCNLP-AACL organizers gratefully acknowledge the support from the following sponsors.

Platinum

vivo

Gold

面壁智能
ModelBest

Silver

translated.

ZHIPU·AI

小牛翻译
NiuTrans.com

Message from the General Chair

Welcome to IJCNLP-AACL 2023, the 17th International Joint Conference on Natural Language Processsing (IJCNLP) and the 3rd Conference of the Asia-Pacific Chapter of the Association for Computational Linguistics (AACL). The conference will be held in Nusa Dua, Bali, Indonesia, during November 1-4, 2023.

The joint conferences of IJCNLP and AACL are organized by alternating leadership in the Asia-Pacific region, in odd years by Asian Federation of Natural Language Processing (AFNLP) and in even years by AACL, except when the annual meetings of ACL are offered in the region every three years, in which case the conferences will be offered and organized solely by ACL. This year, the conference is organized by AFNLP.

As President of AFNLP, I have formed the Conference Coordination Committee (CCC) last year with executive members of AFNLP: Sadao Kurohashi (Vice President), Min Zhang (Secretary), Liang-Chih Yu (Honorary Treasurer), and Minghui Dong (Web Master). Xuanjing Huang has participated in the meetings of the committee as AACL Representative. I am truly thankful for their dedication in the initial stages as CCC members, in particular during the selection of the Local Chairs together with the conference venue and the nomination and appointment of General Chair and Program Committee Chairs, and, after it is decided that I also serve as General Chair of the conference, for their service as respective chairs throughout the conference preparation stages. Their continued support has been of tremendous help and is much appreciated.

I would also like to thank deeply the entire organizing committee of the conference for their hardwork and superb handling of difficult situations, most of all due to the much limited time to address their respective tasks.

- Program Committe Chairs: Yuki Arase, Baotian Hu and Wei Lu have managed the most critical task of establishing the main program of the conference, which includes, among many others, forming and coordinating the Program Committee, constructing the call for papers with a timely theme track, overseeing the review process on both Softconf and ARR, making decisions on paper acceptance, selecting keynote speakers and putting together the program schedule, and most of all communicating with the reviewers, authors, and other committee members over numerous times during the entire process. This is a formidable task, and their efforts for leading to its successful completion are so much appreciated.

- Tutorial Chairs: Yun-Nung (Vivian) Chen and Sadao Kurohashi have gone through the tutorial proposals to select six tutorials that are well balanced both topically and geographically, actively fostering diversity and inclusion.

- Workshop Chairs: Kehai Chen and Lun-Wei Ku have gone over the workshop proposals to select eight strong workshops, NLPMC, WIESP, Eval4NLP, SocialNLP, SEA, FinNLP, NLInt, and ArtOfSafety.

- Demo Chairs: Sriparna Saha and Herry Sujaini have overseen the process of selecting papers among those submitted to the system demonstration session independently of the main program.

- Publication Chairs: Minghui Dong and Kotaro Funakoshi have put together all the documents and articles to construct the conference proceedings expertly, cordially and in a timely manner.

- Sponsorship Chairs: Min Zhang, Satoshi Sekine, Haofeng Wang, and Zhongqing Wang have worked hard to solicit funding to support the conference, and successfully, despite the short time to operate. We are all much grateful to the funding organizations for their generous help.

- Finance Chair: Liang-Chih Yu has always been the person to consult whenever any financial issues arise. Things are not yet fully over at the time of preparing for this message, but are believed to come to self-sustainment, with some room for financial aid as well, thanks to the valiant efforts of all the people involved.
- Website & App Chair: Juntao Li has worked single-handedly and dependably to reflect all the requests to post important news at our conference homepage.
- Publicity & Social Media Chairs: Koustava Goswami and JinYeong Bak have worked to disseminate information over social media as widely as possible whenever there are notable events for the conference.
- Handbook Chairs: Yasuhide Miura and Yunita Sari have worked very hard to meet the deadline for the conference handbook when there is really not much time left. The help of Sonoko Miura as Conference Handbook Designer is also gratefully acknowledged.
- Faculty Advisors to Student Research Workshop (SRW): Hyeju Jang, Yugo Murawaki, and Derek Fai Wong have worked to oversee the SRW, in particular communicating with its chairs, Dongfang Li, Rahmad Mahendra and Zilu Peter Tang. The efforts of the faculty advisors and SRW chairs are much appreciated.
- Diversity & Inclusion Chair: Hwanhee Lee has worked to resolve requests for financial aid, mostly in the form of registration waiver, and as amicably as possible, under a strict limit on granting such requests.
- Registration Chair: Dessi Puji Lestari has worked to oversee the process of registration, together with the kind help of Minghui Dong as the manager of the registration site.
- Local Chairs: Derry Wijaya, Ayu Purwarianti and Adila Alfa Krisnadhi have worked to resolve practically numerous issues, many times beyond the duties of local chairs, after successfully bidding to host the conference in Nusa Dua, Bali, Indonesia. It is with much gratitude and respect that I commend their efforts to the fullest.

In summary, I can only say that their sense of duty and responsibility has been critical to meeting and resolving so many difficulties that we faced along the way. Many, many thanks to all of them.

The mode of the conference has been determined early on to be hybrid, considering the fact that we are not fully over the coronavirus pandemic. However, it has not been quite clear until very recently whether we would need, and can afford, the top-notch professional service of an on-demand video platform such as Underline for a hybrid conference. I am very grateful to all the chairs for the remarkable patience and very happy with the concerted decision to go for the service of Underline, albeit in a limited scope. I wish to thank kindly Damira Mrsic and Sol Rosenberg, representatives of Underline, for the patience and expert help. I also thank Richard Gerber for the help with our use of Softconf.

The Local Chairs made a proposal to host the conference in Nusa Dua early on, but it took all of us a long time to finally come to a decision to choose Grand Hyatt Bali, Nusa Dua, Bali, Indonesia for its exceptional location in the region as the conference venue. Its daytime temperatures are expected to reach 31°C, with the nighttime temperatures of around 24°C. I wish a very pleasant time for all the off-line participants of the conference and an equally memorable time for all the on-line participants.

Welcome to the conference and Nusa Dua!

IJCNLP-AACL 2023 General Chair
Jong C. Park
Korea Advanced Institute of Science and Technology (KAIST)

Message from the Chair of Student Research Workshop

Welcome to the IJCNLP-AACL 2023 Student Research Workshop (SRW)!

The IJCNLP-AACL 2023 SRW is held in conjunction with the 13th International Joint Conference on Natural Langauge Processing (IJCNLP) and the 3rd Conference of the Asia-Pacific Chapter of the Association for Computational Linguistics (AACL)

The IJCNLP-AACL 2023 SRW provides a forum for student researchers who are investigating various areas related to Computational Linguistics and Natural Language Processing. The workshop provides an excellent opportunity for student participants to present their work and receive valuable feedback from the international research community as well as from selected mentors - experienced researchers, specifically assigned according to the topic of their work, who will prepare in-depth comments and questions in advance of the presentation. The workshop's goal is to aid students at multiple stages of their education: including undergraduate, master's, junior, and senior PhD students. This year's IJCNLP-AACL SRW raise a theme of understanding language models, which is reflected in the choice of our keynote speaker (Tom McCoy).

The submissions were organized into two categories, that are general research papers and thesis proposals, following the tradition established by the previous SRWs:

- General research papers: Papers in this category can describe completed work, or work in progress with preliminary results. For these papers, the first author must be a current graduate or undergraduate student.
- Thesis proposals: This category is appropriate for advanced students who have decided on a thesis topic and wish to get feedback on their proposal and broader ideas for their continuing work.

We received a total of 29 submissions: 27 general research papers and 2 thesis proposal. We accepted 11 general research papers and 2 thesis proposal, resulting in an overall acceptance rate of 45%. The decision-making process was competitive, but we were delighted that all accepted submissions have great creativity and make contributions to their fields. The accepted submissions are diverse not only in topics but also in terms of student demographics. Following the tradition established by the previous SRWs, we also provided the pre-submission mentoring program for participants. The mentoring program offers students the opportunity to get feedback by a mentor prior to submitting their work for review. There are 5 papers participated in the pre-submission mentoring program.

We would like to thank the pre-submission mentors that spend their time and effort to help improve the work of the student authors. We would also like to thank all members of the program committee for their in-depth, detailed review and constructive suggestions for each submission. We are especially grateful to all the emergency reviewers who provide timely support and submit their high-quality feedback.

Preparing a workshop is never an easy business. Thanks to Hyeju Jang, Yugo Murawaki, and Derek Fai Wong, who act as the faculty advisors for this year's workshop. Special thanks to Vishakh Padmakumar and Gisela Vallejo, two of the co-chairs of ACL 2023 SRW, and Hanqi Yan, one of the co-chairs of the IJCNLP-AACL 2022 SRW, who shared their invaluable experience in preparing the workshop. We are also grateful to Derry Wijaya for her constant and timely guidance. A huge shout out to Tom McCoy, who agreed to give the SRW keynote. We sincerely appreciate all of the organizers of the IJCNLP-AACL conference for their effort. And of course, we would like to thank all the student authors and participants who submitted their work to the workshop. This workshop cannot be successful without any of them.

We hope you enjoy the IJCNLP-AACL 2023 SRW!

Organizing Committee

Student Research Workshop Co-Chairs

Dongfang Li, Harbin Institute of Technology (Shenzhen), China
Rahmad Mahendra, RMIT University, Australia
Zilu Peter Tang, Boston University, USA

Faculty Advisors

Hyeju Jang, Indiana University Purdue University Indianapolis (IUPUI), USA
Yugo Murawaki, Kyoto University, Japan
Derek Fai Wong, University of Macau, China

Pre-submission Mentors

Raj Dabre
Fajri Koto
Jey Han Lau
Ellie Pavlick
Abhilasha Ravichander

Program Committee

David Ifeoluwa Adelani
Afra Feyza Akyurek
Samuel Cahyawijaya
Ronald Cardenas
Jonathan Chang
Justin Chiu
Chris Develder
Hicham EL BOUKKOURI
Carlos Escolano
Biaoyan Fang
Diana Galvan-Sosa
Ryuichiro Higashinaka
Wen Chin Huang
Muhammad Okky Ibrohim
Shailza Jolly
Muhammed Yusuf Kocyigit

Mamoru Komachi
Fajri Koto
Kemal Kurniawan
Gina-Anne Levow
Sheng Li
Yunxin Li
Jasy Suet Yan Liew
Holy Lovenia
Patrick Lumban Tobing
Adib Mosharrof
Urwa Muaz
Masaaki Nagata
Kiet Nguyen
Vincent Nguyen
Naoki Otani
Rifki Afina Putri
Ivaylo Radev
Mathieu Ravaut
Ade Romadhony
Abulhair Saparov
Isidora Tourni
Bayu Distiawan Trisedya
Thinh Hung Truong
Sowmya Vajjala
Gisela Vallejo
Bailin Wang
Yuxia Wang
Bonnie Webber
Bryan Wilie
Rui Xing
Hanqi Yan
Longfei Yang
Zheng Xin Yong
Zenan Zhai
Junchen Zhao
Rongxin Zhu

Table of Contents

Cross-lingual Transfer Learning for Javanese Dependency Parsing

Fadli Aulawi Al Ghiffari, Ika Alfina, and **Kurniawati Azizah**
Faculty of Computer Science, Universitas Indonesia, Depok, Indonesia
fadli.aulawi@ui.ac.id
{ika.alfina, kurniawati.azizah}@cs.ui.ac.id

Abstract

While structure learning achieves remarkable performance in high-resource languages, the situation differs for under-represented languages due to the scarcity of annotated data. This study focuses on assessing the efficacy of transfer learning in enhancing dependency parsing for Javanese—a language spoken by 80 million individuals but characterized by limited representation in natural language processing. We utilized the Universal Dependencies dataset consisting of dependency treebanks from more than 100 languages, including Javanese. We propose two learning strategies to train the model: transfer learning (TL) and hierarchical transfer learning (HTL). While TL only uses a source language to pre-train the model, the HTL method uses a source language and an intermediate language in the learning process. The results show that our best model uses the HTL method, which improves performance with an increase of 10 % for both UAS and LAS evaluations compared to the baseline model.

1 Introduction

Despite over 80 million native speakers of Javanese (Simons et al., 2023), this language is underrepresented in NLP due to a scarcity of annotated resources. Limited works in Javanese have focused on stemmer (Soyusiawaty et al., 2020), POS tagger (Askhabi et al., 2020), sentiment analysis (Tho et al., 2021), and machine translation (Lesatari et al., 2021). However, few have explored language structure prediction, such as dependency parsing. Dependency parsing is a process that makes a structural representation of a sentence (Kübler et al., 2009) that produces a structure in the form of a dependency tree represented in a graph consisting of several connected links between words in a sentence.

Recent work, Alfina et al. (2023) created a public gold standard dataset for Javanese with 1000 sentences, published as part of the Universal Dependencies dataset (Zeman et al., 2023). This dataset covers annotation for tokenization, POS tagging, morphological features tagging, and dependency parsing tasks. The most recent parser performance (Alfina et al., 2023) using this dataset is not satisfactory, with only 77.08% on Unlabeled Attachment Score (UAS) and 71.21% on Labeled Attachment Score (LAS). The lack of training data is a typical low-resource problem considered one of the biggest NLP research problems (Ruder, 2023).

Transfer learning (TL) involves leveraging a model's knowledge from a high-resource source domain to improve performance on various NLP tasks, particularly in low-resource domains (Weiss et al., 2016), by transferring learned information to target tasks. Inspired by Maulana et al. (2022) that utilizes cross-lingual transfer learning to develop an Indonesian dependency parser, we want to try to replicate its outcome in Javanese with a limited available dataset. Moreover, we also implement hierarchical transfer learning (HTL) with two stages of transfer learning that offer increased flexibility over TL by enabling knowledge transfer between languages with a significant gap (Luo et al., 2019), as demonstrated in diverse applications, including Javanese text-to-speech (Azizah et al., 2020) and biomedical named entity recognition models (Chai et al., 2022).

We build the dependency parser model for Javanese by adopting model (Ahmad et al., 2019) that uses a self-attention encoder and a graph-based decoder. We utilize the Universal Dependency dataset v1.12 (Zeman et al., 2023) that provides dependency treebanks for more than 100 languages, including Javanese. Both TL and HTL use a selection of source languages determined by LangRank (Lin et al., 2020). Specifically, HTL employs Indonesian as an intermediary language, developing from our referenced research (Maulana et al., 2022). The empirical results show that transfer learning improves accuracy with a margin of 10% compared to

Proceedings of the 13th International Joint Conference on Natural Language Processing and the 3rd Conference of the Asia-Pacific Chapter of the Association for Computational Linguistics: Student Research Workshop, pages 1–9

the baseline. We also report the word embedding comparison that fastText performs better than the Javanese BERT, Javanese RoBERTa, and multilingual BERT. In summary, the main contributions of this paper are as follows:

1. Provide the first study of Javanese dependency parsing using TL and HTL strategy. We report that the HTL method can significantly improve performance compared to the training from scratch method.

2. Report the investigation of which source language and word embedding performs best for TL and HTL strategy.

2 Related Works

2.1 Dependency Parser

The dependency parser model can be developed using two methods, the transition-based and graph-based methods (Das and Sarkar, 2020). The transition-based method works by processing the word order one by one in a given sentence (Martin., 2020). Meanwhile, the graph-based method gives a score to each edge of the word relation (Martin., 2020), then looks for the best tree formed from the edges with the best scores.

Apart from these two methods, there is an approach in which the parser is built using an encoder-decoder architecture. It was first developed using a BiLSTM encoder and a deep biaffine decoder (Dozat and Manning, 2017). Encoder variations began to develop using Transformers or self-attention encoders (Vaswani et al., 2017), then subsequent studies modified it using relative positional embedding (Shaw et al., 2018). The first Javanese dependency parser (Alfina et al., 2023) uses UD-Pipe (Straka, 2018), which also utilizes the biaffine attention mentioned before.

In the context of transfer learning, it was found that the best combination is a self-attention encoder and a graph-based decoder (Ahmad et al., 2019), which will be used in this research. This combination has been better than other encoder-decoder combinations in cross-lingual transfer learning.

2.2 Transfer Learning

Transfer learning involves leveraging a pre-trained model's knowledge to enhance the performance of other models (Sarkar and Bali, 2022), addressing resource limitations in low-resource domains. Besides that, hierarchical transfer learning offers a transfer learning method in which a new layer is added before the model is transferred to the low-resource language (Luo et al., 2019). Recent work has shown that transferring multiple times could minimize the dissimilarity between the high-resource and the low-resource domain languages (Azizah et al., 2020).

Transfer learning strategy offers direct capability, which means a model is trained on a source task and then applied without any labeled data from the target task. Specifically on the parsing task, previous research already done by Kurniawan et al. (2021) and Ahmad et al. (2019) for developing an unsupervised parsing model in several languages using only English as its source language. That approach can be improved by adding fine-tuning with the available small dataset from low-resource language. Recent work (Maulana et al., 2022) shows the fine-tuning approach is better than the zero-shot one for building a parsing model in another low-resource language, Indonesian.

3 Method

This section concerns the model's architecture with the addition of the transfer learning method, the dataset and word embedding used to train the model, and the evaluation method of how the model is evaluated.

3.1 Model Architecture

This work uses an encoder-decoder architecture of Ahmad et al. (2019). No parameter modifications were made to maintain the success of the previous work. Because training and fine-tuning the model involves resources from several different languages, only language-independent labels are used where the subtype of the label is not involved.

3.1.1 Encoder

We convert the words and POS tags from the sentence into their embedding form. The self-attention encoder (Vaswani et al., 2017) in this study received an embedding matrix, which concatenates the word and POS embedding matrices. The encoder produces two matrices, M and N. M matrix represents the probability of a word in column j having the head of a word in row i. In comparison, the N matrix represents the probability of a word in column j having a label in row i.

3.1.2 Decoder

The decoder receives the two matrices and processes them in two following processes. First, M is processed with the maximum spanning tree algorithm in the following way:

Let $G = (V, E)$ be a graph constructed using directed weighted graph M. In this case, a vertex is a word representation, and an edge represents the dependency score of the two words. Let $w : E \to \mathbb{R}$ be a function that assigns a weight to each edge in E. Then, the maximum spanning tree problem seeks to find a spanning tree $T = (V, E_T)$ of G such that:

$$T = \arg\max_{T'} \sum_{e \in E_{T'}} w(e) \quad (1)$$

subject to the constraint that T is a tree. Then, a list of head H is generated from all the destination nodes in E_T. It can be denoted as:

$$H = \{d_i \mid \exists (s_i, d_i) \in E_T\}, \;\; i = 1, \ldots, n \quad (2)$$

Meanwhile, N is processed to generate L, containing the list of labels with the highest probability for each word. Finally, the H and L arrays are used to build the final resulting tree from this model.

3.1.3 Word Embedding

This research used two types of word embedding approaches: the static type in the form of fastText and the contextual type in the form of BERT. The two types were selected to compare which type was most suitable for the Javanese parser model.

We chose fastText because of the similarity with that used in the previous research (Maulana et al., 2022). We also used BERT with two scenarios: using a different word embedding for each language (BERT and RoBERTa) and only one word embedding for all languages (multilingual BERT). The BERT and RoBERTa scenario uses all the languages involved except Croatian due to the unavailable resources.

3.2 Training Method

We perform two training methods: transfer learning and hierarchical transfer learning. Each method generates several models based on the number of source languages used. All models are fine-tuned with the Javanese treebank.

Standard transfer learning only uses one transfer stage from high-resource to low-resource language,

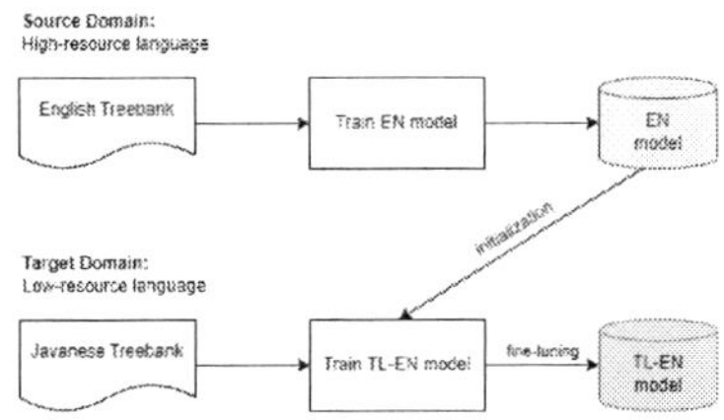

Figure 1: Illustration of standard transfer learning method

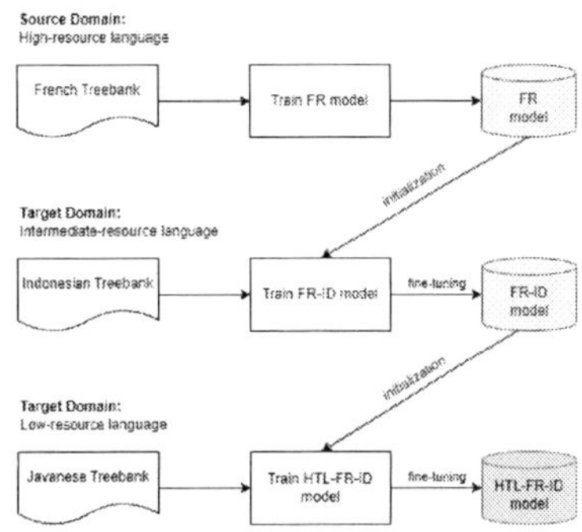

Figure 2: Illustration of hierarchical transfer learning method

as shown in Figure 1. Meanwhile, Figure 2 illustrates a hierarchical transfer learning scenario, where transferring stages are performed twice in hierarchical transfer learning. The first stage is done from a high-source language to an intermediate-resource language, and the second stage is done from an intermediate-resource language to a low-resource language.

3.3 Choosing Source Languages

Some languages are selected as source languages using the help of LangRank (Lin et al., 2020) and references from previous studies. This tool considers combining two main feature groups in each language pair: corpus statistics and typological information.

3.4 Dataset

3.4.1 The Javanese dataset

For the Javanese dataset, we use the only Javanese treebank available in the UD dataset v2.12, the UD_Javanese-CSUI (Alfina et al., 2023). Table 1 shows the statistics of this dataset. The set available for UD_Javanese-CSUI is only a test set because the data size is still relatively small. We do our split process by following the distribution rule of the data into train, dev, and test sets by 80%, 10%, and 10% percentages.

Table 1: The statistics of the Javanese treebank

Description	Statistic
Sentence count	1000
Word count	14344
Unique word count	3793
Average sentence length (in words)	14.32
Universal Part-of-Speech (UPOS) tag count	17
Universal dependency relation count	32
Language-specific dependency relation count	14
Total dependency relation count	46

Table 2: List of treebanks chosen for source languages, with their corresponding size in the number of sentences and words

Treebank	Sentences	Words
UD_Croatian-SET (Agic and Ljubesic, 2015)	9010	199409
UD_English-GUM (Zeldes, 2017)	9124	164396
UD_French-GSD (McDonald et al., 2013)	16341	400232
UD_Indonesian-GSD (McDonald et al., 2013)	5598	122021
UD_Italian-ISDT (Bosco et al., 2022)	14167	298343
UD_Korean-GSD (Chun et al., 2019)	6339	80322

3.4.2 The source language dataset

Langrank recommends the top 3 languages in the following order: Indonesian, Croatian, and Korean. We also use English, one of the important languages in NLP research. These four languages are used in the standard transfer learning scenario.

For the hierarchical transfer learning scenario using Indonesian as the intermediary language, we choose English, French, and Italy as the source languages suggested by Maulana et al. (2022). In total, we use six languages as the source languages.

For each source language, we only use one treebank. If a language has more than one treebank in the UD dataset v2.12, we choose the treebank with the biggest size, as shown in Table 2.

3.5 Experiments Setting

3.5.1 Scenarios

As explained in Section 3.2, we conducted three main scenarios:

1. Training from scratch (FS) or baseline scenario, in which the models are trained only using the target language, Javanese.

2. Standard transfer learning (TL). We construct four distinct models utilizing treebanks from each source language. Then, each model is fine-tuned using the Javanese treebank.

3. Hierarchical transfer learning (HTL). First, we train three different models using treebank from each source language. After that, the models were fine-tuned with the Indonesian treebank before being fine-tuned again with the Javanese treebank.

We also compared the performance of the four types of word embeddings for Javanese: fastText (Grave et al., 2019), Javanese BERT (Wongso et al., 2021), Javanese RoBERTa (Wongso et al., 2021), and multilingual BERT (Devlin et al., 2019).

3.5.2 Environment

Implementation is done in Python environments. The training process is supported by the NVIDIA-DGX server with GPU NVIDIA A100 10GB, RAM of 64GB, and storage of 1 TB.

3.6 Evaluation

All models are evaluated using the unlabeled attachment score (UAS) and labeled attachment score (LAS) metrics, which are the most frequently used for evaluating the dependency parsing model (Nivre and Fang, 2017). The margin of error (MOE) with a 95% confidence level is also used to estimate the range of values within which the true population value is likely to fall.

4 Result and Analysis

The evaluation results for all scenarios are shown in Table 3. Scores in bold are marked as the best model in a particular word embedding type metric.

4.1 Models Comparison: From Scratch (FS) Model, Transfer Learning (TL) Model, and Hierarchical Transfer Learning (HTL) Model

Table 3 shows that the transfer learning model performs better than the baseline model in all word embeddings. The performance increase is quite significant, up to 13% on UAS and 14% on LAS. This verifies previous studies which explain the advantages of using transfer learning (Sarkar and Bali, 2022). The lack of resources in Javanese also indicates that transfer learning is suitable for use.

Figure 3 also shows that the hierarchical transfer learning method consistently outperforms the transfer learning method even though it is not too significant. Specifically, the comparison focused on the TL-ID and HTL models, as all models from the HTL scenario use the TL-ID model as its second base for the transferring method. The difference

Table 3: Evaluation results of all scenarios

Word Embedding	Model	UAS	LAS
fastText	FS	75.87 ± 2.21	68.97 ± 2.39
	TL-ID	84.80 ± 1.85	78.10 ± 2.14
	TL-HR	83.40 ± 1.92	76.57 ± 2.19
	TL-KO	80.68 ± 2.04	74.13 ± 2.26
	TL-EN	83.47 ± 1.92	77.27 ± 2.16
	HTL-EN-ID	84.94 ± 1.85	**79.22 ± 2.10**
	HTL-FR-ID	84.87 ± 1.85	77.55 ± 2.15
	HTL-IT-ID	**85.84 ± 1.80**	78.87 ± 2.11
jv-BERT	FS	74.69 ± 2.25	67.29 ± 2.42
	TL-ID	79.08 ± 2.10	72.32 ± 2.31
	TL-HR	-	-
	TL-KO	77.06 ± 2.17	70.29 ± 2.36
	TL-EN	81.73 ± 2.00	75.52 ± 2.22
	HTL-EN-ID	**83.47 ± 1.92**	**76.64 ± 2.19**
	HTL-FR-ID	81.80 ± 1.99	75.38 ± 2.22
	HTL-IT-ID	81.03 ± 2.02	73.99 ± 2.27
jv-RoBERTa	FS	69.80 ± 2.37	62.97 ± 2.49
	TL-ID	78.45 ± 2.12	72.11 ± 2.32
	TL-HR	-	-
	TL-KO	82.22 ± 1.97	76.22 ± 2.20
	TL-EN	77.13 ± 2.17	70.92 ± 2.35
	HTL-EN-ID	77.41 ± 2.16	70.85 ± 2.35
	HTL-FR-ID	83.05 ± 1.94	77.20 ± 2.17
	HTL-IT-ID	**83.33 ± 1.92**	**77.20 ± 2.17**
multi-BERT	FS	75.80 ± 2.21	69.04 ± 2.39
	TL-ID	82.01 ± 1.98	76.01 ± 2.21
	TL-HR	83.75 ± 1.90	77.68 ± 2.15
	TL-KO	79.78 ± 2.07	73.29 ± 2.28
	TL-EN	80.89 ± 2.03	74.13 ± 2.26
	HTL-EN-ID	82.98 ± 1.94	76.71 ± 2.18
	HTL-FR-ID	83.19 ± 1.93	77.75 ± 2.15
	HTL-IT-ID	**84.45 ± 1.87**	**78.52 ± 2.12**

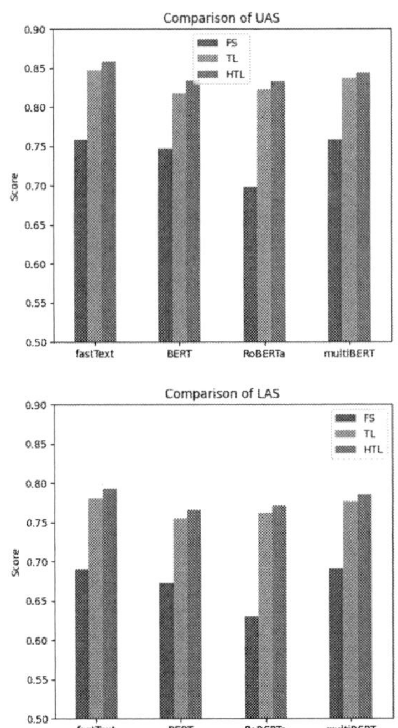

Figure 3: Comparison of the best model evaluation for each scenario

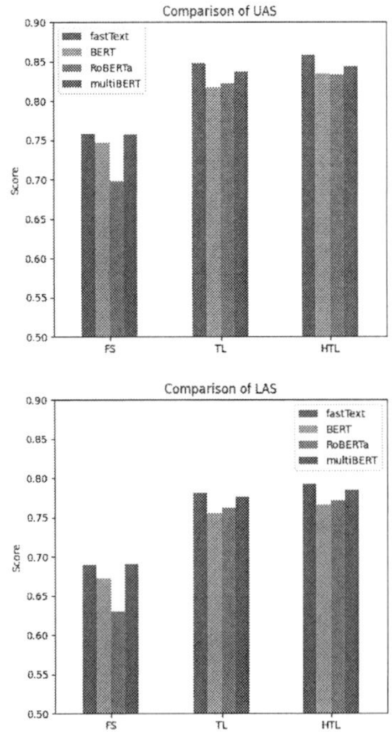

Figure 4: Comparison of the best model evaluation for each word embedding

between these two scenarios shows that adding suitable high-resource language for the initial source model can give a better performance.

4.2 Source Languages Comparison

Table 3 shows that two of the top three recommendations from LangRank have good results. The conclusion is that LangRank can help predict the source language in the Javanese dependency parser. However, it does not rule out the possibility that other languages also have good results. For TL, it cannot be concluded which source language achieves the best performance since different word embedding used by the model gives different results. For HTL using Indonesian as the intermediate language, Italy performs best, followed by English as the source language.

4.3 Word Embeddings Comparison

Figure 4 shows that the model with a higher UAS score was obtained from word embedding fastText, followed by multilingual BERT, Javanese BERT, and Javanese RoBERTa. For LAS evaluation, the sequence is fastText, multilingual BERT, Javanese RoBERTa, and Javanese BERT. Although fastText is slightly superior, the differences are insignificant when considering the models' margin of error.

Table 4: Top 10 errors of the from-scratch model and its comparison with the transfer-learning model

Ground Truth	Prediction	FS	TL	HTL
obl	obj	17	16	15
obl	nsubj	7	3	7
obj	obl	7	13	12
advcl	xcomp	5	5	6
nmod	flat	4	2	1
xcomp	advcl	4	5	5
xcomp	obl	3	3	2
nmod	obl	3	1	1
nsubj	obj	3	1	1
obj	nsubj	2	0	3

4.4 Error Analysis

Table 4 displays more detail about the performance difference. The ten labels taken are obtained from pairs with the highest errors in the from-scratch model. Some pairs significantly reduce error, but there are also pairs with no significant changes and even more errors in scenarios with transfer learning.

One noteworthy insight is the significantly increasing error of words with "obj" label that predicted with "obl". It seems contradictory that model accuracy is increasing simultaneously with the addition of transfer learning. It turns out that there are a few differences in the word labeling of both labels between the source and the target language, so the model could not predict the word label correctly.

5 Conclusions and Future Work

This section explains the conclusion and improvements that can be developed from this work.

5.1 Conclusions

This work investigates whether cross-lingual transfer learning works for dependency parsing tasks of a low-resource language, Javanese. The result shows that the cross-lingual transfer learning model is significantly better than the baseline model. Models with transfer learning can improve performance on UAS and LAS metrics by up to 10%.

The best model was obtained from the hierarchical transfer learning method using Italian and English as the source and Indonesian as the intermediary languages. Meanwhile, the standard transfer learning method achieved the best accuracy using Indonesian as the source language. However, the differences between standard transfer learning and hierarchical learning are insignificant, considering the margin of error from each scenario.

5.2 Future Work

We focused more on the model's learning scheme than the model's development with the highest score. We use architecture from Dozat and Manning (2017) rather than the one built by Mrini et al. (2020), the state-of-the-art dependency parsing task. So, better architecture can be used to produce a model with a higher evaluation score in the future.

Our future works also include further error analysis, especially related to the languages involved that LangRank chose. It could investigate languages with different demography and characteristics (Croatian and Korean) compared to Javanese.

Limitations

The following are the limitations of this research:

1. There is no hyper-parameter tuning treatment in the model creation process.

2. Cross-validation is not performed in the data distribution process.

3. Only one language is used as an intermediary language in hierarchical transfer learning.

Acknowledgements

We thank the Directorate of Research and Development, Universitas Indonesia, under Hibah PUTI 2022 (Grant No. NKB-1384/UN2.RST/HKP.05.00/2022) for funding this research. We also thank Tokopedia-UI AI Center, Faculty of Computer Science Universitas Indonesia, and Program Kompetisi Kampus Merdeka from the Ministry of Education, Culture, Research, and Technology Republic of Indonesia for the NVIDIA-DGX server we used for experiments. We also gratefully acknowledge Dr. Fajri Koto for the insightful feedback during the pre-submission mentorship.

References

Zeljko Agic and Nikola Ljubesic. 2015. Universal Dependencies for Croatian (that work for Serbian, too). In *Proceedings of the Fifth Workshop on Balto-Slavic Natural Language Processing (BSNLP 2015)*.

Wasi Uddin Ahmad, Zhisong Zhang, Xuezhe Ma, Eduard Hovy, Kai Wei Chang, and Nanyun Peng. 2019. On difficulties of cross-lingual transfer with order differences: A case study on dependency parsing. In *NAACL HLT 2019 - 2019 Conference of the North American Chapter of the Association for Computational Linguistics: Human Language Technologies - Proceedings of the Conference*, volume 1.

Ika Alfina, Arlisa Yuliawati, Dipta Tanaya, Arawinda Dinakaramani, and Daniel Zeman. 2023. A gold standard dataset for Javanese tokenization, POS tagging, morphological features analysis, and dependency parsing.

Fa'iq Askhabi, Arie Ardiyanti Suryani, and Moch. Arif Bijaksana. 2020. Part of speech tagging in Javanese using support vector machine method. *e-Proceeding of Engineering*, 7.

Kurniawati Azizah, Mirna Adriani, and Wisnu Jatmiko. 2020. Hierarchical transfer learning for multilingual, multi-speaker, and style transfer DNN-based TTS on low-resource languages. *IEEE Access*, 8.

Cristina Bosco, Felice Dell'Orletta, and Simonetta Montemagni. 2022. *The Evalita 2014 Dependency Parsing Task*. Proceedings of the First Italian Conference on Computational Linguistics CLiC-it 2014 and of the Fourth International Workshop EVALITA 2014 9-11 December 2014, Pisa.

Zhaoying Chai, Han Jin, Shenghui Shi, Siyan Zhan, Lin Zhuo, and Yu Yang. 2022. Hierarchical shared transfer learning for biomedical named entity recognition. *BMC Bioinformatics*, 23.

Jayeol Chun, Na Rae Han, Jena D. Hwang, and Jinho D. Choi. 2019. Building universal dependency treebanks in Korean. In *LREC 2018 - 11th International Conference on Language Resources and Evaluation*.

Ayan Das and Sudeshna Sarkar. 2020. A survey of the model transfer approaches to cross-lingual dependency parsing. *ACM Transactions on Asian and Low-Resource Language Information Processing*, 19.

Jacob Devlin, Ming Wei Chang, Kenton Lee, and Kristina Toutanova. 2019. BERT: Pre-training of deep bidirectional transformers for language understanding. In *NAACL HLT 2019 - 2019 Conference of the North American Chapter of the Association for Computational Linguistics: Human Language Technologies - Proceedings of the Conference*, volume 1.

Timothy Dozat and Christopher D. Manning. 2017. Deep biaffine attention for neural dependency parsing. In *5th International Conference on Learning Representations, ICLR 2017 - Conference Track Proceedings*.

Edouard Grave, Piotr Bojanowski, Prakhar Gupta, Armand Joulin, and Tomas Mikolov. 2019. Learning word vectors for 157 languages. In *LREC 2018 - 11th International Conference on Language Resources and Evaluation*.

Kemal Kurniawan, Lea Frermann, Philip Schulz, and Trevor Cohn. 2021. PPT: Parsimonious parser transfer for unsupervised cross-lingual adaptation. In *EACL 2021 - 16th Conference of the European Chapter of the Association for Computational Linguistics, Proceedings of the Conference*.

Sandra Kübler, Ryan McDonald, and Joakim Nivre. 2009. *Dependency Parsing*, volume 2. Synthesis Lectures on Human Language Technologies.

Aufa Eka Putri Lesatari, Arie Ardiyanti, Arie Ardiyanti, Ibnu Asror, and Ibnu Asror. 2021. Phrase-based statistical machine translation Javanese-Indonesian. *Jurnal Media Informatika Budidarma*, 5.

Yu Hsiang Lin, Chian Yu Chen, Jean Lee, Zirui Li, Yuyan Zhang, Mengzhou Xia, Shruti Rijhwani, Junxian He, Zhisong Zhang, Xuezhe Ma, Antonios Anastasopoulos, Patrick Littell, and Graham Neubig. 2020. Choosing transfer languages for cross-lingual learning. In *ACL 2019 - 57th Annual Meeting of the Association for Computational Linguistics, Proceedings of the Conference*.

Gongxu Luo, Yating Yang, Yang Yuan, Zhanheng Chen, and Aizimaiti Ainiwaer. 2019. Hierarchical transfer learning architecture for low-resource neural machine translation. *IEEE Access*, 7.

Daniel Jurafsky & James H. Martin. 2020. *Speech and Language Processing: An Introduction to Natural Language Processing, Computational Linguistics, and Speech Recognition*. Prentice Hall.

Andhika Yusup Maulana, Ika Alfina, and Kurniawati Azizah. 2022. Building Indonesian dependency parser using cross-lingual transfer learning. In *2022 International Conference on Asian Language Processing (IALP)*, pages 488–493.

Ryan McDonald, Joakim Nivre, Yvonne Quirmbach-Brundage, Yoav Goldberg, Dipanjan Das, Kuzman Ganchev, Keith Hall, Slav Petrov, Hao Zhang, Oscar Täckström, Claudia Bedini, Núria Bertomeu Castelló, and Jungmee Lee. 2013. Universal dependency annotation for multilingual parsing. In *ACL 2013 - 51st Annual Meeting of the Association for Computational Linguistics, Proceedings of the Conference*, volume 2.

Khalil Mrini, Franck Dernoncourt, Quan Tran, Trung Bui, Walter Chang, and Ndapa Nakashole. 2020. Rethinking self-attention: Towards interpretability in neural parsing. In *Findings of the Association for Computational Linguistics Findings of ACL: EMNLP 2020*.

Joakim Nivre and Chiao Ting Fang. 2017. Universal Dependency evaluation. In *Proceedings of the NoDaLiDa 2017 Workshop on Universal Dependencies, UDW 2017*.

Sebastian Ruder. 2023. The 4 biggest open problems in NLP.

Dipanjan Sarkar and Raghav Bali. 2022. *Transfer Learning in Action*, 1 edition. Manning Early Access Program.

Peter Shaw, Jakob Uszkoreit, and Ashish Vaswani. 2018. Self-attention with relative position representations. In *NAACL HLT 2018 - 2018 Conference of the North American Chapter of the Association for Computational Linguistics: Human Language Technologies - Proceedings of the Conference*, volume 2.

Gary Simons, David Eberhard, and Charles Fennig. 2023. *Ethnologue: Languages of the World, 26nd Edition*. SIL International.

Dewi Soyusiawaty, Anna Hendri Soleliza Jones, and Nora Lestari Lestariw. 2020. The stemming application on affixed Javanese words by using Nazief and Adriani algorithm. In *IOP Conference Series: Materials Science and Engineering*, volume 771.

Milan Straka. 2018. UDPIPE 2.0 prototype at Conll 2018 UD Shared Task. In *CoNLL 2018 - SIGNLL Conference on Computational Natural Language Learning, Proceedings of the CoNLL 2018 Shared Task: Multilingual Parsing from Raw Text to Universal Dependencies*, pages 197–207.

C. Tho, Y. Heryadi, L. Lukas, and A. Wibowo. 2021. Code-mixed sentiment analysis of Indonesian language and Javanese language using lexicon-based approach. In *Journal of Physics: Conference Series*, volume 1869.

Ashish Vaswani, Noam Shazeer, Niki Parmar, Jakob Uszkoreit, Llion Jones, Aidan N. Gomez, Łukasz Kaiser, and Illia Polosukhin. 2017. Attention is all you need. In *Advances in Neural Information Processing Systems*, volume 2017-December.

Karl Weiss, Taghi M. Khoshgoftaar, and Ding Ding Wang. 2016. A survey of transfer learning. *Journal of Big Data*, 3.

Wilson Wongso, David Samuel Setiawan, and Derwin Suhartono. 2021. Causal and masked language modeling of Javanese language using transformer-based architectures. In *2021 International Conference on Advanced Computer Science and Information Systems, ICACSIS 2021*.

Amir Zeldes. 2017. The GUM corpus: creating multilayer resources in the classroom. *Language Resources and Evaluation*, 51.

Daniel Zeman, Joakim Nivre, Mitchell Abrams, Elia Ackermann, Noëmi Aepli, Hamid Aghaei, Željko Agić, Amir Ahmadi, Lars Ahrenberg, Chika Kennedy Ajede, Salih Furkan Akkurt, Gabrielė Aleksandravičiūtė, Ika Alfina, Avner Algom, Khalid Alnajjar, Chiara Alzetta, Erik Andersen, Lene Antonsen, Tatsuya Aoyama, Katya Aplonova, Angelina Aquino, Carolina Aragon, Glyd Aranes, Maria Jesus Aranzabe, Bilge Nas Arıcan, Ĥórunn Arnardóttir, Gashaw Arutie, Jessica Naraiswari Arwidarasti, Masayuki Asahara, Katla Ásgeirsdóttir, Deniz Baran Aslan, Cengiz Asmazoğlu, Luma Ateyah, Furkan Atmaca, Mohammed Attia, Aitziber Atutxa, Liesbeth Augustinus, Mariana Avelãs, Elena Badmaeva, Keerthana Balasubramani, Miguel Ballesteros, Esha Banerjee, Sebastian Bank, Verginica Barbu Mititelu, Starkaður Barkarson, Rodolfo Basile, Victoria Basmov, Colin Batchelor, John Bauer, Seyyit Talha Bedir, Shabnam Behzad, Kepa Bengoetxea, Ibrahim Benli, Yifat Ben Moshe, Gözde Berk, Riyaz Ahmad Bhat, Erica Biagetti, Eckhard Bick, Agnė Bielinskienė, Kristín Bjarnadóttir, Rogier Blokland, Victoria Bobicev, Loïc Boizou, Emanuel Borges Völker, Carl Börstell, Cristina Bosco, Gosse Bouma, Sam Bowman, Adriane Boyd, Anouck Braggaar, António Branco, Kristina Brokaitė, Aljoscha Burchardt, Marisa Campos, Marie Candito, Bernard Caron, Gauthier Caron, Catarina Carvalheiro, Rita Carvalho, Lauren Cassidy, Maria Clara Castro, Sérgio Castro, Tatiana Cavalcanti, Gülşen Cebiroğlu Eryiğit, Flavio Massimiliano Cecchini, Giuseppe G. A. Celano, Slavomír Čéplö, Neslihan Cesur, Savas Cetin, Özlem Çetinoğlu, Fabricio Chalub, Liyanage Chamila, Shweta Chauhan, Ethan Chi, Taishi Chika, Yongseok Cho, Jinho Choi, Jayeol Chun, Juyeon Chung, Alessandra T. Cignarella, Silvie Cinková, Aurélie Collomb, Çağrı Çöltekin, Miriam Connor, Daniela Corbetta, Francisco Costa, Marine Courtin, Mihaela Cristescu, Ingerid Løyning Dale, Philemon Daniel, Elizabeth Davidson, Leonel Figueiredo de Alencar, Mathieu Dehouck, Martina de Laurentiis, Marie-Catherine de Marneffe, Valeria de Paiva, Mehmet Oguz Derin, Elvis de Souza, Arantza Diaz de Ilarraza, Carly Dickerson, Arawinda Dinakaramani, Elisa Di Nuovo, Bamba Dione, Peter Dirix, Kaja Dobrovoljc, Adrian Doyle, Timothy Dozat, Kira Droganova, Puneet Dwivedi, Christian Ebert, Hanne Eckhoff, Masaki Eguchi, Sandra Eiche, Marhaba Eli, Ali Elkahky, Binyam Ephrem, Olga Erina, Tomaž Erjavec, Farah Essaidi, Aline Etienne, Wograine Evelyn, Sidney Facundes, Richárd Farkas, Federica Favero, Jannatul Ferdaousi, Marília Fernanda, Hector Fernandez Alcalde, Amal Fethi, Jennifer Foster, Cláudia Freitas, Kazunori Fujita, Katarína Gajdošová, Daniel Galbraith, Federica Gamba, Marcos Garcia, Moa Gärdenfors, Fabrício Ferraz Gerardi, Kim Gerdes, Luke Gessler, Filip Ginter, Gustavo Godoy, Iakes Goenaga, Koldo Gojenola, Memduh Gökırmak, Yoav Goldberg, Xavier Gómez Guinovart, Berta González Saavedra, Bernadeta Griciūtė, Matias Grioni, Loïc Grobol, Normunds Grūzītis, Bruno Guillaume, Céline Guillot-Barbance, Tunga Güngör, Nizar Habash, Hinrik Hafsteinsson, Jan Hajič, Jan Hajič jr., Mika Hämäläinen, Linh Hà Mỹ, Na-Rae Han, Muhammad Yudistira Hanifmuti, Takahiro Harada, Sam Hardwick, Kim Harris, Dag Haug, Johannes Heinecke, Oliver Hellwig, Felix Hennig, Barbora Hladká, Jaroslava Hlaváčová, Florinel Hociung, Petter Hohle, Marivel Huerta Mendez, Jena Hwang, Takumi Ikeda, Anton Karl Ingason, Radu Ion, Elena Irimia, Ọlájídé Ishola, Artan Islamaj, Kaoru Ito, Siratun Jannat, Tomáš Jelínek, Apoorva Jha, Katharine Jiang, Anders Johannsen, Hildur Jónsdóttir, Fredrik Jørgensen, Markus Juutinen, Hüner Kaşıkara, Nadezhda Kabaeva, Sylvain Kahane, Hiroshi Kanayama, Jenna Kanerva, Neslihan Kara, Ritván Karahóǧa, Andre Kåsen, Tolga Kayadelen, Sarveswaran Kengatharaiyer, Václava Kettnerová, Jesse Kirchner, Elena Klementieva, Elena Klyachko, Arne Köhn, Abdullatif Köksal, Kamil Kopacewicz, Timo Korkiakangas, Mehmet Köse, Alexey Koshevoy, Natalia Kotsyba, Jolanta Kovalevskaitė, Simon Krek, Parameswari Krishnamurthy, Sandra Kübler, Adrian Kuqi, Oğuzhan Kuyrukçu, Aslı Kuzgun, Sookyoung Kwak, Kris Kyle, Veronika Laippala, Lorenzo Lambertino, Tatiana Lando, Septina Dian Larasati, Alexei Lavrentiev, John Lee, Phuong Le Hong, Alessandro Lenci, Saran Lertpradit, Herman Leung, Maria Levina, Lauren Levine, Cheuk Ying Li, Josie Li, Keying Li, Yixuan Li, Yuan Li, KyungTae Lim, Bruna Lima Padovani, Yi-Ju Jessica Lin, Krister Lindén, Yang Janet Liu, Nikola Ljubešić, Olga Loginova, Stefano Lusito, Andry Luthfi, Mikko Luukko, Olga Lyashevskaya, Teresa Lynn, Vivien Macketanz, Menel Mahamdi, Jean Maillard, Ilya Makarchuk, Aibek Makazhanov, Michael Mandl, Christopher Manning, Ruli Manurung, Büşra Marşan, Cătălina Mărănduc, David Mareček, Katrin Marheinecke, Stella Markantonatou, Héctor Martínez Alonso, Lorena Martín Rodríguez, André Martins, Cláudia Martins, Jan Mašek, Hiroshi Matsuda, Yuji Matsumoto, Alessandro Mazzei, Ryan McDonald, Sarah McGuinness, Gustavo Mendonça, Tatiana Merzhevich, Niko Miekka, Aaron Miller, Karina Mischenkova, Anna Missilä, Cătălin Mititelu, Maria Mitrofan, Yusuke Miyao, AmirHossein Mojiri Foroushani, Judit Molnár, Amirsaeid Moloodi, Simonetta Montemagni, Amir More, Laura Moreno Romero, Giovanni Moretti, Shinsuke Mori, Tomohiko Morioka, Shigeki Moro, Bjartur Mortensen, Bohdan Moskalevskyi, Kadri Muischnek, Robert Munro, Yugo Murawaki, Kaili Müürisep, Pinkey Nainwani, Mariam Nakhlé, Juan Ignacio Navarro Horñiacek, Anna Nedoluzhko, Gunta Nešpore-Bērzkalne, Manuela Nevaci, Luong Nguyễn Thị, Huyền Nguyễn Thị Minh, Yoshihiro Nikaido, Vitaly Nikolaev, Rattima Nitisaroj, Alireza Nourian, Hanna Nurmi, Stina Ojala, Atul Kr. Ojha, Hulda Óladóttir, Adédayọ Olúòkun, Mai Omura, Emeka Onwuegbuzia, Noam Ordan, Petya Osenova, Robert Östling, Lilja Øvrelid, Şaziye Betül Özateş, Merve Özçelik, Arzucan Özgür, Balkız Öztürk Başaran, Teresa Paccosi, Alessio Palmero Aprosio, Anastasia Panova, Hyunji Hayley Park, Niko Partanen, Elena Pascual, Marco Passarotti, Agnieszka Patejuk, Guilherme Paulino-Passos, Giulia Pedonese, Angelika Peljak-Łapińska, Siyao Peng, Siyao Logan Peng, Rita Pereira, Sílvia Pereira, Cenel-Augusto Perez, Natalia Perkova, Guy Perrier, Slav Petrov, Daria Petrova, Andrea Peverelli, Jason Phelan, Jussi Piitulainen, Yuval Pinter, Clara Pinto, Tommi A Pirinen, Emily Pitler, Magdalena Plamada, Barbara Plank, Thierry Poibeau, Larisa Ponomareva, Martin Popel, Lauma Pretkalniņa, Sophie Prévost, Prokopis Prokopidis, Adam Przepiórkowski, Robert Pugh, Tiina Puolakainen, Sampo Pyysalo, Peng Qi, Andreia Querido, Andriela Rääbis, Alexandre Rademaker, Mizanur Rahoman, Taraka Rama, Loganathan Ramasamy, Joana Ramos, Fam Rashel, Mohammad Sadegh Rasooli, Vinit Ravishankar, Livy Real, Petru Rebeja, Siva Reddy, Mathilde Regnault, Georg Rehm, Arij Riabi, Ivan Riabov, Michael Rießler, Erika Rimkutė, Larissa Rinaldi, Laura Rituma, Putri Rizqiyah, Luisa Rocha, Eiríkur Rögnvaldsson, Ivan Roksandic, Mykhailo Romanenko, Rudolf Rosa, Valentin Roșca, Davide Rovati, Ben Rozonoyer, Olga Rudina, Jack Rueter, Kristján Rúnarsson, Shoval Sadde, Pegah Safari, Aleksi Sahala, Shadi Saleh, Alessio Salomoni, Tanja Samardžić, Stephanie Samson, Manuela Sanguinetti, Ezgi Sanıyar, Dage Särg, Marta Sartor, Mitsuya Sasaki, Baiba Saulīte, Yanin Sawanakunanon, Shefali Saxena, Kevin Scannell, Salvatore Scarlata, Nathan Schneider, Sebastian Schuster, Lane Schwartz, Djamé Seddah, Wolfgang Seeker, Mojgan Seraji, Syeda Shahzadi, Mo Shen, Atsuko Shimada, Hiroyuki Shirasu, Yana Shishkina, Muh Shohibussirri, Maria Shvedova, Janine Siewert, Einar Freyr Sigurdsson, João Silva, Aline Silveira, Natalia Silveira, Sara Silveira, Maria Simi, Radu Simionescu, Katalin Simkó, Mária Šimková, Haukur Barri Símonarson, Kiril Simov, Dmitri Sitchinava, Ted Sither, Maria Skachedubova, Aaron Smith, Isabela Soares-Bastos, Per Erik Solberg, Barbara Sonnenhauser, Shafi Sourov, Rachele Sprugnoli, Vivian Stamou, Steinhór Steingrímsson, Antonio Stella, Abishek Stephen, Milan Straka, Emmett Strickland, Jana Strnadová, Alane Suhr, Yogi Lesmana Sulestio, Umut Sulubacak, Shingo Suzuki, Daniel Swanson, Zsolt Szántó, Chihiro Taguchi, Dima Taji, Fabio Tamburini, Mary Ann C. Tan, Takaaki Tanaka, Dipta Tanaya, Mirko Tavoni, Samson Tella, Isabelle Tellier, Marinella Testori, Guillaume Thomas, Sara Tonelli, Liisi Torga, Marsida Toska, Trond Trosterud, Anna Trukhina, Reut Tsarfaty, Utku Türk, Francis Tyers, Sveinbjörn Hórarson, Vilhjálmur Horsteinsson, Sumire Uematsu, Roman Untilov, Zdeňka Urešová, Larraitz Uria, Hans Uszkoreit, Andrius Utka, Elena Vagnoni, Sowmya Vajjala, Socrates Vak, Rob van der Goot, Martine Vanhove, Daniel van Niekerk, Gertjan van Noord, Viktor Varga, Uliana Vedenina, Giulia Venturi, Veronika Vincze, Natalia Vlasova, Aya Wakasa, Joel C. Wallenberg, Lars Wallin, Abigail Walsh, Jonathan North Washington, Maximilan Wendt, Paul Widmer, Shira Wigderson, Sri Hartati Wijono, Seyi Williams, Mats Wirén, Christian Wittern, Tsegay Woldemariam, Tak-sum Wong, Alina Wróblewska, Mary Yako, Kayo Yamashita, Naoki Yamazaki, Chunxiao Yan, Koichi Yasuoka, Marat M. Yavrumyan, Arife Betül Yenice, Olcay Taner Yıldız, Zhuoran Yu, Arlisa Yuliawati, Zdeněk Žabokrtský, Shorouq Zahra, Amir Zeldes, He Zhou, Hanzhi Zhu, Yilun Zhu, Anna Zhuravleva, and Rayan Ziane. 2023. Universal Dependencies 2.12. LINDAT/CLARIAH-CZ digital library at the Institute of Formal and Applied Linguistics (ÚFAL), Faculty of Mathematics and Physics, Charles University.

An Investigation of Warning Erroneous Chat Translations in Cross-lingual Communication

Yunmeng Li[1] **Jun Suzuki**[1,3] **Makoto Morishita**[2] **Kaori Abe**[1*] **Kentaro Inui**[4,1,3]
[1]Tohoku University [2]NTT [3]RIKEN [4]MBZUAI
li.yunmeng.r1@dc.tohoku.ac.jp

Abstract

Machine translation models are still inappropriate for translating chats, despite the popularity of translation software and plug-in applications. The complexity of dialogues poses significant challenges and can hinder cross-lingual communication. Instead of pursuing a flawless translation system, a more practical approach would be to issue warning messages about potential mistranslations to reduce confusion. However, it is still unclear how individuals perceive these warning messages and whether they benefit the crowd. This paper tackles to investigate this question and demonstrates the warning messages' contribution to making chat translation systems effective.

1 Introduction

Globalization has led to the popularity of neural machine translation (Bahdanau et al., 2014; Vaswani et al., 2017; Gehring et al., 2017). Applications like Google Translate[1] and DeepL[2] have become essential tools in people's lives (Medvedev, 2016; Patil and Davies, 2014). Chat software such as WeChat and LINE also integrates built-in translation features to facilitate cross-lingual communication. Plug-in translating applications like UD Talk[3] and Hi Translate[4] have become popular as well with the rise of online communication.

However, while machine translation technologies have demonstrated sound performance in translating documents (Barrault et al., 2019, 2020; Nakazawa et al., 2019; Ma et al., 2020; Maruf and Haffari, 2018), current methods are not always suitable for translating conversations (Uthus and Aha, 2013), especially colloquial dialogues such as chats (Läubli et al., 2018; Toral et al., 2018; Farajian et al., 2020; Liang et al., 2021a). When a translation system generates erroneous translations, people unable to read the other language may not recognize such errors, leading to confusion.

Achieving a perfect error-free chat translation system is challenging due to the unique characteristics of chat (Tiedemann and Scherrer, 2017; Maruf et al., 2018; Liang et al., 2021a,b), making it impractical to aim for perfection. Instead, a viable alternative approach is to enhance translation software by providing warnings about possible mistranslations to reduce confusion. However, the perception and effects of such warning messages remain unclear. To investigate this, we proposed to provide a warning message for erroneous translations during the cross-lingual chat and conducted a survey to explore how such warnings help people communicate. The survey design is shown in Figure 1. Participants engage in a simulated cross-lingual chat scenario, where they have to select the most reasonable response from three options. Whenever a translation error occurs, a warning message is displayed. At the end of the chat, participants answer corresponding questions regarding their perceptions of the warning messages.

We conducted the survey and collected responses through crowdsourcing. The results indicate that warning messages (1) are helpful in cross-lingual chats and (2) potentially encourage users to change their chat behavior. Moreover, the survey reveals the crowd's desired features for the warning messages. This is the first study of its kind to explore the impacts of warning users about erroneous translations in cross-lingual chat. The findings are valuable for developing an assistant function that detects and warns users of erroneous chat translations.

2 Related Work

Previous studies have pointed out the potential benefits of incorporating machine translation in chat, despite its imperfections (Uthus and Aha, 2013).

*Currently affiliated with Machine Learning Solutions Inc.

[1]https://translate.google.com/

[2]https://www.deepl.com/translator

[3]https://udtalk.jp/

[4]https://bit.ly/3pWhz9T

Proceedings of the 13th International Joint Conference on Natural Language Processing and the 3rd Conference of the Asia-Pacific Chapter of the Association for Computational Linguistics: Student Research Workshop, pages 10–16
November 1–4, 2023.

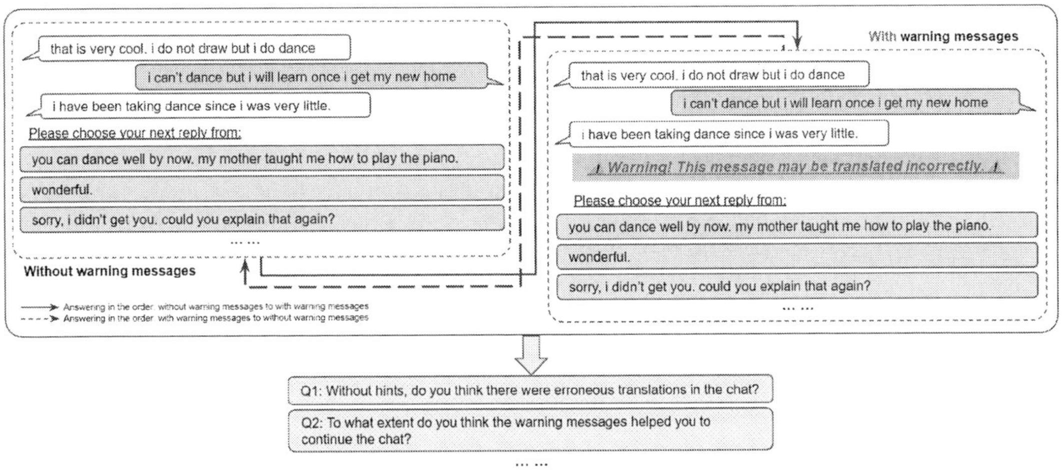

Figure 1: An illustration of the designed survey. Participants will engage in two rounds of chat in the survey: one without warning messages (left) and one with warning messages (right). The content and response options are the same in both rounds. The order of the two rounds, either "without-with" (solid line) or "with-without" (dotted line), will be randomly assigned to participants.

Several researchers have trained models using different methods to enhance chat translation performance (Maruf et al., 2018; Farajian et al., 2020; Liang et al., 2021a). However, features such as ambiguity, omissions, and multi-speakers make it challenging to improve translation accuracy in chat (Tiedemann and Scherrer, 2017; Liang et al., 2021a,b). In contrast to existing studies of training chat translation models, we focus on acknowledging the imperfect nature of machine translation (Uthus and Aha, 2013) and aim to enhance people's experience of chat translation through an alternative approach. We propose the warning message of erroneous translation and thus improve people's experience in cross-lingual chat. A chat translation error detector discussed in a recent study provides a binary assessment of the coherence and correctness of chat translations (Li et al., 2022b). If the error detector's predictions are transformed into warning messages, our survey could be instrumental in assessing the error detector's practical effectiveness. To the best of our knowledge, the study is the first to investigate the crowd's acceptance of such chat translation error detection tasks.

3 Survey Design

We propose an alternative strategy to improve translation software's performance by integrating cautionary alerts for potential mistranslations to reduce confusion. We designed a warning message and executed a survey to evaluate its effectiveness. Figure 1 illustrates the survey process, including two simulated chat rounds: one devoid of warning messages and the other incorporating them.

3.1 Simulated Cross-lingual Chat Scenarios

Since dynamic real-time chats are relatively uncontrollable and high-cost, we simulated a chat scenario with a foreign partner based on chat data from Persona-chat (Zhang et al., 2018). In the simulation, participants are presented with three initial chat turns as historical chat logs at the beginning.Participants choose the most contextually fitting response from the three provided options each time their scripted partners respond iteratively. To explore the cognitive processes of individuals lacking proficiency in a foreign language, we operated under the assumption that participants would receive translated messages generated by the machine translation system from their partners. Hence, all texts within the survey are presented to participants in their native language.

3.2 Chat Data

We prepared the simulated scenarios with the Persona-chat dataset, containing multi-turn chat data about various personality traits with assumed personas in English. To ensure the quality of the data, we eliminated incoherent and unnatural chat data from Persona-chat through crowdsourcing at Amazon Mechanical Turk [5]. We defined "inco-

[5] https://requester.mturk.com/

herence" as questions being ignored, the presence of unnatural topic changes, one speaker not addressing what the other speaker said, responses appearing to be out of order or generally difficult to follow. We scored each chat according to the workers' answers and selected 6 of $1,500$ chats marked as accurate and coherent by at least seven of the ten workers. The chosen chats were used as the base of the simulated scenarios in the survey.

Similarly, we required proficient English speakers to continue the chat with given personas and topics from Persona-chat for other branching options and extended chats triggered by the options.

3.3 Erroneous Translations

To provide the chat data that were supposed to be erroneous translations, we translated the prepared chat data with a low-quality machine translation model that achieved a considerably low BLEU score (Papineni et al., 2002) of 4.9 on the English-Japanese chat translation evaluation dataset BPersona-chat (Li et al., 2022a). Consequently, we transformed the low-quality translations twenty times through Google Translate into different languages and finally translated them back to the source language of the survey. To ensure the final translations could serve as erroneous translations, we manually confirmed that the texts included significant syntax issues, incorrect emotional expressions, incoherence, or other errors that led to confusion. We designed that at least one of the three turns of the simulated chat would include erroneous translations. We required proficient English speakers to continue the chat based on the erroneous translations to prepare the extended chat.

3.4 Warning Messages

We designed the warning message to notify participants of erroneous translations in the chat. When the current text is assumed to be the erroneous translation, participants are presented with a warning message alerting them of the mistranslation, as shown in Figure 1. We structured the warning messages into two types since receiving and sending are both essential in a conversation. One type alerts participants of erroneous translations in the messages they received, while the other type indicates potential errors in the last message they sent.

3.5 Corresponding Questions

After the chat, participants are asked to answer if they notice erroneous translations without hints. If participants answer yes, they rate their experience on two Likert Scale questions (Joshi et al., 2015; Nemoto and Beglar, 2014). The first question assesses the extent to which the errors prevented them from continuing the chat, while the second question asks to what extent they could grasp exactly where the erroneous translations were in the message. Participants will use 1-5 to score their perceptions, with higher numbers indicating a greater awareness or understanding of the errors.

Participants must also rate on a Likert Scale question the extent to which they think the warning helped them continue the chat. Further, they check the plural options of additional features they find helpful if added to the warnings. Selectable features include: *indicating the correctness rate of the translation, providing alternative translation suggestions, showing specific errors in the translation,* and *suggesting the emotion of their partner.*[6]

4 Crowdsourcing Experiments

We prepared the survey in English, Chinese, and Japanese to observe the possible difference between languages. Professional translators translated the data from English to Chinese and Japanese to ensure quality. We prepared three sets of chat data for each type of warning message and two types of warnings; hence, we provided six sets of chat and collected the responses through crowdsourcing. We provided instructions for participants on how the chat would be presented and what they should do to attend the chat at the beginning of the task. Participants would be acknowledged that (1) their partner would speak to them in a language other than their native language, (2) the system would translate their partners' messages and the chat would only be presented in their language, (3) they would read the chat log and choose the most reasonable of the three options, (4) the message sent to them would be displayed on the odd-numbered lines, and their answer would be displayed on the even-numbered lines.

To minimize any possible influence of showing warnings first or later, we provided each chat in two orders. Participants answer either without warning messages first or with warning messages first. At the round of warning messages, we would explain the role of warning messages to participants and inform them that they could refer to the warnings

[6]Participants can fill in their comments or skip if they do not have any specific wanting features.

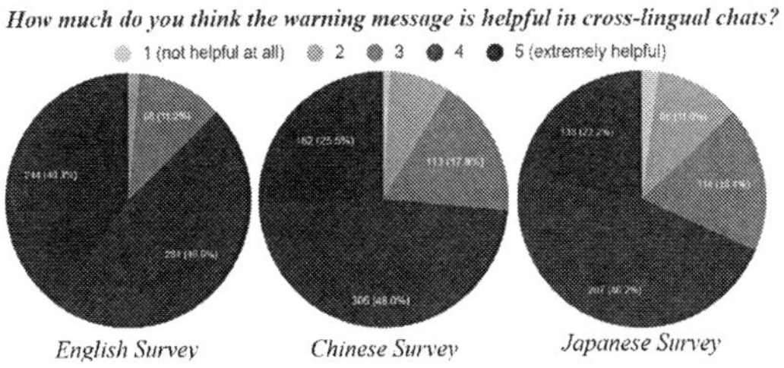

Figure 2: The responses to how participants think the warning messages helped them continue the chat.

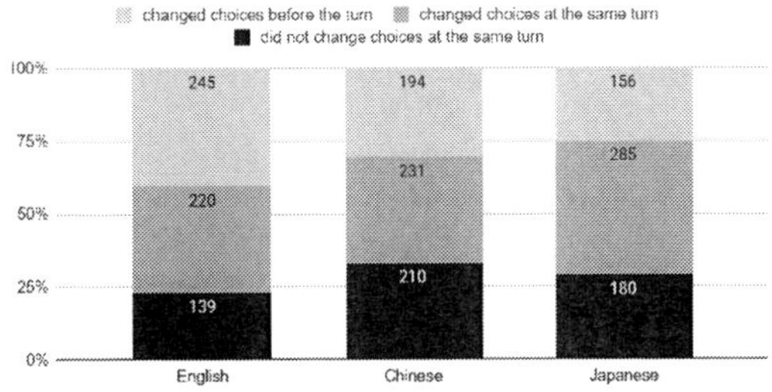

Figure 3: The results that whether participants changed their choices with the help of warning messages.

to help them make choices.

We invited at least 50 participants for each order and ensured they could not join both orders through the crowdsourcing platforms' features. Crowdworkers were unaware of the fact that there were two orders, and they did not know which order they would join. Ultimately, we invited at least 100 participants for each set of chats.

The surveys were conducted on Amazon Mechanical Turk[7] for English participants, WenJuanXing[8] for Chinese participants, and CrowdWorks[9] for Japanese participants. Workers participated anonymously and were informed that the results would be used for academic purposes. Classification rounds were held in advance for efficiency.

5 Results and Analysis

Under the different policies of crowdsourcing platforms, we finally gathered 604 English, 635 Chinese, and 621 Japanese responses. Figure 2 displays the overall summaries. Around 70% of participants across three languages rated the warning messages as *"4 - helpful"* or above in the chat. Most participants view the warning messages as helpful in cross-lingual chats, aligned with Likert Scale analysis (Amidei et al., 2019).

With or without warning messages The results of *"Without hints, do you think there were erroneous translations in the chat"* based on the order in which participants answered the survey are listed in Table 1. The percentages of noticing erroneous translations without hints remain consistent, regardless of participants answering with warning messages first or after. Hence, we conclude that the impact of answering orders on the crowds appears minimal. Moreover, considering a score greater or equal to 4 suggests the positivity of a Likert Scale question, we conclude that most participants who noticed erroneous translations also considered those errors as obstacles.

It is worth noting that while the English and Chinese results are relatively similar, Japanese results differ slightly. The recognition of erroneous translations without hints is notably lower in Japanese than in English and Chinese contexts. Participants' feedback suggests this may be related to Japanese linguistic specificity in "omission." Participants considered erroneous translations as omissions, aligning with Japanese conversational patterns where subjects or objects are often omitted. The warning messages helped them realize that the expression was not omitted but errors for the better continuation of the chat.

Additionally, English and Chinese participants also remarked that the warnings clarified unusual expressions as translation errors rather than humor or slang. The feedback helped state the usefulness of warning messages and the consideration for future differentiation between translation errors and humorous terms or buzzwords.

Impact of warning messages on modifying user's chat behavior We analyzed participants' choices in relation to warning messages, categorizing them into three cases: (1) entered the same scenario in both the round with warnings and the round without warnings and did not change their choices, (2) entered the same scenario in both rounds and changed their choices, and (3) did not change their choices due to entering other branches in advance. We believe that the first case demonstrates that participants were not influenced by warnings, while the second case shows that they were influenced. In the third case, although it is impossible to compare whether participants changed their choices in the same scenario since they changed earlier, we still view it as an indirect influence due to the equiv-

[7]`https://requester.mturk.com/`

[8]`https://www.wjx.cn/`

[9]`https://crowdworks.jp/`

	Without Warning Messages First					With Warning Messages First				
English	**Noticing mistranslations without hints**					**Noticing mistranslations without hints**				
	234 of 303 (77.2%)					234 of 302 (77.4%)				
	Considering mistranslations to be barriers					**Considering mistranslations to be barriers**				
	Score=1	*Score=2*	*Score=3*	*Score=4*	*Score=5*	*Score=1*	*Score=2*	*Score=3*	*Score=4*	*Score=5*
	2	11	56	126	39	5	17	55	108	49
Chinese	**Noticing the erroneous translations without hints**					**Noticing the erroneous translations without hints**				
	228 of 325 (70.2%)					241 of 310 (77.7%)				
	Considering mistranslations to be barriers					**Considering mistranslations to be barriers**				
	Score=1	*Score=2*	*Score=3*	*Score=4*	*Score=5*	*Score=1*	*Score=2*	*Score=3*	*Score=4*	*Score=5*
	2	26	45	112	53	2	26	62	115	36
Japanese	**Noticing the erroneous translations without hints**					**Noticing the erroneous translations without hints**				
	175 of 321 (54.5%)					158 of 300 (52.7%)				
	Considering mistranslations to be barriers					**Considering mistranslations to be barriers**				
	Score=1	*Score=2*	*Score=3*	*Score=4*	*Score=5*	*Score=1*	*Score=2*	*Score=3*	*Score=4*	*Score=5*
	3	21	29	89	33	1	17	29	86	25

Table 1: The results of the questions about noticing erroneous translations without hints in the two different answering orders. Participants who answered yes to the question continued to rate the extent they considered the erroneous translations to be barriers in the chat. The higher the score was, the more confused the participant felt.

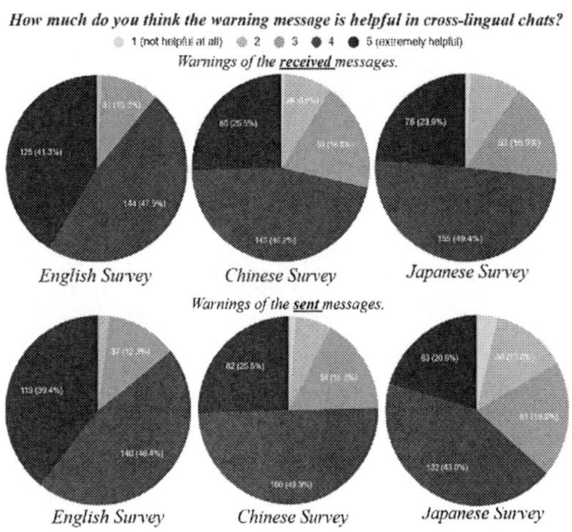

Figure 4: The responses to how participants think the warnings of the **received/sent** messages helped them continue the chat.

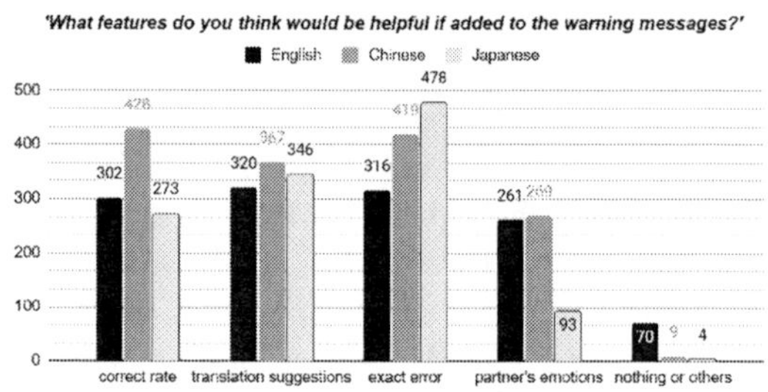

Figure 5: The results about expected additional features to the warning messages.

alence between having no warning messages and having no erroneous translations. Indeed, 103 participants stated they changed their choices as they ensured there were no erroneous translations.

Survey results shown in Figure 3 indicate that approximately 25% participants remained unchanged, while about 75% changed their choices, either directly or indirectly, due to the warning messages. We confirm that the participants were genuinely influenced by warning messages and participated in the subsequent feedback.

Warnings on the received messages or the sent messages The collected responses of different types of warning messages are summarized in Figure 4. Regardless of whether the warning messages indicated translation errors in the message received or sent, over 60% of the participants found the warning messages helpful (rating with a score-4 or higher) in all three languages.

Expected features of the warning message The results of expected additional information of the warning message are presented in Figure 5.

Chinese and Japanese participants showed a greater expectation for warning messages to indicate the exact error of their partners' messages. In addition, Chinese participants prefer to know the correct rate. Feedback from participants indicated that the correctness rate would better assist them in determining whether they needed to reinterpret. Japanese participants consider having other translation suggestions as references. English survey participants voted on all the listed features on average, but knowing their partner's emotions were still lower than others. In summary, to enhance the warning messages, the focus may better be on highlighting the exact errors in the translations.

6 Conclusions

We conducted a survey to investigate the effectiveness of warning about possible mistranslations in chat as an alternative approach to enhance the experience of cross-lingual communication. Through crowdsourcing, we collected responses and concluded that such warning messages are helpful. By comparing the participants' choices with and without warning messages, we found that the warning messages did encourage participants to change their behaviors. We also found the crowd expects the warning message to (1) show the specific error in the translation, (2) indicate the correctness rate of the translation, and (3) provide alternative translation suggestions.

This survey is the first to explore the effects of warning about erroneous translations in cross-lingual chat, providing valuable insights for developing an assistant function that detects and warns people of erroneous chat translations.

Limitations

During the survey design phase, diligent measures were taken to minimize potential leading effects on the participants' judgment by randomly switching the order and neutralizing the questioning style. Despite the conscientious efforts, we must acknowledge the inherent challenges in completely eliminating all influences on the people who participated in the survey. With this realization, we recognize the need for further optimization to guarantee the fairness and validity of the responses. Refinement is warranted to minimize the biases further.

Ethics

The crowdsourcing survey employed in this study adheres to stringent ethical guidelines to ensure participant privacy and data protection. The survey design deliberately avoids collecting any personally identifiable information from the participants. No restrictions or enforcement of work hours were imposed upon participants, thereby eliminating undue influence or coercion. Given the absence of personal data collection and voluntary participation, the data is not subject to ethics review at the organization. Consequently, the survey design and data collection procedures adhere to the ethical standards and regulations governing research practices.

Acknowledgements

This work was supported by JST (the establishment of university fellowships towards the creation of science technology innovation) Grant Number JPMJFS2102, JST CREST Grant Number JPMJCR20D2 and JST Moonshot R&D Grant Number JPMJMS2011 (fundamental research). The crowdsourcing was supported by Amazon Mechanical Turk (`https://www.mturk.com/`), WenJuanXing (`https://www.wjx.cn/`) and Crowdworks (`https://crowdworks.jp/`).

References

Jacopo Amidei, Paul Piwek, and Alistair Willis. 2019. The use of rating and Likert scales in natural language generation human evaluation tasks: A review and some recommendations. In *Proceedings of the 12th International Conference on Natural Language Generation*, pages 397–402, Tokyo, Japan. Association for Computational Linguistics.

Dzmitry Bahdanau, Kyunghyun Cho, and Yoshua Bengio. 2014. Neural machine translation by jointly learning to align and translate. *arXiv preprint arXiv:1409.0473*.

Loïc Barrault, Magdalena Biesialska, Ondřej Bojar, Marta R. Costa-jussà, Christian Federmann, Yvette Graham, Roman Grundkiewicz, Barry Haddow, Matthias Huck, Eric Joanis, Tom Kocmi, Philipp Koehn, Chi-kiu Lo, Nikola Ljubešić, Christof Monz, Makoto Morishita, Masaaki Nagata, Toshiaki Nakazawa, Santanu Pal, Matt Post, and Marcos Zampieri. 2020. Findings of the 2020 conference on machine translation (WMT20). In *Proceedings of the Fifth Conference on Machine Translation*, pages 1–55, Online. Association for Computational Linguistics.

Loïc Barrault, Ondřej Bojar, Marta R. Costa-jussà, Christian Federmann, Mark Fishel, Yvette Graham, Barry Haddow, Matthias Huck, Philipp Koehn, Shervin Malmasi, Christof Monz, Mathias Müller, Santanu Pal, Matt Post, and Marcos Zampieri. 2019. Findings of the 2019 conference on machine translation (WMT19). In *Proceedings of the Fourth Conference on Machine Translation (Volume 2: Shared Task Papers, Day 1)*, pages 1–61, Florence, Italy. Association for Computational Linguistics.

M. Amin Farajian, António V. Lopes, André F. T. Martins, Sameen Maruf, and Gholamreza Haffari. 2020. Findings of the WMT 2020 shared task on chat translation. In *Proceedings of the Fifth Conference on Machine Translation*, pages 65–75, Online. Association for Computational Linguistics.

Jonas Gehring, Michael Auli, David Grangier, Denis Yarats, and Yann N Dauphin. 2017. Convolutional sequence to sequence learning. In *International conference on machine learning*, pages 1243–1252. PMLR.

Ankur Joshi, Saket Kale, Satish Chandel, and D Kumar Pal. 2015. Likert scale: Explored and explained. *British journal of applied science & technology*, 7(4):396.

Samuel Läubli, Rico Sennrich, and Martin Volk. 2018. Has machine translation achieved human parity? a case for document-level evaluation. In *Proceedings of the 2018 Conference on Empirical Methods in Natural Language Processing*, pages 4791–4796, Brussels, Belgium. Association for Computational Linguistics.

Yunmeng Li, Jun Suzuki, Makoto Morishita, Kaori Abe, Ryoko Tokuhisa, Brassard Ana, and Inui Kentaro. 2022a. Bpersona-chat: A coherence-filtered english-japanese dialogue corpus. In *Proceedings of NLP2022*, pages E7–3.

Yunmeng Li, Jun Suzuki, Makoto Morishita, Kaori Abe, Ryoko Tokuhisa, Ana Brassard, and Kentaro Inui. 2022b. Chat translation error detection for assisting cross-lingual communications. In *Proceedings of the 3rd Workshop on Evaluation and Comparison of NLP Systems*, pages 88–95, Online. Association for Computational Linguistics.

Yunlong Liang, Fandong Meng, Yufeng Chen, Jinan Xu, and Jie Zhou. 2021a. Modeling bilingual conversational characteristics for neural chat translation. In *Proceedings of the 59th Annual Meeting of the Association for Computational Linguistics and the 11th International Joint Conference on Natural Language Processing (Volume 1: Long Papers)*, pages 5711–5724, Online. Association for Computational Linguistics.

Yunlong Liang, Chulun Zhou, Fandong Meng, Jinan Xu, Yufeng Chen, Jinsong Su, and Jie Zhou. 2021b. Towards making the most of dialogue characteristics for neural chat translation. In *Proceedings of the 2021 Conference on Empirical Methods in Natural Language Processing*, pages 67–79, Online and Punta Cana, Dominican Republic. Association for Computational Linguistics.

Shuming Ma, Dongdong Zhang, and Ming Zhou. 2020. A simple and effective unified encoder for document-level machine translation. In *Proceedings of the 58th Annual Meeting of the Association for Computational Linguistics*, pages 3505–3511, Online. Association for Computational Linguistics.

Sameen Maruf and Gholamreza Haffari. 2018. Document context neural machine translation with memory networks. In *Proceedings of the 56th Annual Meeting of the Association for Computational Linguistics (Volume 1: Long Papers)*, pages 1275–1284, Melbourne, Australia. Association for Computational Linguistics.

Sameen Maruf, André F. T. Martins, and Gholamreza Haffari. 2018. Contextual neural model for translating bilingual multi-speaker conversations. In *Proceedings of the Third Conference on Machine Translation: Research Papers*, pages 101–112, Brussels, Belgium. Association for Computational Linguistics.

Gennady Medvedev. 2016. Google translate in teaching english. *Journal of teaching English for specific and academic purposes*, 4(1):181–193.

Toshiaki Nakazawa, Nobushige Doi, Shohei Higashiyama, Chenchen Ding, Raj Dabre, Hideya Mino, Isao Goto, Win Pa Pa, Anoop Kunchukuttan, Yusuke Oda, Shantipriya Parida, Ondřej Bojar, and Sadao Kurohashi. 2019. Overview of the 6th workshop on Asian translation. In *Proceedings of the 6th Workshop on Asian Translation*, pages 1–35, Hong Kong, China. Association for Computational Linguistics.

Tomoko Nemoto and David Beglar. 2014. Likert-scale questionnaires. In *JALT 2013 conference proceedings*, pages 1–8.

Kishore Papineni, Salim Roukos, Todd Ward, and Wei-Jing Zhu. 2002. Bleu: a method for automatic evaluation of machine translation. In *Proceedings of the 40th Annual Meeting of the Association for Computational Linguistics*, pages 311–318, Philadelphia, Pennsylvania, USA. Association for Computational Linguistics.

Sumant Patil and Patrick Davies. 2014. Use of google translate in medical communication: evaluation of accuracy. *Bmj*, 349.

Jörg Tiedemann and Yves Scherrer. 2017. Neural machine translation with extended context. In *Proceedings of the Third Workshop on Discourse in Machine Translation*, pages 82–92, Copenhagen, Denmark. Association for Computational Linguistics.

Antonio Toral, Sheila Castilho, Ke Hu, and Andy Way. 2018. Attaining the unattainable? reassessing claims of human parity in neural machine translation. In *Proceedings of the Third Conference on Machine Translation: Research Papers*, pages 113–123, Brussels, Belgium. Association for Computational Linguistics.

David C Uthus and David W Aha. 2013. Multiparticipant chat analysis: A survey. *Artificial Intelligence*, 199:106–121.

Ashish Vaswani, Noam Shazeer, Niki Parmar, Jakob Uszkoreit, Llion Jones, Aidan N Gomez, Łukasz Kaiser, and Illia Polosukhin. 2017. Attention is all you need. *Advances in neural information processing systems*, 30.

Saizheng Zhang, Emily Dinan, Jack Urbanek, Arthur Szlam, Douwe Kiela, and Jason Weston. 2018. Personalizing dialogue agents: I have a dog, do you have pets too? In *Proceedings of the 56th Annual Meeting of the Association for Computational Linguistics (Volume 1: Long Papers)*, pages 2204–2213, Melbourne, Australia. Association for Computational Linguistics.

Gender Inflected or Bias Inflicted: On Using Grammatical Gender Cues for Bias Evaluation in Machine Translation

Pushpdeep Singh
National Institute of Technology, Hamirpur
Anu, Hamirpur, India
pushpdeep30@gmail.com

Abstract

Neural Machine Translation (NMT) models are state-of-the-art for machine translation. However, these models are known to have various social biases, especially gender bias. Most of the work on evaluating gender bias in NMT has focused primarily on English as the source language. For source languages different from English, most of the studies use gender-neutral sentences to evaluate gender bias. However, practically, many sentences that we encounter do have gender information. Therefore, it makes more sense to evaluate for bias using such sentences. This allows us to determine if NMT models can identify the correct gender based on the grammatical gender cues in the source sentence rather than relying on biased correlations with, say, occupation terms. To demonstrate our point, in this work, we use Hindi as the source language and construct two sets of gender-specific sentences: *OTSC-Hindi* and *WinoMT-Hindi* that we use to evaluate different Hindi-English (HI-EN) NMT systems automatically for gender bias. Our work highlights the importance of considering the nature of language when designing such extrinsic bias evaluation datasets.

1 Introduction

Various models trained to learn from data are susceptible to picking up spurious correlations in their training data, which can lead to multiple social biases. In NLP, such biases have been observed in different forms: Bolukbasi et al. (2016) found that word embeddings exhibit gender stereotypes, Zhao et al. (2017) observed that models for visual semantic role labelling aggrandize existing gender bias present in data, similar biased behaviour had been observed in NLP tasks like coreference resolution (Lu et al., 2019) and Natural Language Inference (Rudinger et al., 2017).

Even state-of-the-art NMT models develop such biases (Prates et al., 2019). These models can express gender bias in different ways. One is when due to their poor coreference resolution ability, they rely on biased associations with, say, occupation terms to disambiguate the gender of pronouns (Stanovsky et al., 2019; Saunders et al., 2020). Another is when these models translate gender-neutral sentences into gendered ones (Prates et al., 2019; Cho et al., 2019). In many cases, NMT models give a 'masculine default' translation.

This problem also exists for HI-EN Machine Translation (Ramesh et al., 2021). When put to use, such systems can cause various harms (Savoldi et al., 2021). Thus, evaluating and mitigating such biases from NMT models is critical to ensure fairness.

Prior research evaluating gender bias in machine translation has predominantly centered around English as the source language (Stanovsky et al., 2019). However, these evaluation methods or benchmarks don't seamlessly extend to other source languages, especially the ones with grammatical gender. For instance, in Hindi, elements like pronouns, adjectives, and verbs are often inflected with gender. Nonetheless, prior studies in other source languages often utilize gender-neutral sentences (Cho et al., 2019; Ramesh et al., 2021) for bias evaluation. Yet, in practice, many sentences inherently possess gender information.

Therefore, in this work, we propose to evaluate NMT models for bias using sentences with grammatical gender cues of the source language. This allows us to ascertain whether NMT models can discern the accurate gender from context or if they depend on biased correlations. In this work, we contribute the following :

- Using Hindi as source language in NMT, we highlight the limitations of existing bias evaluation methods that use gender-neutral sentences.
- Additionally, we propose to use context-based

Proceedings of the 13th International Joint Conference on Natural Language Processing and the 3rd Conference of the Asia-Pacific Chapter of the Association for Computational Linguistics: Student Research Workshop, pages 17–23
November 1–4, 2023. ©2023 Association for Computational Linguistics

gender bias evaluation using grammatical gender markers of the source language. We construct two evaluation sets for bias evaluation of NMT models: Occupation Testset with Simple Context (*OTSC-Hindi*) and *WinoMT-Hindi*.

- Using these evaluation sets, we evaluate various blackbox and open-source HI-EN NMT models for gender bias.
- We highlight the importance of creating such benchmarks for source languages with expressive gender markers.

Code and data are publicly available[1].

2 Experimental Setup

NMT Models : We test HI-EN NMT models which are widely popular and represent state-of-the-art in both commercial or academic research : (1) IndicTrans (Ramesh et al., 2022), (2) Google Translate[2], (3) Microsoft Translator[3], and (4) AWS Translate[4]. IndicTrans is an academic, open-source multilingual NMT model, while the latter four are commercial NMT systems available via APIs.

Hindi as Source Language : We create bias evaluation sentences in Hindi to evaluate HI-EN NMT Models. We choose Hindi due to two reasons. First, only limited research has been done on evaluating gender bias in Hindi translation. Previous work by Ramesh et al. (2021) focused only on the gender-neutral side of Hindi by evaluating simple sentences with gender-neutral, third person pronouns like "वह(vah)", "वे(ve)" and "वो(vo)". Second, choosing Hindi allows us to demonstrate bias evaluation using sentences with a diverse range of gender markers. In Hindi, verbs, adjectives and possessive pronouns often carry gender indicators. The grammatical gender system in Hindi is exclusively rooted in biological gender (Agnihotri, 2007). However, the variety of gender markers can be different for different languages. Therefore it's essential to study gender-related rules of the specific language for creating benchmarks for such tasks.

[1] https://github.com/iampushpdeep/Gender-Bias-Hi-En-Eval

[2] https://translate.google.com/

[3] https://www.bing.com/translator

[4] https://aws.amazon.com/translate/

3 TGBI Evaluation using Gender-Neutral Sentences

Cho et al. (2019) introduced *translation gender bias index* (TGBI) as a metric to measure bias in NMT systems using gender-neutral source language sentences, originally for the Korean language. Ramesh et al. (2021) showed that the TGBI metric can be applied to Hindi too. They constructed seven sets (P_1 to P_7) of gender-neutral sentences in Hindi which included: formal (S1), impolite (S2), informal (S3), occupation (S4), negative (S5), polite (S6), and positive (S7) versions.

For translation into English, TGBI uses the fraction of sentences in a sentence set S translated as "masculine", "feminine" or "neutral" in the target , i.e., p_m, p_f and p_n, respectively to calculate P_S as :

$$P_S = \sqrt{(p_m p_f + p_n)} \quad (1)$$

P_i is calculated for each sentence set S_i (S_1 to S_n) to finally calculate TGBI = avg(P_i). Using lists from Ramesh et al. (2021), we evaluate four HI-EN NMT models using the TGBI score to create a comparison for our evaluation methods.

Often, using a metric like TGBI is not very practical. For example, when the original intent is not gender-neutral but constraints of the source language make it gender-neutral, then showing all versions[5] or *random guessing*, with a 50% chance of choosing one gender in translation, are more practical. Also, gender-specific sentences are more common and making errors in such sentences makes for a more unfair system. Hence, we propose to expose gender bias by evaluating NMT models on such source language sentences.

4 Approach

We construct two sets of sentences, one with a simple gender-specified context and another with a more complex context. In creating these sets, we focus on the gender markers of the source language, i.e. Hindi. Also, we use template sentences which can help to automatically evaluate bias without using additional tools at the target side.

4.1 OTSC-Hindi

Escudé Font and Costa-jussà (2019) created a test set with custom template sentences to evaluate the

[5] https://ai.googleblog.com/2020/04/a-scalable-approach-to-reducing-gender.html

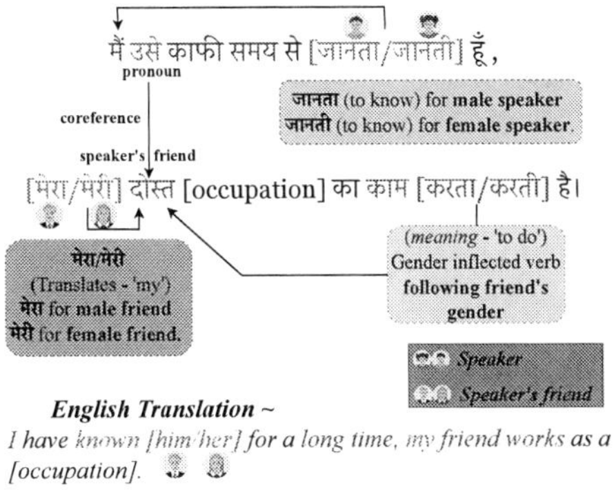

Figure 1: OTSC-Hindi sample template sentence along with its English translation. Gender of the speaker is specified by gender-inflected verb, i.e. "जानता" or "जानती". The possessive pronoun "मेरा" or "मेरी" and the verb "करता" or "करती" specify friend's gender. Here, the pronoun "उसे" references speaker's friend.

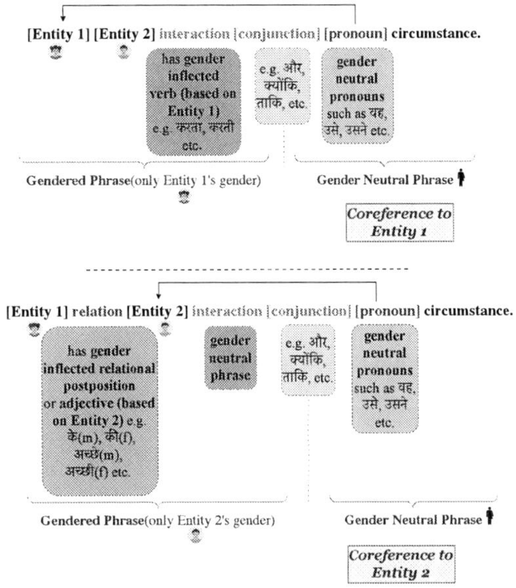

Figure 2: Sentence Template for WinoMT-Hindi. When Entity 1 is referenced, we use gender-inflected verb to specify its gender. When Entity 2 is referenced, its gender is specified using gender-inflected relational postposition or an adjective. Phrase after the conjuction (containing the pronoun which refers to either entity) is gender neutral.

gender bias for English to Spanish Translation. Inspired by this template, we create a Hindi version with grammatical gender cues: " मैं उसे काफी समय से {जानता,जानती} हूँ,{मेरा,मेरी} दोस्त **[occupation]** का काम {करता,करती} है।" (*I have known [him/her] for a long time, my friend works as a [occupation].*) Figure 1 explains the template and gender-related information. Note that, unlike the English version, this template specifies the gender of the speaker (first person) using a gender-inflected verb, i.e. "जानता(*jaanta*)" for male while "जानती(*jaanti*)" for female. The possessive pronoun is also gender inflected based on the gender of the speaker's friend. In Hindi, the possessive pronoun is gender inflected based on the word following it, here "मेरा(*mera*)" is used for male friend while "मेरी(*meri*)" is used for female friend. Based on the use of "मेरा(*mera*)" or "मेरी(*meri*)", the verb "करता(*karta*)" and "करती(*karti*)" is used for a male friend and female friend, respectively. So in this template, there are four possibilities based on the gender of the speaker and the gender of the speaker's friend. Using 1071 occupations, we construct these four sets with 1071 sentences each and check the percentage of sentences where the speaker's friend is translated as male or female. This is because English translation only specifies the gender of the friend while the gender of the speaker is lost in translation.

4.2 WinoMT-Hindi

In the real world, NMT models deal with more complex sentences: long sentences with further context,

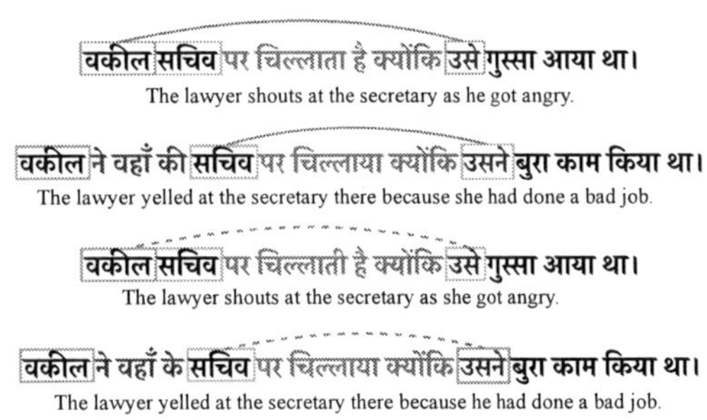

Figure 3: Sample Sentences in WinoMT-Hindi. The solid line shows pro-stereotypical coreference, while the dashed line shows anti-stereotypical coreference. Male and female (stereotypically) entities are marked in blue and orange boxes, respectively. Hindi pronouns are marked in blue or orange box based on the actual gender of their referred entity according to the grammatical context.

more entities, and complex coreferences. A model not good at coreference resolution becomes gender-biased when it relies on biased correlations to ascertain gender. Stanovsky et al. (2019) composed a challenge set called *WinoMT* for evaluating gender bias in NMT models. This set combined gender-balanced *Winogender* (Rudinger et al., 2018) and

WinoBias (Zhao et al., 2018) coreference test sets. However, since it is in English, using it for evaluating bias for other source languages is not possible. Therefore we contextualize this test set for the evaluation of bias in HI-EN Translation by manually creating "WinoMT-Hindi", which consists of 704 WinoBias-like sentences in Hindi, but modified to include gender cues of the language, mainly: gender-inflected adjectives, postpositions, and verbs.

Construction of "WinoMT-Hindi" is explained in Figure 2. Sample sentences are shown in Figure 3. In Winobias, only the English pronoun carries the gender of referenced entity, but here, to provide the gender of the referenced entity, we use gender-inflected verbs for Entity 1 and postpositions or adjectives for Entity 2. The phrase after the conjunction is gender-neutral, challenging the model to look for a more extended context. We only specify the gender of the referenced entity to avoid confusing the model with too much information.

We don't need reference translations in English, as automatic evaluation is possible. Due to the nature of our source sentences, we can mark the gender of the target by simply checking for the presence of male pronouns (he, him or his) or female pronouns (she or her) in the translation. Interestingly, we also observe that few sentences are translated into gender-neutral form. For example, the sentence: "सचिव मूवर से पूछता है कि वह मदद के लिए क्या करे" (Secretary asks mover what he should do to help) is translated as "The secretary asks the mover what to do to help" by Google Translate. While there is an increased interest in promoting Gender-Neutral translation for inclusivity (Piergentili et al., 2023), others call for gender preservation in translation (Cabrera and Niehues, 2023). The presence of neutral output sentences can be modelled as *false negatives* or *true positives* depending upon the goals of the evaluation. For this study, we model their presence as *false negatives* for male and female class, i.e. equivalent to misgendering sentences. Nonetheless, due to the limited fraction of such sentences, metrics largely reflect bias due to misgendering.

For gender bias evaluation, we use the metrics: *Acc*, Δ_G and Δ_S given by Stanovsky et al. (2019). For measuring the difference in F_1 score between male and female classes, i.e. Δ_G, we use class-wise F_1 score. We have divided our sentences into pro-stereotypical and anti-stereotypical sets using translated and transliterated versions of the occupations list by Zhao et al. (2018). This was done manually to ensure gender-neutrality of these occupation terms (and avoid their gender-inflected versions) in Hindi. To measure the difference in overall performance between pro-stereotypical and anti-stereotypical groups, i.e., Δ_S, we use *macro-F_1* score by averaging F_1 for male and female class only. We also report the percentage of sentences translated as gender-neutral, i.e. *N* for each NMT system.

	IT	GT	MS	AWS
S1	0.787	0.708	**0.724**	0.691
S2	0.620	0.534	0.394	0.656
S3	0.623	0.623	0.467	0.682
S4	0.569	0.531	0.574	0.411
S5	**0.819**	**0.763**	0.673	**0.803**
S6	**0.926***	**0.862***	**0.951***	**0.725**
S7	**0.848**	**0.788**	**0.720**	**0.845***
TGBI	0.742	0.687	0.643	0.688

Table 1: TGBI Evaluation of IndicTrans (IT), Google Translate (GT), Microsoft Translator (MS) and AWS Translate (AWS). The table contains the P values (higher is better) and their average, i.e. TGBI at the bottom. Bold represents the top three highest P values. * represent set with highest P value. The highlighted cell represents the highest TGBI value.

5 Results and Discussion

5.1 TGBI Evaluation

The results are shown in Table 1. For most translation systems, sentences in "Negative (S5)", "Polite (S6)" and "Positive (S7)" sets have higher P values. With the highest TGBI score, "IndicTrans" performs better at translating gender-neutral Hindi sentences into English with minimum gender bias. The problem with the TGBI metric is that it may not accurately capture the true fairness of an NMT system since evaluation is only done on gender-neutral sentences.

5.2 Evaluation using OTSC-Hindi

The results are shown in Table 2. Based on these results, the IndicTrans system shows heavy bias against the feminine gender. Even though it has the highest TGBI score, IndicTrans fails to use the given context to disambiguate the gender of occupation terms and gives "male default" for most

Sentence Set	IT		GT		MS		AWS	
	p_m	p_w	p_m	p_w	p_m	p_w	p_m	p_w
Female Speaker, Female Friend	**98.41**	1.59*	1.68	**98.32***	**98.97**	1.03*	**95.61**	4.39*
Female Speaker, Male Friend	**99.25***	0.75	**90.66***	9.34	**99.72***	0.28	**95.70***	4.30
Male Speaker, Female Friend	**99.35**	0.65*	2.43	**97.57***	**66.01**	33.99*	**99.29**	2.71*
Male Speaker, Male Friend	**99.91***	0.09	**96.45***	3.55	**98.60***	1.40	**97.48***	2.52

Table 2: Evaluation of IndicTrans(IT), Google Translate(GT), Microsoft Translator(MS) and AWS Translate(AWS) using the OTSC-Hindi test set. Here p_m and p_w are the percentage of sentences translated as male and female, respectively for the speaker's friend. $*$ corresponds to the percentage of sentences translated into the true label for each sentence set. Bold values indicate the maximum percentage of sentences translated into a single gender class.

	Acc	Δ_G	Δ_S	N
IndicTrans	48.9	48.5	-0.1$^\bullet$	6.2
Google Translate	69.0*	10.6$^\diamond$	-3.8	5.3
Microsoft Translator	57.7	32.9	0.2$^\bullet$	4.1
AWS Translate	49.9	51.9	-0.2$^\bullet$	2.8

Table 3: Comparison of performance of various NMT Models on WinoMT-Hindi on Acc, Δ_G, Δ_S and N (all in %) measures. $\star$ indicates significantly highest value, $\diamond$ indicates significantly lowest value, $\bullet$ indicates near about values for Acc, Δ_G and Δ_S, respectively.

of the translations. Similarly, Microsoft and AWS Translate systems also show bias against women by translating most of the sentences into their "male default" versions. Out of all the NMT models, Google Translate performs best at disambiguating gender from the given context. This shows that using such a set of sentences and extrinsic metrics, which take into account the gendered nature of the source sentence, is better at exposing the gender bias of an NMT system otherwise hidden by a metric such as TGBI.

5.3 Evaluation using WinoMT-Hindi

The results are shown in Table 3. Since *Acc* i.e. Accuracy should be high while Δ_G and Δ_S values should be low, Google Translate outperforms other models as being the least gender-biased model. IndicTrans and AWS Translate are heavily biased toward a particular gender. These models have lower *Acc* values (almost equal to the probability of a random guess, i.e. 50%) and higher Δ_G values indicating that the F_1 score for the male class is very large in comparison to the F_1 score for female.

We also observe that Δ_S values are very low for all NMT systems. There are two potential reasons. First, it is observed that these HI-EN NMT systems strongly prefer masculine outputs irrespective of occupation stereotypes. Hence they give the "masculine default" in most cases leading to a similar performance on pro-stereotypical and anti-stereotypical sentences. Another reason can be the poor contextualisation of occupation stereotype. We rely on stereotype labels provided by original English occupation lists by Zhao et al. (2018) to divide the occupations into pro-stereotypical and anti-stereotypical sets. However, these lists were based on data from US Department of Labor. This might not contextualise well for Hindi. Culturally relevant occupation related statistics is required for creating these stereotype labels for different occupations in Hindi which was difficult to obtain in our case.

However, WinoMT-Hindi provides a way to generalise and motivate the creation of such evaluation benchmarks for other languages.

6 Related Work

Many works have focused on evaluating gender translation accuracy by creating various benchmarks. **WinoMT** benchmark by Stanovsky et al. (2019) is widely used for gender bias evaluation. It contains sentences from WinoBias (Zhao et al., 2018) and Winogender (Rudinger et al., 2018) coreference test sets in English. Without reference translations, it devises an automatic translation evaluation method for eight diverse target languages.

Other benchmarks include **MuST-SHE** (Bentivogli et al., 2020), **GeBioCorpus** (Costa-jussà et al., 2020), **MT-GenEval** (Currey et al., 2022), **GATE** (Rarrick et al., 2023) etc. MT-GenEval provides gender-balanced, counterfactual sentences in eight language pairs with English as the source. Therefore, most of the benchmarks focus on English as the source language.

Bias evaluation of NMT models on source languages other than English has mainly focused on the translation of gender-neutral sentences. Cho et al. (2019) proposed *TGBI* measure to evaluate gender bias in the translation of gender-neutral Korean sentences to English. Ramesh et al. (2021) used TGBI measure for Hindi-English machine translation. Our work emphasises on creation of gender unambiguous evaluation benchmarks for source languages other than English by accounting for gender inflections in the language to test the model's ability to find these gender-related cues.

7 Conclusion and Future Work

To conclude our study, we highlighted the need for contextualising NMT bias evaluation for non-English source languages, especially for languages that capture gender-related information in different forms. We demonstrated this using Hindi as a source language by creating evaluation benchmarks for HI-EN Machine Translation and comparing various state-of-the-art translation systems. In future, we plan to extend our evaluation to more languages and use natural sentences for evaluation without following a particular template. We are also looking forward to developing evaluation methods that are more inclusive of all gender identities.

References

R.K. Agnihotri. 2007. *Hindi: An Essential Grammar*. Essential grammar. Routledge.

Luisa Bentivogli, Beatrice Savoldi, Matteo Negri, Mattia A. Di Gangi, Roldano Cattoni, and Marco Turchi. 2020. Gender in danger? evaluating speech translation technology on the MuST-SHE corpus. In *Proceedings of the 58th Annual Meeting of the Association for Computational Linguistics*, pages 6923–6933, Online. Association for Computational Linguistics.

Tolga Bolukbasi, Kai-Wei Chang, James Y. Zou, Venkatesh Saligrama, and Adam Tauman Kalai. 2016. Man is to computer programmer as woman is to homemaker? debiasing word embeddings. In *NIPS*.

Lena Cabrera and Jan Niehues. 2023. Gender lost in translation: How bridging the gap between languages affects gender bias in zero-shot multilingual translation.

Won Ik Cho, Ji Won Kim, Seok Min Kim, and Nam Soo Kim. 2019. On measuring gender bias in translation of gender-neutral pronouns. In *Proceedings of the First Workshop on Gender Bias in Natural Language Processing*, pages 173–181, Florence, Italy. Association for Computational Linguistics.

Marta R. Costa-jussà, Pau Li Lin, and Cristina España-Bonet. 2020. GeBioToolkit: Automatic extraction of gender-balanced multilingual corpus of Wikipedia biographies. In *Proceedings of the Twelfth Language Resources and Evaluation Conference*, pages 4081–4088, Marseille, France. European Language Resources Association.

Anna Currey, Maria Nadejde, Raghavendra Reddy Pappagari, Mia Mayer, Stanislas Lauly, Xing Niu, Benjamin Hsu, and Georgiana Dinu. 2022. MT-GenEval: A counterfactual and contextual dataset for evaluating gender accuracy in machine translation. In *Proceedings of the 2022 Conference on Empirical Methods in Natural Language Processing*, pages 4287–4299, Abu Dhabi, United Arab Emirates. Association for Computational Linguistics.

Joel Escudé Font and Marta R. Costa-jussà. 2019. Equalizing gender bias in neural machine translation with word embeddings techniques. In *Proceedings of the First Workshop on Gender Bias in Natural Language Processing*, pages 147–154, Florence, Italy. Association for Computational Linguistics.

Kaiji Lu, Piotr Mardziel, Fangjing Wu, Preetam Amancharla, and Anupam Datta. 2019. Gender bias in neural natural language processing.

Andrea Piergentili, Dennis Fucci, Beatrice Savoldi, Luisa Bentivogli, and Matteo Negri. 2023. Gender neutralization for an inclusive machine translation: from theoretical foundations to open challenges.

Marcelo O. R. Prates, Pedro H. C. Avelar, and Luis Lamb. 2019. Assessing gender bias in machine translation – a case study with google translate.

Gowtham Ramesh, Sumanth Doddapaneni, Aravinth Bheemaraj, Mayank Jobanputra, Raghavan AK, Ajitesh Sharma, Sujit Sahoo, Harshita Diddee, Mahalakshmi J, Divyanshu Kakwani, Navneet Kumar, Aswin Pradeep, Srihari Nagaraj, Kumar Deepak, Vivek Raghavan, Anoop Kunchukuttan, Pratyush Kumar, and Mitesh Shantadevi Khapra. 2022. Samanantar: The largest publicly available parallel corpora collection for 11 Indic languages. *Transactions of the Association for Computational Linguistics*, 10:145–162.

Krithika Ramesh, Gauri Gupta, and Sanjay Singh. 2021. Evaluating gender bias in Hindi-English machine translation. In *Proceedings of the 3rd Workshop on Gender Bias in Natural Language Processing*, pages 16–23, Online. Association for Computational Linguistics.

Spencer Rarrick, Ranjita Naik, Varun Mathur, Sundar Poudel, and Vishal Chowdhary. 2023. Gate: A challenge set for gender-ambiguous translation examples.

Rachel Rudinger, Chandler May, and Benjamin Van Durme. 2017. Social bias in elicited natural language inferences. In *Proceedings of the First ACL Workshop on Ethics in Natural Language Processing*, pages 74–79, Valencia, Spain. Association for Computational Linguistics.

Rachel Rudinger, Jason Naradowsky, Brian Leonard, and Benjamin Van Durme. 2018. Gender bias in coreference resolution. In *Proceedings of the 2018 Conference of the North American Chapter of the Association for Computational Linguistics: Human Language Technologies, Volume 2 (Short Papers)*, pages 8–14, New Orleans, Louisiana. Association for Computational Linguistics.

Danielle Saunders, Rosie Sallis, and Bill Byrne. 2020. Neural machine translation doesn't translate gender coreference right unless you make it. In *Proceedings of the Second Workshop on Gender Bias in Natural Language Processing*, pages 35–43, Barcelona, Spain (Online). Association for Computational Linguistics.

Beatrice Savoldi, Marco Gaido, Luisa Bentivogli, Matteo Negri, and Marco Turchi. 2021. Gender bias in machine translation. *Transactions of the Association for Computational Linguistics*, 9:845–874.

Gabriel Stanovsky, Noah A. Smith, and Luke Zettlemoyer. 2019. Evaluating gender bias in machine translation. In *Proceedings of the 57th Annual Meeting of the Association for Computational Linguistics*, pages 1679–1684, Florence, Italy. Association for Computational Linguistics.

Jieyu Zhao, Tianlu Wang, Mark Yatskar, Vicente Ordonez, and Kai-Wei Chang. 2017. Men also like shopping: Reducing gender bias amplification using corpus-level constraints. In *Proceedings of the 2017 Conference on Empirical Methods in Natural Language Processing*, pages 2979–2989, Copenhagen, Denmark. Association for Computational Linguistics.

Jieyu Zhao, Tianlu Wang, Mark Yatskar, Vicente Ordonez, and Kai-Wei Chang. 2018. Gender bias in coreference resolution: Evaluation and debiasing methods. In *Proceedings of the 2018 Conference of the North American Chapter of the Association for Computational Linguistics: Human Language Technologies, Volume 2 (Short Papers)*, pages 15–20, New Orleans, Louisiana. Association for Computational Linguistics.

Exploring Automatic Evaluation Methods based on a Decoder-based LLM for Text Generation

Tomohito Kasahara, Daisuke Kawahara
Waseda University
{tomo_k@ruri.,dkw@}waseda.jp

Abstract

Automatic evaluation of text generation is essential for improving the accuracy of generation tasks. In light of the current trend towards increasingly larger decoder-based language models, we investigate automatic evaluation methods based on such models for text generation. This paper compares various methods, including tuning with encoder-based models and large language models under equal conditions, on two different tasks, machine translation evaluation and semantic textual similarity, in two languages, Japanese and English. Experimental results show that compared to the tuned encoder-based models, the tuned decoder-based models perform poorly. The analysis of the causes for this suggests that the decoder-based models focus on surface word sequences and do not capture meaning. It is also revealed that in-context learning of very large decoder-based models such as ChatGPT makes it difficult to identify fine-grained semantic differences.

1 Introduction

Neural network-based text generation models are used in various natural language processing tasks, including machine translation, dialogue systems, and text summarization. However, the outputs from these models are open-ended, and there is no single correct answer, making the evaluation of generations difficult. Manual evaluation is often used due to its high accuracy but incurs significant temporal and financial costs. Therefore, automatic evaluation is essential for the rapid development of text generation models.

Automatic evaluation methods for text generation, such as BLEU (Papineni et al., 2002) and ROUGE (Lin, 2004), have been based mainly on surface word overlaps between the generated text and the reference text. In recent years, with the development of self-supervised models such as BERT (Devlin et al., 2019) and BART (Lewis et al., 2020), more accurate automatic evaluation methods have been proposed. For example, BERTScore (Zhang et al., 2020) uses word embeddings obtained by these models. Such methods can be classified along two axes: whether the model used is an encoder-based, decoder-based, or encoder-decoder-based architecture of Transformer (Vaswani et al., 2017), and whether tuning is performed. While encoder-based methods with tuning are reported to be highly accurate (Rei et al., 2020), in-context learning without tuning is the mainstream in decoder-based methods.

In recent years, self-supervised decoder-based models have become larger and larger, as seen in GPT-4 (OpenAI, 2023), Megatron-Turing (Smith et al., 2022), and PaLM (Chowdhery et al., 2022). These decoder-based self-supervised large language models are referred to as **LLMs** in this paper. However, encoder-based models have remained relatively smaller than decoder-based ones.

Based on the above situation, this paper compares various methods, including tuning with encoder-based models and LLMs under equal conditions, on two different tasks, machine translation evaluation and semantic textual similarity (STS), in two languages, Japanese and English. The results revealed the following three observations.

1. When a decoder-based model is tuned, the accuracy is proportional to the model size up to a certain model size, but it reaches a ceiling.
2. Compared to tuned encoder-based models, tuned decoder-based models perform poorly.
3. In-context learning of very large decoder-based models such as ChatGPT[1] makes it difficult to identify fine-grained semantic differences.

The analysis of the causes for the poor performance of the tuned decoder-based models suggests

[1] https://openai.com/chatgpt

Proceedings of the 13th International Joint Conference on Natural Language Processing and the 3rd Conference of the Asia-Pacific Chapter of the Association for Computational Linguistics: Student Research Workshop, pages 24–31
November 1–4, 2023.

that they focus on surface word sequences and do not capture meaning. Note that our study focuses on evaluation methods under the assumption that reference text is available.

2 Related Work

Automatic evaluation of text generation mainly requires the text generated by a model and the reference text. The classic automatic evaluation metrics, such as BLEU, ROUGE, METEOR (Banerjee and Lavie, 2005), and CIDEr (Vedantam et al., 2015), are based on the n-gram overlap between these two texts. The biggest disadvantage of these metrics is that they do not score well even when synonyms are included, as the n-grams must match exactly for a higher score. TER (Snover et al., 2006) and others that base their evaluation on edit distance have similar drawbacks. METEOR aims to overcome this drawback by using a synonym dictionary, but it is unable to perform context-sensitive synonym evaluation.

Using embeddings derived from self-supervised models, synonyms can be judged to be similar based on their context. BERTScore (Zhang et al., 2020) is a method that embeds the generated text and the reference text respectively by an encoder-based model and calculates a score based on their similarity. BARTScore (Yuan et al., 2021) and T5Score (Qin et al., 2022) input the source text to the encoder and the target text to the decoder, and calculate a score based on the generation probability of the target text. GPTScore (Fu et al., 2023) calculates a score based on the generation probability of the target text by applying in-context learning (Brown et al., 2020) to an LLM. G-Eval (Liu et al., 2023) proposes a method to have an LLM generate scores directly. In addition, Chen et al. (2023) show that directly generated scores are more accurate than generation probability-based ones when using LLMs.

Other evaluation methods increase accuracy by fine-tuning a self-supervised model using datasets consisting of text pairs and their similarity labels. Models trained on translation evaluation datasets include BLEURT (Sellam et al., 2020) and COMET (Rei et al., 2020), while models trained on STS datasets include Sentence-BERT (Reimers and Gurevych, 2019). There are also methods such as SimCSE (Gao et al., 2021) that learn sentence embeddings by contrastive learning on natural language inference datasets and use them to calculate text pair similarity. Most of these self-supervised methods use encoder-based models. InstructScore (Xu et al., 2023) is a method of fine-tuning LLaMA (Touvron et al., 2023). However, Xu et al. (2023)'s experiments did not involve tuned LLMs on the target datasets and did not compare them to encoder-based models under equal conditions. In this study, we compare LLMs, which do not have bidirectional attention but larger model size, with encoder-based models, which have bidirectional attention but smaller model size, by tuning them under equal conditions.

3 Experimental Setup

We compare various methods for text generation evaluation, including tuned encoder-based models and LLMs on equal conditions, on two different tasks, machine translation evaluation and STS, in two languages, Japanese and English.

3.1 Datasets

3.1.1 Datasets in English

For the experiments in English, we use WMT20 (Mathur et al., 2020) and WMT21 (Freitag et al., 2021) as the translation evaluation datasets, and STS-B (Cer et al., 2017) and SICK (Marelli et al., 2014) as the datasets for STS. WMT20 and WMT21 include human-translated texts, machine-translated texts, and their evaluation labels of Direct Assessment (DA) and Multidimensional Quality Metrics (MQM). In our experiments, we adopted the MQM labels that were evaluated by experts and native speakers. Since only the Chinese-to-English translation task is labeled with MQM, we use its datasets (WMT20 MQM and WMT21 MQM). STS and SICK consist of sentence pairs and their similarity labels. Note that for WMT20 and WMT21, the datasets were not pre-separated into train, valid, and test, and we randomly split these datasets with a ratio of 8:1:1.

3.1.2 Datasets in Japanese

The datasets used in the experiments in Japanese are the WMT20 English to Japanese translation task (WMT20 en-ja) and JSTS included in the Japanese General Language Understanding Evaluation (JGLUE) (Kurihara et al., 2022) benchmark. The WMT20 dataset includes human-translated texts, machine-translated texts, and their evaluation labels (Direct Assessment). JSTS is an STS dataset for Japanese, consisting of sentence pairs and their

Method	Model	Architecture	Size	WMT20	WMT21	STS-B	SICK
No-Tuning Methods							
BLEU	-	-	-	0.109	0.120	0.244	0.354
Edit Distance	-	-	-	0.345	0.340	0.089	0.278
BERTScore	RoBERTa-large	Encoder	355M	0.306	0.294	0.405	0.455
BARTScore CNN+Para	BART-large	Enc-Dec	406M	0.225	0.219	0.475	0.505
OpenAI Embeddings	text-embedding-ada-002	Encoder	?	0.184	0.181	0.655	0.627
ChatGPT Zero-Shot	gpt-3.5-turbo	Decoder	?	0.113	0.097	0.669	0.622
ChatGPT Few-Shot	gpt-3.5-turbo	Decoder	?	0.175	0.136	0.618	0.656
Tuning Methods (Not Target Dataset)							
BLEURT-20	RemBERT	Encoder	576M	0.345	0.323	0.620	0.574
InstructScore	LLaMA	Decoder	6.7B	0.439	0.345	0.471	0.526
Tuning Methods (Target Dataset)							
COMET (WMT21 MQM)	XLM-RoBERTa-large	Encoder	560M	0.506	0.362	–	–
RoBERTa Fine-Tuning	RoBERTa-large	Encoder	355M	**0.699**	**0.391**	**0.737**	**0.658**
LLM LoRA-Tuning	Cerebras-GPT	Decoder	111M	0.589	0.362	0.540	0.425
			256M	0.634	0.378	0.585	0.462
			590M	0.654	0.371	0.616	0.486
			1.3B	0.663	0.383	0.625	0.483
			2.7B	0.671	0.377	0.661	0.512
			6.7B	0.665	0.370	0.681	0.530

Table 1: Kendall's correlation coefficients between the predictions by the automatic evaluation metrics and the labels in the experiments in English.

similarity labels. Note that WMT20 en-ja was randomly split at a ratio of train:valid:test=8:1:1 as in the English datasets.

3.2 Tuning of LLMs

For the method by LLM tuning, we performed LoRA-tuning of LLMs using datasets of text pairs and their evaluation or similarity labels. We chose LoRA-tuning because it can achieve competitive accuracy with fine-tuning at a lower cost (Hu et al., 2021).

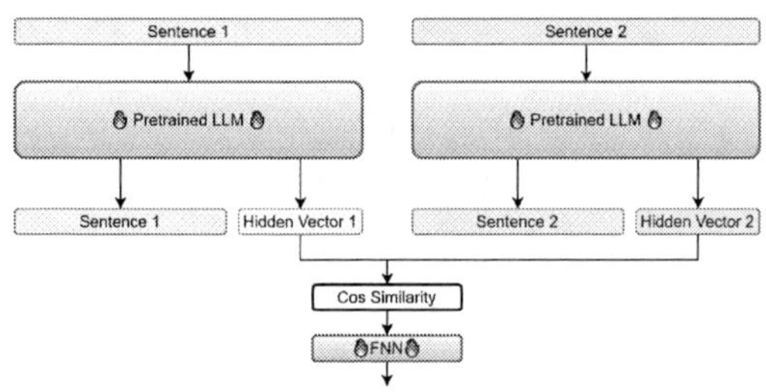

Figure 1: The architecture and input-output overview of the LLM's tuning.

3.2.1 Architecture and Input-Output Relationships

The architecture and input-output relationship of the LLM's tuning are shown in Figure 1. Given a text pair as an input to the model, their similarity value is returned as an output. The following procedure is used to calculate the similarity.

1. Feed each text of a text pair into an LLM.

2. Obtain the embedding corresponding to the token at the end of each text (the preceding token of the EOS token).

3. Calculate the cosine similarity between the two embeddings.

4. Pass the cosine similarity to a 1-layer FNN and regard its output as the similarity of the text pair.

The FNN layer is used to convert the cosine similarity values into a label distribution of the dataset. Based on the results of our preliminary experiments, we decided to use the embedding of the token at the end of a text instead of the special EOS token.

3.2.2 Training Method

The gold labels (similarity values) in the dataset are normalized between 0 and 1 in advance. We calculate the similarity of a text pair using the procedure described in Section 3.2.1. Next, only the parameters newly added to the model (including the parameters of the FNN) are updated based on the mean squared error between the predictions and the gold labels. Furthermore, the initial values of the FNN are set to 1 for weight and 0 for bias. We employ LoRA-tuning as the tuning method of the LLM for its high performance.

For experiments in English, we use the Cerebras-

Method	Model	Architecture	Size	WMT20	JSTS
No-Tuning Methods					
BLEU	-	-	-	0.226	0.353
Edit Distance	-	-	-	0.242	0.321
BERTScore	Waseda RoBERTa-large	Encoder	337M	0.319	0.558
OpenAI Embeddings	text-embedding-ada-002	Encoder	?	0.237	0.611
ChatGPT Zero-Shot	gpt-3.5-turbo	Decoder	?	0.187	0.709
ChatGPT Few-Shot	gpt-3.5-turbo	Decoder	?	0.205	0.690
Tuning Methods (Not Target Dataset)					
BLEURT-20	RemBERT	Encoder	576M	0.315	0.569
Tuning Methods (Target Dataset)					
RoBERTa Fine-Tuning	Waseda RoBERTa-large	Encoder	337M	**0.396**	**0.729**
LLM LoRA-Tuning	Rinna-gpt	Decoder	37M	0.342	0.600
			110M	0.378	0.644
			336M	**0.396**	0.677
			1.3B	0.370	0.659
			3.6B	0.380	0.687

Table 2: Kendall's correlation coefficients between the predictions by the automatic evaluation metrics and the labels in the experiments in Japanese.

GPT models[2] with parameter sizes ranging from 111M to 6.7B. These models are tuned on WMT20 MQM for the translation evaluation task and on STS-B for the STS tasks, respectively. In other words, the models trained with WMT20 MQM are evaluated on WMT20 MQM and WMT21 MQM, and the models trained with STS-B are evaluated on STS-B and SICK.

For experiments in Japanese, we use the GPT-2 and GPT-NeoX models developed by rinna[3], ranging from the 37M model to the 3.6B model. We trained models on each of the two datasets in Section 3.1.2.

3.3 Baselines

For comparison, we adopt the following baselines: BLEU, character edit distance, fine-tuned RoBERTa-large (Liu et al., 2019), BERTScore[4], BARTScore[5], OpenAI Embeddings (Neelakantan et al., 2022), in-context learning of ChatGPT (gpt-3.5-turbo), BLEURT[6], COMET[7] and InstructScore[8]. For fine-tuned RoBERTa, as described in Section 3.2.2, we trained models on WMT20 MQM and STS-B for the English experiments and on the two datasets shown in Section 3.1.2 for the Japanese experiments, respectively. For BERTScore, the training data is used to select the best output layer to obtain the embeddings. For OpenAI Embeddings, the scores are the cosine similarity of the obtained embeddings. The prompt used in ChatGPT's in-context learning is shown in Appendix A. We also had a preliminary experiment with in-context learning of Cerebras-GPT as well as ChatGPT, but were unable to generate scores successfully. It is assumed that the model size of few billion is too small for in-context learning. We do not tune BLEURT, but instead use BLEURT-20 (Pu et al., 2021), which is trained in multiple languages. For COMET, we use the model trained on WMT21 MQM. We do not apply COMET to the STS datasets because COMET is a metric for automatic translation evaluation and requires three inputs: pre-translated text, human-translated text, and machine-translated text. Our hyperparameters for training are shown in Appendix B.

Note that BARTScore, COMET, and InstructScore, only support English and hence are not used for experiments in Japanese.

4 Experimental Results and Analysis

4.1 Main Results

Kendall's correlation coefficients between the predictions by the automatic evaluation metrics and the gold labels in English and Japanese are shown in Tables 1 and 2, respectively. For all datasets in both languages, RoBERTa-large with fine-tuning achieved the highest accuracy. For LoRA-tuned LLMs, there is a tendency for the accuracy to be proportional to the model size up to a certain model size, but it reaches a ceiling. Also, even models with overwhelmingly larger parameter sizes than

[2] https://huggingface.co/cerebras
[3] https://huggingface.co/rinna
[4] https://github.com/Tiiiger/bert_score
[5] https://github.com/neulab/BARTScore
[6] https://github.com/google-research/bleurt
[7] https://unbabel.github.io/COMET
[8] https://github.com/xu1998hz/SEScore3

Model	Size	BLEU				Edit Distance			
		WMT20	WMT21	STS-B	SICK	WMT20	WMT21	STS-B	SICK
RoBERTa-large	355M	0.126	0.127	0.237	0.363	0.394	0.511	0.046	0.262
Cerebras-GPT	111M	0.213	0.212	0.281	0.553	0.491	0.612	0.077	0.491
	256M	0.192	0.216	0.292	0.553	0.455	0.615	0.081	0.486
	590M	0.187	0.211	0.268	0.559	0.432	0.583	0.087	0.487
	1.3B	0.175	0.225	0.277	0.545	0.425	0.574	0.096	0.483
	2.7B	0.178	0.231	0.263	0.549	0.428	0.567	0.058	0.478
	6.7B	0.181	0.205	0.259	0.552	0.441	0.522	0.068	0.472

Table 3: Kendall's correlations between the metrics based on superficial word sequences and the predictions by models with tuning in the experiments in English.

RoBERTa-large showed low accuracy. For ChatGPT's in-context learning, the accuracy on the STS datasets was comparable to that of the tuning-based methods, but its accuracy on the translation evaluation datasets was low. Note that most of the p-values were very close to 0.

4.2 Analysis of Why Tuned LLMs are Inferior

From Tables 1 and 2, we observe that LoRA-tuned LLMs, which have by far a larger number of parameters than RoBERTa-large, are inferior in terms of performance. We analyze the causes of this from the experimental results in English.

The most significant difference between the two models is that RoBERTa, an encoder-based model, has bidirectional attention, while an LLM has unidirectional attention. Here, we hypothesized that unidirectional attention focuses more on surface word sequences as opposed to bidirectional attention. To confirm this hypothesis, we calculated the correlations of the predictions of RoBERTa and LLMs to BLEU and character edit distance, which are the metrics based on superficial word sequences. The results are shown in Table 3. As hypothesized, the results show that the correlations to both BLEU and edit distance are stronger for LLMs than the encoder-based model. The fact that the correlation decreases as the model size increases in LLMs suggests that the larger the model size, the better the prediction is able to capture not only the surface word sequences but also the meaning of the text. However, even with a model size of 6.7B, the LLM is still not as accurate as RoBERTa.

4.3 Analysis of the Inability of ChatGPT's In-context Learning

While ChatGPT's in-context learning showed high accuracy on the STS datasets, it did not perform well on the translation evaluation datasets. We analyze the causes of this from the experimental results in English.

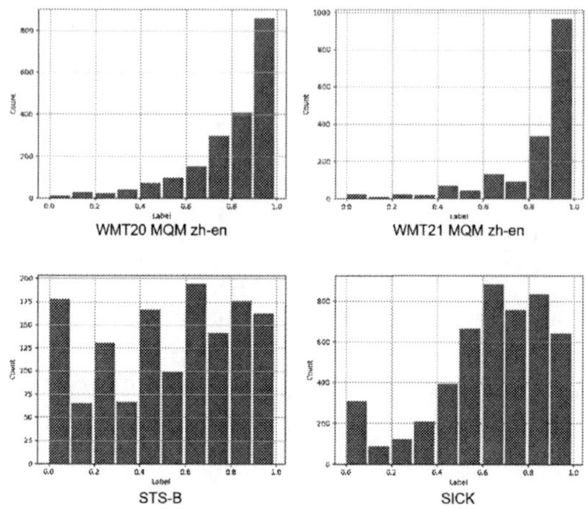

Figure 2: Label distribution of the test datasets used in the English experiments.

In our experiments, the prompts were created to score on a scale of 0 to 100. However, in the output scores, there were many cases where the last digit was 0 or 5 in both zero-shot and few-shot settings. Also, as shown in Figure 2, the label distributions of the translation evaluation datasets are skewed between 0.9 and 1.0, compared to the STS datasets, which have gently sloping distributions. Therefore, most of the predictions in the translation evaluation datasets are 95, etc., and this is thought to have caused the accuracy drop. Thus, it is clear that ChatGPT's in-context learning has difficulty in identifying fine-grained semantic differences.

5 Conclusion

In this paper, we compared various automatic evaluation methods for text generation in two languages, Japanese and English. We showed that fine-tuned encoder-based models are the strongest when training data is available, and in-context learning of ChatGPT is equally accurate when the variance of scores is large. Our analysis also revealed that tuned LLMs are less accurate than tuned encoder-based models because of their focus on surface word sequences.

Limitations

Our experiments assume the presence of a training dataset. If no dataset for training exists, refer to the results without the **Tuning Method (Target Dataset)** to compare the metrics in Tables 1 and 2.

Acknowledgements

This work was supported by a joint research grant from LINE Corporation.

References

Satanjeev Banerjee and Alon Lavie. 2005. METEOR: An automatic metric for MT evaluation with improved correlation with human judgments. In *Proceedings of the ACL Workshop on Intrinsic and Extrinsic Evaluation Measures for Machine Translation and/or Summarization*, pages 65–72, Ann Arbor, Michigan. Association for Computational Linguistics.

Tom Brown, Benjamin Mann, Nick Ryder, Melanie Subbiah, Jared D Kaplan, Prafulla Dhariwal, Arvind Neelakantan, Pranav Shyam, Girish Sastry, Amanda Askell, et al. 2020. Language models are few-shot learners. *NeurIPS2020*, 33:1877–1901.

Daniel Cer, Mona Diab, Eneko Agirre, Iñigo Lopez-Gazpio, and Lucia Specia. 2017. SemEval-2017 task 1: Semantic textual similarity multilingual and crosslingual focused evaluation. In *Proceedings of the 11th International Workshop on Semantic Evaluation (SemEval-2017)*, pages 1–14, Vancouver, Canada. Association for Computational Linguistics.

Yi Chen, Rui Wang, Haiyun Jiang, Shuming Shi, and Ruifeng Xu. 2023. Exploring the use of large language models for reference-free text quality evaluation: A preliminary empirical study. *arXiv preprint arXiv:2304.00723*.

Aakanksha Chowdhery, Sharan Narang, and Jacob Devlin et al. 2022. Palm: Scaling language modeling with pathways. arXiv. Abs/2204.02311.

Jacob Devlin, Ming-Wei Chang, Kenton Lee, and Kristina Toutanova. 2019. BERT: Pre-training of deep bidirectional transformers for language understanding. In *Proceedings of the 2019 Conference of the North American Chapter of the Association for Computational Linguistics: Human Language Technologies, Volume 1 (Long and Short Papers)*, pages 4171–4186, Minneapolis, Minnesota. Association for Computational Linguistics.

Markus Freitag, Ricardo Rei, Nitika Mathur, Chi-kiu Lo, Craig Stewart, George Foster, Alon Lavie, and Ondřej Bojar. 2021. Results of the WMT21 metrics shared task: Evaluating metrics with expert-based human evaluations on TED and news domain. In *Proceedings of the Sixth Conference on Machine Translation*, pages 733–774, Online. Association for Computational Linguistics.

Jinlan Fu, See-Kiong Ng, Zhengbao Jiang, and Pengfei Liu. 2023. Gptscore: Evaluate as you desire. *arXiv preprint arXiv:2302.04166*.

Tianyu Gao, Xingcheng Yao, and Danqi Chen. 2021. SimCSE: Simple contrastive learning of sentence embeddings. In *Proceedings of the 2021 Conference on Empirical Methods in Natural Language Processing*, pages 6894–6910, Online and Punta Cana, Dominican Republic. Association for Computational Linguistics.

Edward J Hu, Yelong Shen, Phillip Wallis, Zeyuan Allen-Zhu, Yuanzhi Li, Shean Wang, Lu Wang, and Weizhu Chen. 2021. Lora: Low-rank adaptation of large language models. arXiv. Abs/2106.09685.

Kentaro Kurihara, Daisuke Kawahara, and Tomohide Shibata. 2022. JGLUE: Japanese general language understanding evaluation. In *LREC2022*, pages 2957–2966, Marseille, France. European Language Resources Association.

Mike Lewis, Yinhan Liu, Naman Goyal, Marjan Ghazvininejad, Abdelrahman Mohamed, Omer Levy, Veselin Stoyanov, and Luke Zettlemoyer. 2020. BART: Denoising sequence-to-sequence pre-training for natural language generation, translation, and comprehension. In *Proceedings of the 58th Annual Meeting of the Association for Computational Linguistics*, pages 7871–7880, Online. Association for Computational Linguistics.

Chin-Yew Lin. 2004. ROUGE: A package for automatic evaluation of summaries. In *Text Summarization Branches Out*, pages 74–81, Barcelona, Spain. Association for Computational Linguistics.

Yang Liu, Dan Iter, Yichong Xu, Shuohang Wang, Ruochen Xu, and Chenguang Zhu. 2023. Gpteval: Nlg evaluation using gpt-4 with better human alignment. *arXiv preprint arXiv:2303.16634*.

Yinhan Liu, Myle Ott, Naman Goyal, Jingfei Du, Mandar Joshi, Danqi Chen, Omer Levy, Mike Lewis, Luke Zettlemoyer, and Veselin Stoyanov. 2019. Roberta: A robustly optimized bert pretraining approach. arXiv. Abs/1907.11692.

Marco Marelli, Stefano Menini, Marco Baroni, Luisa Bentivogli, Raffaella Bernardi, and Roberto Zamparelli. 2014. A SICK cure for the evaluation of compositional distributional semantic models. In *Proceedings of the Ninth International Conference on Language Resources and Evaluation (LREC'14)*, pages 216–223, Reykjavik, Iceland. European Language Resources Association (ELRA).

Nitika Mathur, Johnny Wei, Markus Freitag, Qingsong Ma, and Ondřej Bojar. 2020. Results of the WMT20 metrics shared task. In *Proceedings of the Fifth Conference on Machine Translation*, pages 688–725, Online. Association for Computational Linguistics.

Arvind Neelakantan, Tao Xu, Raul Puri, Alec Radford, Jesse Michael Han, Jerry Tworek, Qiming Yuan, Nikolas Tezak, Jong Wook Kim, Chris Hallacy, et al. 2022. Text and code embeddings by contrastive pretraining. *arXiv preprint arXiv:2201.10005*.

OpenAI. 2023. Gpt-4 technical report.

Kishore Papineni, Salim Roukos, Todd Ward, and Wei-Jing Zhu. 2002. Bleu: a method for automatic evaluation of machine translation. In *Proceedings of the 40th Annual Meeting of the Association for Computational Linguistics*, pages 311–318, Philadelphia, Pennsylvania, USA. Association for Computational Linguistics.

Amy Pu, Hyung Won Chung, Ankur Parikh, Sebastian Gehrmann, and Thibault Sellam. 2021. Learning compact metrics for MT. In *Proceedings of the 2021 Conference on Empirical Methods in Natural Language Processing*, pages 751–762, Online and Punta Cana, Dominican Republic. Association for Computational Linguistics.

Yiwei Qin, Weizhe Yuan, Graham Neubig, and Pengfei Liu. 2022. T5score: Discriminative fine-tuning of generative evaluation metrics. *arXiv preprint arXiv:2212.05726*.

Ricardo Rei, Craig Stewart, Ana C Farinha, and Alon Lavie. 2020. COMET: A neural framework for MT evaluation. In *Proceedings of the 2020 Conference on Empirical Methods in Natural Language Processing (EMNLP)*, pages 2685–2702, Online. Association for Computational Linguistics.

Nils Reimers and Iryna Gurevych. 2019. Sentence-BERT: Sentence embeddings using Siamese BERT-networks. In *Proceedings of the 2019 Conference on Empirical Methods in Natural Language Processing and the 9th International Joint Conference on Natural Language Processing (EMNLP-IJCNLP)*, pages 3982–3992, Hong Kong, China. Association for Computational Linguistics.

Thibault Sellam, Dipanjan Das, and Ankur Parikh. 2020. BLEURT: Learning robust metrics for text generation. In *Proceedings of the 58th Annual Meeting of the Association for Computational Linguistics*, pages 7881–7892, Online. Association for Computational Linguistics.

Shaden Smith, Mostofa Patwary, Brandon Norick, Patrick LeGresley, Samyam Rajbhandari, Jared Casper, Zhun Liu, Shrimai Prabhumoye, George Zerveas, Vijay Korthikanti, et al. 2022. Using deepspeed and megatron to train megatron-turing nlg 530b, a large-scale generative language model. arXiv. Abs/2201.11990.

Matthew Snover, Bonnie Dorr, Rich Schwartz, Linnea Micciulla, and John Makhoul. 2006. A study of translation edit rate with targeted human annotation. In *Proceedings of the 7th Conference of the Association for Machine Translation in the Americas: Technical Papers*, pages 223–231, Cambridge, Massachusetts, USA. Association for Machine Translation in the Americas.

Hugo Touvron, Thibaut Lavril, Gautier Izacard, Xavier Martinet, Marie-Anne Lachaux, Timothée Lacroix, Baptiste Rozière, Naman Goyal, Eric Hambro, Faisal Azhar, et al. 2023. Llama: Open and efficient foundation language models. *arXiv preprint arXiv:2302.13971*.

Ashish Vaswani, Noam Shazeer, Niki Parmar, Jakob Uszkoreit, Llion Jones, Aidan N Gomez, Łukasz Kaiser, and Illia Polosukhin. 2017. Attention is all you need. *NeurIPS2017*.

Ramakrishna Vedantam, C Lawrence Zitnick, and Devi Parikh. 2015. Cider: Consensus-based image description evaluation. In *Proceedings of the IEEE conference on computer vision and pattern recognition*, pages 4566–4575.

Wenda Xu, Danqing Wang, Liangming Pan, Zhenqiao Song, Markus Freitag, William Yang Wang, and Lei Li. 2023. Instructscore: Towards explainable text generation evaluation with automatic feedback. *arXiv preprint arXiv:2305.14282*.

Weizhe Yuan, Graham Neubig, and Pengfei Liu. 2021. Bartscore: Evaluating generated text as text generation. *NeurIPS2021*, 34:27263–27277.

Tianyi Zhang, Varsha Kishore, Felix Wu, Kilian Q Weinberger, and Yoav Artzi. 2020. Bertscore: Evaluating text generation with bert. *ICLR2020*.

A Prompt Used in Experiments with ChatGPT

The following text is an example of the prompt used in our experiments with ChatGPT, which was created by referring to the prompt used in Chen et al. (2023)'s experiments.

```
Score the following text pair on a continual scale from 0 (worst) to 100 (best), where score of 0 means "the meaning of the text pair is completely different" and score of 100 means "the meaning of the text pair is completely identical".

Text 1: There is no boy playing outdoors and there is no man smiling

Text 2: A group of kids is playing in a yard and an old man is standing in the background

Score:
```

B Hyperparameters

The hyperparameters that we used for training models in our experiments are shown in Table 4. Note that the GPU used in our experiments is the NVIDIA A100 SXM4 GPU with a GPU memory size of 40 GB.

Hyperparameters	RoBERTa Fine-Tuning	LLM LoRA-Tuning
Learning Rate	2e-5	2e-4, 1e-4, 5e-5, 1e-5
Epoch Num	10	10
LoRA Dim	-	4
LoRA Alpha	-	32
LoRA Dropout	-	0.1

Table 4: Hyperparameters for training in the experiments.

Style-sensitive Sentence Embeddings for Evaluating Similarity in Speech Style of Japanese Sentences by Contrastive Learning

Yuki Zenimoto **Shinzan Komata** **Takehito Utsuro**
Degree Programs in Systems and Information Engineering,
Graduate School of Science and Technology, University of Tsukuba
{s2220753, s2320742}_@_u.tsukuba.ac.jp
utsuro_@_iit.tsukuba.ac.jp

Abstract

Since dialogue systems are required to keep its speech style consistency, evaluating the similarity of speech styles is an important task. However, the Japanese language has a wide variety of speech styles, and also for each speech style, huge variety of vocabulary and word usage characteristics are observed, making it difficult to evaluate the similarity of speech styles. This study proposes a speech style embedding model that produces a style-sensitive sentence embedding of Japanese sentences. The speech style embedding model is constructed by fine-tuning a pre-trained BERT model. Here, sentence pairs with similar/dissimilar speech styles are automatically collected on a large scale using a sequence of sentences in web novels, with which constrastive learning is performed for the training of the speech style embedding model. Using the Ward's hierarchical clustering method, we also analyze the clusters of speech styles and the characteristic vocabulary/word usage of each speech style. Finally, we focus on the variation in speech styles of each person depending on the situation, and further analyze the variation in style-sensitive embeddings of each character in the novel.

1 Introduction

The speech style of a dialogue system plays a crucial role in user interaction, and dialogue systems are expected to keep its speech style consistency (Zhou et al., 2020). Therefore, a mechanism for evaluating the similarity of speech styles across entire utterances is necessary. However, the Japanese language has a diverse range of speech styles (Kinsui, 2003; Akama et al., 2018), and a vast variety of characteristic expressions exist for each speech style, making it difficult to evaluate the similarity of speech styles across entire utterances.

In this study, we propose a simple speech style sentence embedding method, which can produce embeddings capable of evaluating the similarity of speech styles by fine-tuning a pre-trained BERT model (Devlin et al., 2019) using contrastive learning (Gao et al., 2021). The training dataset consists of positive instances collected from pairs of utterances estimated to be by an identical character and negative instances from pairs of utterances estimated to be by distinct characters. This data collection method is based on the observation that the utterances by an identical character have a consistent speech style, whereas those from different characters have distinct speech styles. Through this training, it is expected that the embeddings can be obtained for evaluating the similarity of speech styles rather than the content similarity of sentences. Furthermore, we revealed characteristic words of various speech styles through unsupervised clustering of style-sensitive sentence embeddings. Finally, we focused on utterances by specific characters within a novel and conducted an analysis of variations in the speech styles of an identical character.

The results contribute to confirming the following insights:

1. The consecutive utterances in novels are effective in training the embeddings of speech style by the proposed approach using contrastive learning.
2. The style-sensitive sentence embeddings correctly capture various speech styles including those representing politeness, gender, and typical fictional character.
3. Even for an identical character, the speech style can vary significantly depending on conversation partners and surrounding situations, where this variation in speech styles constitutes the characteristic of the character.

Proceedings of the 13th International Joint Conference on Natural Language Processing and the 3rd Conference of the Asia-Pacific Chapter of the Association for Computational Linguistics: Student Research Workshop, pages 32–39
November 1–4, 2023.

2 Related Work

Numerous prior studies have targeted English speech styles, investigating various aspects such as politeness (Rao and Tetreault, 2018; Danescu-Niculescu-Mizil et al., 2013) and sarcasm (Khodak et al., 2018). Previous research has been conducted on a diverse range of speech styles, and datasets have also been constructed. In contrast to previous research, Kang and Hovy (2021) proposed a novel approach to comprehensively grasping the phenomenon of cross-stylistic language variation. The primary emphasis lies in examining the interdependence of diverse styles within written text, elucidating the interplay between these styles, and systematically deconstructing their composition in text generation.

Japanese speech styles rely on various characteristics of the entire sentence, such as first-person pronouns and sentence-ending expressions (Kinsui, 2003; Matsuyoshi et al., 2006; Miyazaki et al., 2016). Consequently, it is desirable to evaluate the similarity of speech styles across an entire sentence. Akama et al. (2018) proposed an unsupervised learning method of style-sensitive word vector that evaluates the similarity of speech styles. However, Akama's method focuses on the speech style of individual words and does not evaluate the similarity of speech styles across an entire sentence. To evaluate the similarity of speech styles across an entire sentence, Miyazaki et al. (2021a); Zenimoto and Utsuro (2022) proposed a method that utilizes a speech style classification model built with training data containing sentences in specific speech styles. However, these methods are not adaptable to the speech styles of unknown characters. In contrast, our method can be adapted to the speech styles of unknown characters. Furthermore, prior researches utilize undisclosed datasets for training and evaluation, making it difficult to conduct comparative experiments.

3 Japanese Speech Style

This section describes the characteristics of Japanese speech styles, which the proposed model are expected to capture. In the Japanese language, first-person pronouns, particles, and auxiliary verbs in utterances differ depending on the speaker's trait, such as gender, age, and role (Kinsui, 2003; Matsuyoshi et al., 2006; Miyazaki et al., 2016). For example, the utterance "俺はこれが好きだぜ (I like it)" is reminiscent of a masculine person because the characteristic words "俺 (I)" and "だぜ (*daze*)" are used predominantly by males. In contrast, the utterance "私はこれが好きですわ (I like it)", which has the same meaning as the utterance "俺はこれが好きだぜ (I like it)", is reminiscent of a female person because the characteristic words "私 (I)" and "ですわ (*desuwa*)" are used predominantly by females. As mentioned above, the Japanese language has numerous expressions that, while conveying the same meaning, are reminiscent of significantly different persons. The proposed model is expected to capture the speech style of utterances that elicit such specific personal associations.

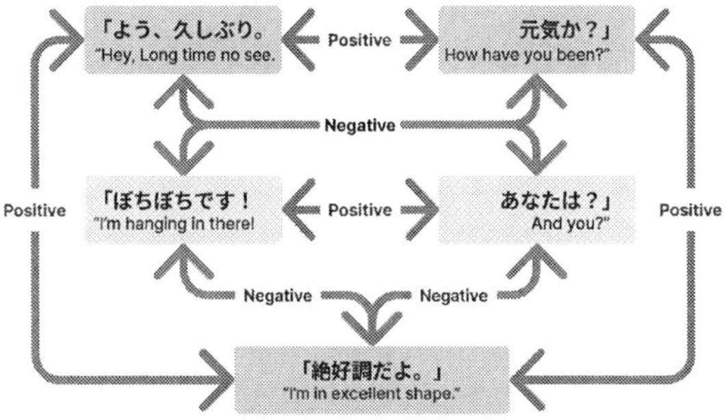

Figure 1: Procedures of Creating Positive and Negative Instances from Consecutive Utterances ("Positive" indicates the pairs of utterances estimated to be by an identical character. "Negative" indicates the pairs of utterances estimated to be by distinct characters.)

Data type	Positive	Negative	Total
Training	51.3M	53.2M	105M
Validation	259K	269K	528K
Test	259K	269K	528K
Total	51.8M	53.8M	105M

Table 1: Statistics of Experimental Data

4 Dataset Construction

4.1 The Procedure

For the training of speech style embedding model using contrastive learning, it is required to prepare pairs of sentences with similar speech styles as positive instances and pairs of sentences with dissimilar speech styles as negative instances. This study proposes a method to automatically collect a large amount of positive and negative instances from consecutive utterances in novels. In general, speakers alternate in consecutive utterances in novels. Therefore, in consecutive utterances, the following pairs of sentences can be considered as positive and negative instances:

Positive instance 1 Pairs of the n-th and n+2-th utterances in consecutive utterances.

Positive instance 2 Pairs of sentences in an utterance obtained by splitting an utterance with specific symbols ("!", "?" and "。").

Negative instance Pairs of the n-th and n+1-th utterances in consecutive utterances.

Figure 1 shows examples of positive and negative instances. As the resource for the dataset, we collected about 9,000 novels published on the novel posting site called "小説家になろう (Aim to be a novelist)"[1], and collected approximately 50 million pairs of positive and negative instances. Of this total of approximately 100 million pairs dataset, 99% is used as training data, and the remaining 0.5% each as validation and test data. The statistics of positive and negative instances are shown in Table 1.

4.2 Evaluation of the Dataset

To verify the correctness of the automatically collected positive and negative instances, we manually annotated the 5-level scale of similarity grade from -2 to 2 to each of randomly selected utterance pairs (250 pairs each)[2]. Table 2 shows that 62.4% of the automatically collected positive instances correctly have *similar* (i.e., the grades of 2 and 1) speech styles, while 58.8% of the negative instances correctly have *dissimilar* (i.e., the grades of -2 and -1) speech styles. When we consider the pairs of the similarity grade 0 as correct instances, the proportion of data that can be properly used for the training exceeds 70% for both positive and negative instances, indicating that these automatically collected data are sufficiently useful for constructing a speech style embedding model. The inter-annotator agreement of the annotation was evaluated using the Quadratic Weighted Kappa (QWK) score (Cohen, 1968), which ranges from 0 to 1, with a higher value indicating better agreement. Our annotation achieved a QWK score of 0.763, suggesting that there were no significant disagreement between the two annotators.

[1] https://syosetu.com/

[2] The annotation work was done by the first and second authors, where each pair is annotated with "—" when either of the two sentences is not an utterance, but an emphasis or a quotation.

sim. grade	Comparison with それは安心ね / sore wa anshin ne / That's a relief (female speech style)	avg. sim. grade of two annotators	ratio (%)	
			pos.	neg.
2	The two sentences are completely with an equivalent speech style, containing identical characteristic words. すごいわね / sugoi wa **ne** / That's great (female speech style)	2.0, 1.5	34.8	12.4
1	The two sentences are with an equivalent speech style, but containing distinct characteristic words. どうかしら / do **kashira** / I'm not sure (female speech style)	1.0, 0.5	27.6	12.4
0	Either of the two sentences is an utterance that could be uttered by anyone. それは... / sore wa / That is ... (common speech style)	0	15.6	14.4
-1	The two sentences are not equivalent speech style, but are utterances that could be used by an identical person in some situations. すごいよ / sugoi **yo** / It's great (kind male speech style)	−0.5, −1.0	7.2	18.0
-2	The two sentences are completely dissimilar. 俺の版だぜ / ore no ban **daze** / It's my turn (masculine speech style)	−1.5, −2.0	7.2	40.8
—	Either of the two sentences is not an utterance, but an emphasis or a quotation. 洞窟 / dokutsu / The Cave	—	4.8	2.0

Table 2: Evaluation of Automatically Collected Positive/Negative Instances

5 Speech Style Embedding Model

5.1 Model Configuration

For the construction of the speech style embedding model, we utilize the Sentence-BERT architecture (Reimers and Gurevych, 2019), and Tohoku University's Japanese version of BERT-base[3] as pre-trained BERT model. The batch size is set to 128 sentences, and the maximum input token length is set to 64 tokens. The utilized loss function is defined by the Contrastive Loss equation (Hadsell et al., 2006) as presented below:

$$L = \frac{1}{2} Y D^2 + (1 - Y) \max(margin - D, 0)^2$$

Here, Y represents the label where 1 indicates a positive instance and 0 indicates a negative instance. Following (Gao et al., 2021), we use D as the cosine distance between the two utterances of positive/negative instances, and the $margin$ is set to 1. Through this training process, we anticipate that the speech style of the input utterance will be embedded in the 768-dimensional output vector for the CLS token of the speech style embedding model.

[3] https://github.com/cl-tohoku/bert-japanese

Target Utterance	Example Utterances to Compare Similarities	Similarity
(1) 俺はこれが好きだぜ / *ore wa kore ga suki* ***da ze*** / I like it / (a masculine speech style utterance)	いいじゃねえの / *ii* ***ja ne no*** / That's good, isn't it? / (masculine)	0.839
	ちょうどよかったぜ / *cho do yokatta* ***ze*** / Just in time / (masculine)	0.770
	すごいだろ！ / *sugoi* ***da ro*** / It's great! / (masculine)	0.502
	すごいだろ? / *sugoi* ***da ro*** / It's great? / (masculine)	0.390
	すごいだろ... / *sugoi* ***da ro*** / It's great... / (masculine)	0.367
	すごいだろ / *sugoi* ***da ro*** / It's great / (masculine)	0.345
(2) どういたしましょうか / *do* ***itashi masyo ka*** / what should I do? / (a strong polite speech style utterance reminiscent of a maid or servant)	いかがしますか / ***ikaga shimasu ka*** / What would you like? / (strong polite)	0.924
	申し訳ありません / ***moshi wake ari mase n*** / I'm so sorry / (strong polite)	0.830
	お願い致します / *onegai* ***itashi masu*** / I'm begging you / (strong polite)	0.456
	お願いします / *onegai* ***shi masu*** / I'm begging you / (polite)	0.480
	お願いだよ / *onegai* ***da yo*** / I'm begging you / (casual)	-0.514
	田中様 / *tanaka* ***sama*** / Mr.Tanaka / (strong polite)	0.844
	田中殿 / *tanaka* ***dono*** / Mr.Tanaka / (classical polite)	0.536
	田中 / tanaka / *Tanaka* / (informal)	-0.116
(3) ふなっしーはこれが好きなっしー / *funassyi wa kore ga suki* ***nassyi*** / I like it / (a speech style used only by the fictional mascot character "ふなっしー (Funassyi)"	お疲れ様なっしー / *otsukare sama* ***nassyi*** / You must be tired / (Funassyi)	0.758
	よろしくなっしなー / *yoroshiku* ***nassyina*** / Nice to meet you / (Funassyi)	0.451
	危なかったー / *abuna katta* / That was close / (childish)	0.756
	誰だろー / *dare daro* / I wonder who it is / (childish)	0.670
	私はこれが好きです / *watashi wa kore ga suki* ***desu*** / I like it / (formal)	0.259
	俺はこれが好きだぜ / *ore wa kore ga suki* ***daze*** / I like it / (masculine)	0.096
	儂はこれが好きなんじゃ / *watashi wa kore ga suki* ***desu*** / I like it / (classical)	0.039

Table 3: Examples of Comparing Speech Style Similarities

5.2 Dimensionality Reduction

Using 768-dimensional vectors directly as style-sensitive sentence embeddings could be considered excessive in terms of the complexity of speech styles. Therefore, we attempt to convert them into smaller-dimensional vectors through dimensionality reduction using Principal Component Analysis (PCA).

The result of PCA shows that the cumulative proportion exceeds 99.8% with the first 32 principal components, indicating that 32 dimensions are sufficient to retain speech style information. Consequently, we treat the vectors with their dimensionality reduced to 32 dimensions as the final style-sensitive sentence embedding.

6 Analysis of Style-sensitive Sentence Embeddings

6.1 Comparison of Similar Utterances

We verify whether the speech style embedding model appropriately captures speech style expressions. Table 3 shows examples of comparing speech style similarities. In the comparison between (1) a masculine speech style utterance "俺はこれが好きだぜ (I like this)" and other utterances, it can be seen that the similarities with other masculine speech style utterances such as with "ねえの (*ne no*)" and "よかったぜ (*yokatta ze*)" are appropriately high. Moreover, it is evident that the similarity varies significantly depending on the specific symbols ("!", "?", and "···"). Furthermore, in the comparison between (2) a strong polite speech style utterance reminiscent of a maid or servant "どういたしましょうか (What should I do?)" and other utterances, it can be seen that the similarities are higher with utterances containing strong polite expressions like "致します (*itashi masu*)" and "様 (*sama*)" whereas they decrease significantly for casual speech styles and utterances without honorifics. These results indicate that the speech style embedding model can effectively distinguish distinct speech styles and understand various nuances in the Japanese language.

Finally, we conduct a comparison between (3) a unique speech style utterance "ふなっしーはこれが好きなっしー (I like this)" and other utterances. This speech style is used only by the fictional mascot character "ふなっしー (Funassy)"[4]. This character, "ふなっしー (Funassy)" usually appends words such as "なっしー (*nassyi*)" or its variant "なっしなー (*nassyina*)" at the end of sentences. From the comparison results, the similarity with the utterances ending with "なっしー (*nassyi*)" is appropriately high, and the utterances with distinctly different speech styles, such as the formal speech style "私はこれが好きです (I like this)" or the masculine speech style "俺はこれが好きだぜ (I like this)", are appropriately low. It is important to note that the training data does not include the speech style of "ふなっしー (Funassy)", suggesting that the speech style embeddings model can

[4] https://274ch.com/

ID speech style	Top 5 bi-grams by tf-idf
46 housemaid	(ました / *mashi ta*), (んです / *n desu*) (ません / *mase n*), (のです / *no desu*) (して / *shi te*)
35 ninja	(でござる / *de gozaru*), (ござるよ / *gozaru yo*) (とは / *to wa*), (ですな / *desu na*) (ござるか / *gozaru ka*)
31 boss	(ように / *yo ni*), (して / *shi te*) (ている / *te iru*), (だから / *da kara*) (しなさい / *shi nasai*)
12 king	(ておる / *te oru*), (して / *shi te*) (では / *de wa*), (ている / *te iru*) (お主 / *o nushi*)
13 female	(のよ / *no yo*), (わよ / *wa yo*) (して / *shi te*), (ないわ / *nai wa*) (たの / *ta no*)
33 masculine	(んだ / *n da*), (か？ / *ka ?*) (のか / *no ka*), (ぜ！ / *ze !*) (だぜ / *da ze*)
10 cat	(にゃ！ / *nya !*), (にゃ？ / *nya ?*) (たにゃ / *ta nya*), (かにゃ / *ka nya*) (によ / *ni yo*)
22 kind male	(だね / *da ne*), (かい？ / *kai ?*) (んだ / *n da*), (だよ / *da yo*) (のかい / *no kai*)

Table 4: Example Clusters and their Characteristic Expressions

correctly evaluate unknown speech styles. However, the similarity with the utterance containing "なっしなー (*nassyina*)" as well as with the variant of "なっしー (*nassyi*)" is incorrectly low, suggesting that the speech style embeddings model cannot correctly evaluate the variant of unknown speech styles. In addition, the similarity with the different speech style utterance containing only a prolonged sound "ー" at the end of sentence is incorrectly high. While the model can correctly identify and evaluate distinct speech styles, there is room for improvement in capturing the variants of unknown speech styles.

6.2 Analyzing Speech Styles through Clustering

To analyze the clusters of speech styles and their characteristics, we conduct clustering on approximately 820,000 unique utterances in the test data, which have been converted into style-sensitive sentence embeddings. To analyze the clustering process, we attempt hierarchical clustering using the Ward's method (Ward Jr., 1963). Due to computational limitation, it is not feasible to cluster all 820,000 style-sensitive sentence embeddings using the Ward's method, so we first classify them into 10,000 clusters using the k-means method, and then cluster the centroid vectors of k-means clusters using the Ward's method[5].

Figure 2 shows the dendrogram of the uppermost 50 clusters in the Ward's method clustering results. Next, we extract bi-grams for each sentence within a cluster and calculate their tf-idf values. Then, we extract the top-5 bi-grams with the highest tf-idf values as the characteristic expressions of each cluster. Table 4 shows the characteristic expressions for the sample 8 clusters. From Figure 2 and Table 4, it is evident that various interesting clusters are observed, such as "masculine" speech styles, "housemaid" speech styles, and "cat" speech styles. In the cluster "ID=33", expressions like "んだ (*n da*)" and "だぜ (*da ze*)" are ranked at the top, suggesting that "masculine" speech styles are grouped together. On the other hand, clusters around "ID=26" and "ID=21" also contain "masculine" speech styles, indicating that the utterances with closely related speech styles distributed in distinct clusters. Furthermore, within the clusters grouped together around "boss" ("ID=31") speech styles, there are clusters of more unique "king" speech styles that use expressions like "ておる (*te oru*)" and "お主 (*o nushi*)". Therefore, it is observed that, while the expressions that should ideally be in an identical cluster are somehow closely distributed but still dispersed, clusters that should be farther apart are relatively close together. In order to handle these issues, it is necessary to devise ways to lower the similarity between different speech styles during the learning process or to remove wrong data from the training data.

7 Analysis of Variation in Speech Styles of an Identical Character

It can be assumed that even for an identical person, their speech style may change depending on conversation partners and surrounding situations. Therefore, we analyze the variation in speech styles embeddings of the utterances of three main characters in a romance novel[6] published on "小説家になろう (Aim to be a novelist)". Table 5 shows the character names, speech styles, and number of utterances of the three characters.

Figure 3 shows the scatter plot of the first

[5]While our style-sensitive embeddings are based on cosine distance, the k-means and the Ward' methods use euclidean distance. Therefore, we normalized the speech style embeddings prior to the application of k-means and Ward's methods.

[6]`https://ncode.syosetu.com/n1860fv/`

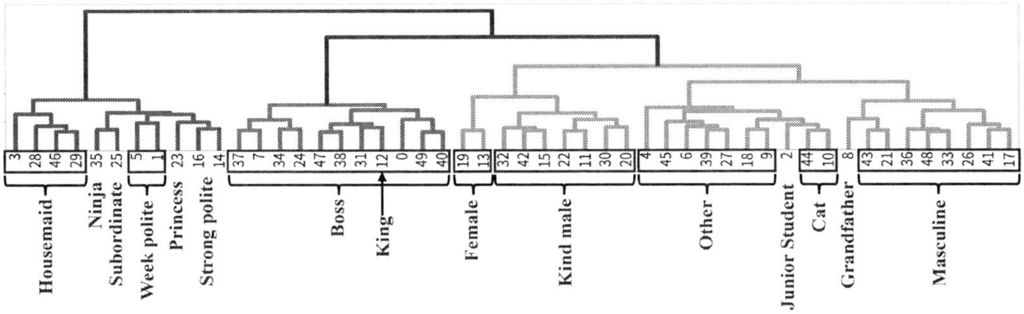

Figure 2: Dendrogram of the Results of Clustering Speech Style Vectors using the Ward's Method.

Character (traits)	Speech Style	#Utterance
Marie (aristocratic woman)	casual female, polite	1,177
Kyuros (aristocratic man)	only male	1,030
Mio (housemaid)	only housemaid	450

Table 5: Speech Style and Number of Utterances of the Three Characters in a Novel

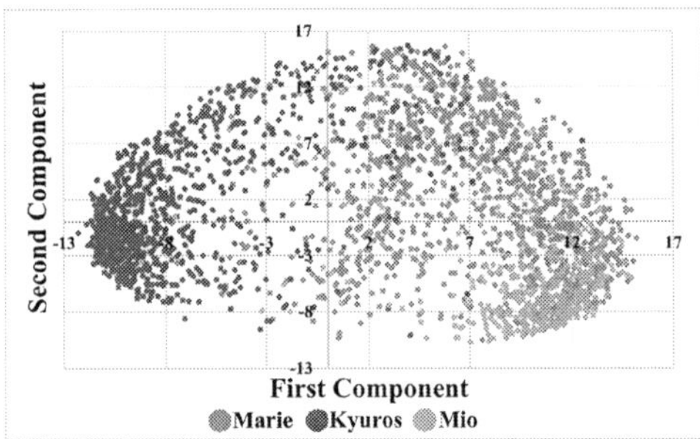

Figure 3: Scatter Plot of the Style-sensitive Sentence Embeddings of the Three Characters in a Novel

and second principal components[7] of the style-sensitive sentence embeddings for all utterances of three characters. While utterances from the identical character tend to cluster together, it is evident that the distribution of the embeddings is scattered to some extent even for an identical character.

Focusing on the variation of the distribution for each character, it is evident that the variation in Mio's style-sensitive sentence embeddings, who always uses typical polite speech reminiscent of a housemaid's speech, is small, while the variation in Marie's style-sensitive sentence embeddings, who switches between "casual female" and "polite" depending on the conversation partner, is larger. In other words, the distribution of the style-sensitive sentence embeddings can be considered as a characteristic of the character's speech style.

8 Conclusion

In this study, we proposed a speech style embedding model that produces style-sensitive sentence embeddings capable of evaluating the similarity of speech styles. The speech style embedding model was constructed using contrastive learning with training data consisting of pairs of utterances with similar/dissimilar speech styles collected from consecutive dialogues in novels. We demonstrated that this speech style embedding model not only captures the similarity of speech styles, but also the strength of politeness, masculinity, and femininity. Furthermore, we confirmed the formation of characteristic speech style clusters such as female and ninja speech styles through clustering of style-sensitive sentence embeddings using the Ward's method. In addition, we analyzed the variation of style-sensitive sentence embeddings across the entire utterances of all the characters in a novel.

Future challenges include constructing a dataset for evaluating speech style similarity with multiple annotators and generating style-sensitive sentence embeddings that take into account the conversation partners and surrounding situations. Additionally, it is necessary to incorporate training methodologies such as the triplet objective function (Reimers and Gurevych, 2019) and in-batch negatives (Gao et al., 2021) to improve model performance. It is equally essential to conduct performance comparison experiments with preceding studies (Akama et al., 2018; Miyazaki et al., 2021b) and verify the usefulness of style-sensitive embeddings in downstream tasks such as controlling the speech style of dialogue systems.

[7]The cumulative proportion up to the second principal component is 41.9%.

References

Reina Akama, Kento Watanabe, Sho Yokoi, Sosuke Kobayashi, and Kentaro Inui. 2018. Unsupervised learning of style-sensitive word vectors. In *Proceedings of the 56th Annual Meeting of the Association for Computational Linguistics (Volume 2: Short Papers)*, pages 572–578, Melbourne, Australia. Association for Computational Linguistics.

Jacob Cohen. 1968. Weighted kappa: Nominal scale agreement provision for scaled disagreement or partial credit. *Psychological Bulletin*, 70:213–220.

Cristian Danescu-Niculescu-Mizil, Moritz Sudhof, Dan Jurafsky, Jure Leskovec, and Christopher Potts. 2013. A computational approach to politeness with application to social factors. In *Proceedings of the 51st Annual Meeting of the Association for Computational Linguistics (Volume 1: Long Papers)*, pages 250–259, Sofia, Bulgaria. Association for Computational Linguistics.

Jacob Devlin, Ming-Wei Chang, Kenton Lee, and Kristina Toutanova. 2019. BERT: Pre-training of deep bidirectional transformers for language understanding. In *Proceedings of the 2019 Conference of the North American Chapter of the Association for Computational Linguistics: Human Language Technologies, Volume 1 (Long and Short Papers)*, pages 4171–4186, Minneapolis, Minnesota. Association for Computational Linguistics.

Tianyu Gao, Xingcheng Yao, and Danqi Chen. 2021. SimCSE: Simple contrastive learning of sentence embeddings. In *Proceedings of the 2021 Conference on Empirical Methods in Natural Language Processing*, pages 6894–6910, Online and Punta Cana, Dominican Republic. Association for Computational Linguistics.

Raia Hadsell, Sumit Chopra, and Yann LeCun. 2006. Dimensionality reduction by learning an invariant mapping. In *2006 IEEE Computer Society Conference on Computer Vision and Pattern Recognition (CVPR'06)*, volume 2, pages 1735–1742.

Dongyeop Kang and Eduard Hovy. 2021. Style is NOT a single variable: Case studies for cross-stylistic language understanding. In *Proceedings of the 59th Annual Meeting of the Association for Computational Linguistics and the 11th International Joint Conference on Natural Language Processing (Volume 1: Long Papers)*, pages 2376–2387, Online. Association for Computational Linguistics.

Mikhail Khodak, Nikunj Saunshi, and Kiran Vodrahalli. 2018. A large self-annotated corpus for sarcasm. In *Proceedings of the Eleventh International Conference on Language Resources and Evaluation (LREC 2018)*, Miyazaki, Japan. European Language Resources Association (ELRA).

Satochi Kinsui. 2003. *Vaacharu nihongo: yakuwari-go no nazo (In Japanese)*. Iwanami, Tokyo, Japan.

Suguru Matsuyoshi, Satoshi Sato, and Takehito Utsuro. 2006. Compilation of a dictionary of japanese functional expressions with hierarchical organization. In *Proceedings of the 21st International Conference on Computer Processing of Oriental Languages: Beyond the Orient: The Research Challenges Ahead*, ICCPOL'06, page 395–402, Berlin, Heidelberg. Springer-Verlag.

Chiaki Miyazaki, Toru Hirano, Ryuichiro Higashinaka, and Yoshihiro Matsuo. 2016. Towards an entertaining natural language generation system: Linguistic peculiarities of Japanese fictional characters. In *Proceedings of the 17th Annual Meeting of the Special Interest Group on Discourse and Dialogue*, pages 319–328, Los Angeles. Association for Computational Linguistics.

Chiaki Miyazaki, Saya Kanno, Makoto Yoda, Junya Ono, and Hiromi Wakaki. 2021a. Fundamental exploration of evaluation metrics for persona characteristics of text utterances. In *Proceedings of the 22nd Annual Meeting of the Special Interest Group on Discourse and Dialogue*, pages 178–189, Singapore and Online. Association for Computational Linguistics.

Chiaki Miyazaki, Saya Kanno, Makoto Yoda, Junya Ono, and Hiromi Wakaki. 2021b. Fundamental exploration of evaluation metrics for persona characteristics of text utterances. In *Proceedings of the 22nd Annual Meeting of the Special Interest Group on Discourse and Dialogue*, pages 178–189, Singapore and Online. Association for Computational Linguistics.

Sudha Rao and Joel Tetreault. 2018. Dear sir or madam, may I introduce the GYAFC dataset: Corpus, benchmarks and metrics for formality style transfer. In *Proceedings of the 2018 Conference of the North American Chapter of the Association for Computational Linguistics: Human Language Technologies, Volume 1 (Long Papers)*, pages 129–140, New Orleans, Louisiana. Association for Computational Linguistics.

Nils Reimers and Iryna Gurevych. 2019. Sentence-BERT: Sentence embeddings using Siamese BERT-networks. In *Proceedings of the 2019 Conference on Empirical Methods in Natural Language Processing and the 9th International Joint Conference on Natural Language Processing (EMNLP-IJCNLP)*, pages 3982–3992, Hong Kong, China. Association for Computational Linguistics.

Joe H. Ward Jr. 1963. Hierarchical grouping to optimize an objective function. *Journal of the American Statistical Association*, 58(301):236–244.

Yuki Zenimoto and Takehito Utsuro. 2022. Speaker identification of quotes in Japanese novels based on gender classification model by BERT. In *Proceedings of the 36th Pacific Asia Conference on Language, Information and Computation*, pages 126–136, Manila, Philippines. De La Salle University.

Li Zhou, Jianfeng Gao, Di Li, and Heung-Yeung Shum. 2020. The design and implementation of XiaoIce, an empathetic social chatbot. *Computational Linguistics*, 46(1):53–93.

Intermediate-Task Transfer Learning for Peer Review Score Prediction

Panitan Muangkammuen[1], Fumiyo Fukumoto[2], Jiyi Li[2], and Yoshimi Suzuki[2]
[1]Integrated Graduate School of Medicine, Engineering, and Agricultural Sciences
[2]Interdisciplinary Graduate School
University of Yamanashi, Kofu, Japan
{g21dts04,fukumoto,jyli,ysuzuki}@yamanashi.ac.jp

Abstract

Peer review is a fundamental component of the academic publishing process, ensuring the quality and validity of research findings. However, predicting peer-review aspect scores accurately can be challenging due to the small size of publically available datasets on the target aspect of scores. To address this issue, we propose an intermediate-task transfer learning method to further improve the performance of pre-trained models. The method assumes an intermediate task that is related to the target task to learn beneficial features before fine-tuning it on a target task. Our experiments demonstrate that intermediate-task transfer learning helps improve the performance of the pre-trained model on peer review score prediction. Our code is available at https://github.com/panitan-m/peerreview-intermediate-trans.

1 Introduction

In recent years, there has been a surge volume of submissions to AI-related international conferences and journals. This upsurge has consequently intensified the difficulties of the review process. To alleviate the burgeoning reviewers' workload, employing an approach to reject papers with evidently low quality serves as a practical strategy. On the other hand, constructive critique extended to authors about the shortcomings in their submissions can encourage refinement and enhancement of their work. In response to this challenge, the development of automatic Peer Review Score Prediction systems has emerged. These systems score a numerical evaluation of academic papers, assessing a spectrum of aspects like "*clarity*" and "*originality*".

A pioneering contribution to the field comes in the form of the PeerRead dataset. This publicly accessible corpus of scientific peer reviews, introduced by Kang et al. (2018), serves as a valuable resource for researchers with diverse objectives. These objectives are ranging from classification of paper acceptance (Ghosal et al., 2019; Deng et al., 2020; Maillette de Buy Wenniger et al., 2020; Fytas et al., 2021), prediction of review aspect scores (Li et al., 2020; Wang et al., 2020; Muangkammuen et al., 2022), to citation recommendation (Jeong et al., 2019), and predicting citation counts (van Dongen et al., 2020). In this paper, we focus on review aspect score prediction.

Unsupervised pre-training SciBERT (Beltagy et al., 2019) was utilized on various downstream scientific NLP tasks, including biomedical domain (Li et al., 2016; Nye et al., 2018), computer science domain (Luan et al., 2018; Jurgens et al., 2018), and multiple domains (Cohan et al., 2019). One promising approach for further enhancing pretrained models that have been shown to be broadly helpful is to first fine-tune a pre-trained model on an intermediate task, before fine-tuning again on the target task, also referred to as *Supplementary Training on Intermediate Labeled-data Tasks* (STILTs) (Phang et al., 2019; Pruksachatkun et al., 2020). STILTs explore the potential of incorporating a secondary phase of pre-training using data-rich intermediate supervised tasks, with the aim of improving the effectiveness of the resulting target task model. In this work, we perform comprehensive experiments using the Aspect-enhanced Peer Review (ASAP-Review) dataset (Yuan et al., 2022) that we extract review aspect sentiments for our intermediate task training. The ASAP-Review dataset is a collection of peer-reviews with fine-grained annotations of review aspect information. For example, *"The paper is well-written and easy to follow"* shows a positive sentiment of *clarity* aspect and a high score of clarity aspect. These aspect sentiments can be beneficial for the review aspect score prediction. We extract the review aspect sentiment from the review texts of a paper and use it as a target label for that given paper. We ran our experiments on 6 intermediate tasks and 7 target tasks, resulting in a total of 42 intermediate-target task pairs.

Proceedings of the 13th International Joint Conference on Natural Language Processing and the 3rd Conference of the Asia-Pacific Chapter of the Association for Computational Linguistics: Student Research Workshop, pages 40–47
November 1–4, 2023.

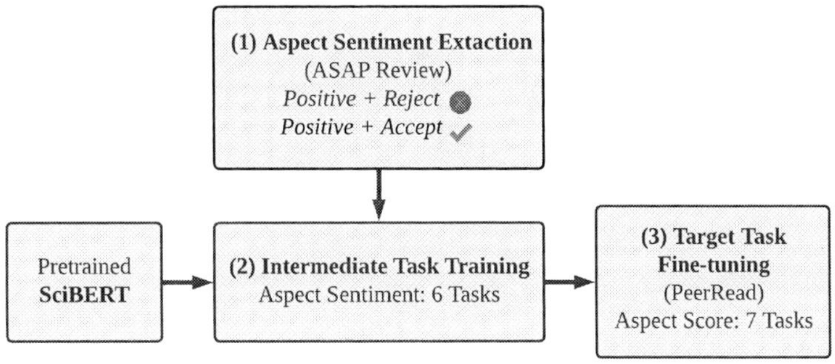

Figure 1: Overview of our pipeline framework. It comprises aspect sentiment extraction, intermediate-task training, and fine-tuning on the target task.

In summary, our main contributions are:

- This work is the first to introduce an intermediate-task transfer learning method to peer-review score prediction.
- We propose a method to extract aspect sentiments for intermediate-task training for peer-review score prediction.
- We conduct experiments to demonstrate the efficacy of each intermediate task, resulting in performance gains across every review aspect score prediction.

2 Related Work

Artificial Intelligence is a crucial tool for academic peer review, and it is a rapidly growing field that demands more attention from the academic community. The renowned Toronto Paper Matching system, developed by Charlin and Zemel (2013), was designed to match papers with appropriate reviewers. Notably, Price and Flach (2017) conducted an in-depth examination of the diverse methods for harnessing computational support in the peer review system. Mrowinski et al. (2017) explored the application of evolutionary algorithms to enhance editorial strategies within the peer review process. Ghosal et al. (2018a,b) delved into an investigation of the impact of various features in the editorial pre-screening process. Wang and Wan (2018) explored a multi-instance learning framework for conducting sentiment analysis on peer review texts. Ghosal et al. (2019) investigated the impact of reviewer sentiment expressed in peer review texts on the outcome of the review process. Li et al. (2020) proposed a multi-task learning approach that automatically selects shared structures and auxiliary resources for peer review prediction. More recently, Muangkammuen et al. (2022) explored a semi-supervised learning for improving peer review score prediction.

Our investigations are currently centered on a portion of the PeerRead dataset that has been made available to the public (Kang et al., 2018). Our approach achieves performance improvement on the peer review aspect score prediction task compared to Kang et al. (2018). We attribute this to the use of intermediate task training and the extraction of aspect sentiment in our approach.

3 Methods

We present a simple intermediate-task transfer learning for peer review score prediction. Figure 1 illustrates the method pipeline that consists of the following steps: *aspect sentiment extraction*, *intermediate-task training*, and *fine-tuning on the target task*.

3.1 Aspect Sentiment Extraction

To further train the pre-trained model SciBERT on the intermediate tasks, we extract aspect sentiments from the ASAP-Review dataset (Yuan et al., 2022) to utilize them for our intermediate-task training. The ASAP-Review dataset comprises peer-review data from ICLR and NeurIPS. We use only ICLR data as it contains both accepted and rejected papers which are the same as the target task dataset, PeerRead.

Originally, this dataset contained review texts with sequence labels of fine-grained annotation of aspect information. An example of the review annotations is shown in Table 1. We utilize 6 aspects in the dataset, which are Clarity (CLA-*i*), Meaningful Comparison (COM-*i*), Motivation/Impact (MOT-*i*), Originality (ORI-*i*), Soundness/Correctness (SOU-

Summary	Soundness +	Motivation +	Clarity +

The authors prove a generalization guarantee for deep neural networks with ReLU activations, in terms of margins of the classifications and norms of the weight matrices. They compare this bound with a similar recent bound proved by Bartlett, et al. While strictly speaking, the bounds are incomparable in strength, the authors of the submission make a convincing case that their new bound makes stronger guarantees under some interesting conditions. The analysis is elegant. It uses some existing tools but brings them to bear in an important new context, with substantive new ideas needed. The mathematical writing is excellent. Very nice paper. I guess that networks including convolutional layers are covered by their analysis. It feels to me that these tend to be sparse, but that their analysis still my provides some additional leverage for such layers. Some explicit discussion of convolutional layers may be helpful.

Table 1: An example of review annotations of ASAP-Review dataset. "+" denotes positive sentiment. Negative sentiment does not occur in this example.

Aspects	Negative	Positive	Total
CLA-*i*	1,560	1,003	2,563
COM-*i*	1,738	180	1,918
MOT-*i*	525	1,453	1,978
ORI-*i*	1,257	1,186	2,443
SOU-*i*	1,789	933	2,722
SUB-*i*	1,726	505	2,231

Table 2: Statistics of the aspect sentiments of ASAP-Review dataset for the intermediate-task training.

Aspects	Total
Clarity (CLA)	136
Meaningful Comparison (COM)	132
Impact (IMP)	132
Originality (ORI)	136
Soundness/Correctness (SOU)	136
Substance (SUB)	136
Overall Recommendation (REC)	136

Table 3: Statistics of the PeerRead ACL 2017 dataset for the target tasks.

i), and Substance (SUB-*i*). Each aspect is also marked with a sentiment, *positive* or *negative*. We count the number of positives and negatives of each aspect in the reviews. We use the majority polarity as a label for the reviewed paper since one paper consists of multiple reviews. We further remove the samples having a positive aspect label with a reject decision and having a negative aspect label with an accept decision to amplify the characteristic in the data. The statistics of the ASAP-Review dataset after aspect sentiment extraction are shown in Table 2. To distinguish it from the target tasks, i.e., review aspect score predictions, we add *"-i"* to each intermediate task.

3.2 Intermediate Task Training

We fine-tune SciBERT model on each intermediate task, following the standard procedure of fine-tuning a pre-trained model on a target task as described in Devlin et al. (2019). Instead of multi-task training (Liu et al., 2019), we use single intermediate-task training to examine the effect of each intermediate task independently. The objective of these intermediate tasks is to predict the sentiment for each review aspect. We train the model to minimize the *Binary Cross-Entropy* loss.

3.3 Target Task Fine-tuning

After intermediate-task training, we fine-tune our models on each target task individually. Our target task is peer-review score prediction, which consists of 7 aspects shown in Table 3. The PeerRead dataset contains peer-review datasets from several conferences. Among them, we chose the ACL 2017 dataset for our experiment as it includes aspect scores that are fully annotated. In this dataset, an input paper has multiple review scores, we use the rounded average score of each aspect as the target score ranging from 1 to 5. We fine-tune the models to minimize the *Categorical Cross-Entropy* loss of five classes.

4 Experiments

4.1 Experimental settings

We used the pre-trained model `scibert-scivocab-uncased` in all experiments. For each intermediate and target task, we used a peak learning rate at 5×10^{-5} and a dropout rate of 0.1. We used a batch size of 8 and a maximum se-

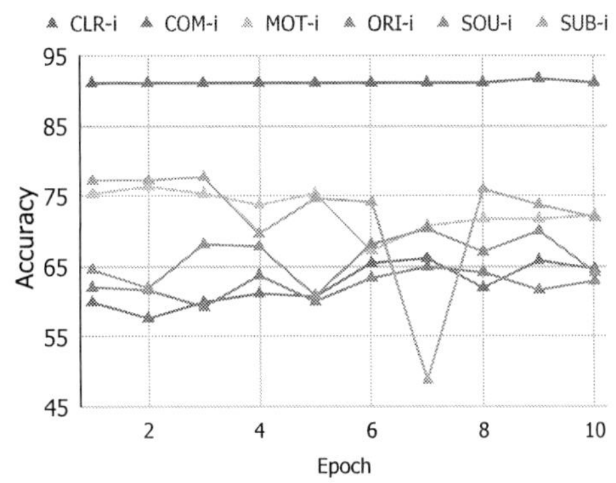

Figure 2: Performances on intermediate tasks in accuracy at each checkpoint.

quence length of 512. We trained our models using the AdamW (Loshchilov and Hutter, 2019) with linear decay and 0.2 warm-up ratio. We performed our experiments on NVIDIA GeForce RTX 3090 GPUs.

A pipeline with one intermediate task works as follows: First, we split the extracted ASAP-Review data into training and validation sets with a 9:1 ratio. We fine-tuned SciBERT on the intermediate task for 10 epochs and saved a checkpoint at the end of each epoch, resulting in 10 checkpoints. The performance of each intermediate task evaluated on the validation set is shown in Figure 2. The performances were quite stable during fine-tuning, except for SUB-*i*. We then fine-tuned copies of the resulting models separately on each of the 7 target tasks. We chose the result of the checkpoint that performs best on the target task. Because the test set of the PeerRead dataset is very small, i.e., only 7 samples, most of the results reported by Wang et al. (2020) can be obtained by just using the majority score as a prediction, and it could lead to inappropriate evaluation. Instead of using the original sets to perform the experiments, we ran the same pipeline on 5-fold cross-validation three times. This gave us 15 observations for each result in our experiments.

We compared our method to the PeerRead (Kang et al., 2018). We re-implemented their model based on CNN and kept the same hyperparameters. GloVe 840B embeddings (Pennington et al., 2014) were utilized as input word representations, without tuning. The outputs from the CNN model are fed into a max pooling layer and the final linear layer. We evaluated their model in our experimental settings.

Aspects	PeerRead	Ours
CLA	67.4 (22.5)	**69.3 (27.4)**
COM	55.0 (20.4)	**62.1 (33.9)**
IMP	80.2 (30.3)	**82.0 (37.2)**
ORI	47.8 (21.5)	**56.9 (50.7)**
SOU	50.2 (21.6)	**60.5 (41.9)**
SUB	67.1 (21.1)	**68.6 (31.2)**
REC	58.8 (23.5)	**64.0 (36.4)**
Avg.	60.9 (23.0)	**66.2 (37.0)**

Table 4: Results compared with the method in PeerRead (Kang et al., 2018). Each cell indicates accuracy (macro F1). **Bold** indicates the best result.

4.2 Results and Discussion

Figure 3 shows the differences in target task performances between the baselines and models trained with intermediate-task training, each averaged across three 5-fold cross-validations. A positive result indicates a successful transfer.

We observed that transfer learning, almost every intermediate-task training, helps improve the performance of the target task. The *Soundness/Correctness* score prediction gains more performance from intermediate-task training with around 10% on both accuracy and macro F1. Overall our best results are better than those of the baselines around 4.1% and 8.4% on average, in accuracy and macro F1, respectively. The best improvements in accuracy are from ORI-*i* on *Soundness/Correctness* at 9.6%. The best improvement in macro F1 score is up to 13.9% from ORI-*i* on *Overall Recommendation*. On average across every target task, the ORI-*i* is the most successful intermediate task that increases 3.7% and 5.8% in accuracy and macro F1, respectively.

Interestingly, we did not find the largest improvement from the same aspect of the intermediate task (sentiment prediction) and the target task (score prediction), except for the *Originality* on the accuracy metric. Instead, the score prediction task gains more performance from other aspects of the intermediate task.

We also compared our method to the PeerRead (Kang et al., 2018) which is shown in Table 4. Our method performed better than the PeerRead model on every task and increased 5.3% and 14% on average, in accuracy and macro F1, respectively. It outperformed the PeerRead model by 10.3% on *Soundness/Correctness* in term of accuracy and by 29.2% on *Originality* in term of macro F1.

Target \ Intermediate	CLR	COM	MOT	ORI	SOU	SUB	Baseline	Our Best
CLR	0.9	0.7	0.4	0.0	0.4	1.6	67.7	69.3
COM	0.5	0.7	-0.3	3.5	2.7	1.0	58.6	62.1
IMP	1.5	1.3	0.8	1.0	1.0	1.0	80.5	82.0
ORI	2.9	1.7	3.7	7.1	5.1	2.0	49.8	56.9
SOU	5.4	4.5	4.4	9.6	4.2	5.2	50.9	60.5
SUB	0.5	0.7	0.2	0.5	0.1	0.7	67.9	68.6
REC	1.4	0.9	3.9	4.1	2.7	4.9	59.1	64.0
Avg. Target	1.9	1.5	1.9	3.7	2.3	2.3	62.1	66.2

(a) Accuracy

Target \ Intermediate	CLR	COM	MOT	ORI	SOU	SUB	Baseline	Our Best
CLR	2.5	1.1	2.3	0.4	3.1	3.6	23.8	27.4
COM	5.1	2.5	0.3	7.2	6.6	2.6	26.7	33.9
IMP	5.2	4.9	2.3	5.5	5.0	3.5	31.7	37.2
ORI	5.6	-0.2	2.1	9.6	10.3	0.9	40.4	50.7
SOU	9.8	4.3	7.0	10.2	5.1	7.3	31.7	41.9
SUB	3.4	1.7	1.9	3.9	8.0	2.8	23.2	31.2
REC	4.9	2.8	10.0	13.9	11.1	12.7	22.5	36.4
Avg. Target	5.2	2.4	3.7	5.8	5.8	3.7	28.6	37.0

(b) Macro F1

Figure 3: Transfer learning results between intermediate and target tasks. Baselines on the second rightmost column are models that are fine-tuned without intermediate-task training. Our best results from the models with intermediate-task training are on the rightmost column. Each cell shows the difference in performance between the baseline and model with intermediate-task training. The cool and warm tone colors indicate improvement, and deterioration, respectively.

4.3 Ablation Study

Our approach to extracting the ASAP-Review dataset for intermediate-task training contains two strategies, i.e., aspect sentiment extraction from review text and removing a sample that has a positive label with a reject decision and vice versa. To examine how each strategy contributes to the performance of the target task, we consider the following variants of our intermediate task:

a) **Decision** - Using decision prediction as an intermediate task. Here, the decision prediction task predicts whether a paper gets *accepted* or *rejected.* The statistics of decision data are shown in Table 5.

b) **Aspect** - Using aspect sentiment data without removing a sample. Here, the sample has a positive label with a reject decision and vice versa. The statistics of the data are shown in Table 6.

c) **Aspect + Decision** - Our full method using two strategies altogether. By incorporating two strategies, the quantity of data is decreased by over 30% from the **Aspect**.

Accept	Reject	Total
3,295	1,855	5,150

Table 5: Statistics of the decision data.

Aspects	Negative	Positive	Total
CLA-*i*	2,430	1,626	4,056
COM-*i*	2,889	264	3,153
MOT-*i*	773	2,655	3,428
ORI-*i*	1,837	1,984	3,821
SOU-*i*	2,700	1,357	4,057
SUB-*i*	2,901	760	3,661

Table 6: Statistics of the aspect polarity data without removing a sample that has a positive label with a reject decision and vice versa.

Table 7 shows the results of different strategies of the intermediate task training. We can see that **Decision** helps improve the pre-trained model performance in almost every target task except *Substance* on macro F1. **Aspect** further improves the pre-trained model compared to **Decision** in almost

Target Task	Baseline	Intermediate Task		
		Decision	Aspects	Aspects + Decision
CLR	66.7 (23.8)	+0.4 (+1.4)	+0.4 (+1.3)	**+1.6 (+3.6)**
COM	58.6 (26.7)	+1.2 (+4.8)	+2.3 (+6.4)	**+3.5 (+7.2)**
IMP	80.5 (31.7)	+1.3 (+5.8)	**+2.0 (+7.7)**	+1.5 (+5.5)
ORI	49.8 (40.4)	+4.2 (+5.1)	+3.0 (+3.7)	**+7.1 (+10.3)**
SOU	50.9 (31.7)	+5.2 (+6.8)	+4.2 (+6.4)	**+9.6 (+10.2)**
SUB	67.9 (23.2)	+0.2 (-0.2)	**+1.4** (+4.3)	+0.7 **(+8.0)**
REC	59.1 (22.5)	+1.9 (+7.1)	+3.2 (+9.2)	**+4.9 (+13.9)**
Avg.	62.1 (28.6)	+2.1 (+4.4)	+2.4 (+5.6)	**+4.1 (+8.4)**

Table 7: Results on the variants of the intermediate task. The baseline column indicates the results without intermediate-task training. The other columns show the difference in performance between the baseline and model with intermediate-task training. Each cell indicates an improvement in accuracy (macro F1 score) compared with the baseline. **Bold** indicates the best result.

every target task and has a better performance on accuracy and macro F1 on average. This indicates that the aspect sentiment data contains richer information for review aspect score prediction compared to the decision data. In contrast, the decision data shows more relevance on the *Originality* and *Soundness/Correctness* score predictions than aspect sentiment data. One possible reason for this is that they are the main aspect of the reviewer's judgment.

As we can see from Table 7 that combining aspect polarity data with a decision strategy leads to a better result on almost every target task and the best result on average in both accuracy and macro F1 score. Although the data size of **Aspect + Decision** is smaller than that of **Aspect**, the average result of **Aspect + Decision** is still better. This shows that the characteristic is more important than the quantity of the data for intermediate-task training.

4.4 Error Analysis

We plot the confusion matrix between truth and model prediction on test data in Figure 4, which shows that the prediction scores of our model tend to be close to the true values. The model tends to be biased to a score of 4, which is the most common score in the dataset. The model was able to classify some papers with a score of 2 or 3 correctly. In contrast, it was unable to correctly classify papers with a score of 1 or 5. However, it still rated papers with a score of 5 higher than a score of 1. The shortage of training samples for scores 1 and 5 (less than 5 samples) complicates its prediction. Incorporating techniques to handle imbalanced datasets is an interesting direction for future work.

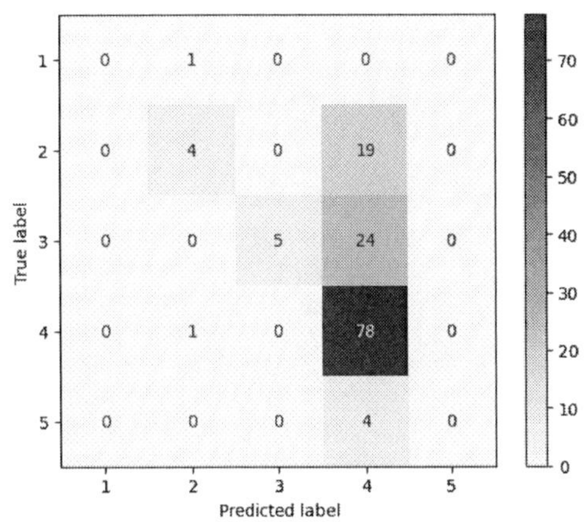

Figure 4: Confusion matrix of true and prediction of *Overall Recommendation* scores.

5 Conclusion

In this study, we investigated the impact of intermediate-task transfer learning on peer-review score prediction. Specifically, we fine-tuned a pre-trained model SciBERT on an intermediate task before fine-tuning again on the target task. We proposed a method to extract the ASAP-Review dataset for intermediate-task training to improve peer-review score prediction. The experimental results showed the effectiveness of the intermediate-task training as it attained a better result than the baseline on every target task in both accuracy and macro F1. Future work will include (1) extending the method to process longer sequences to cover the full length of the paper, and (2) incorporating multiple tasks for the intermediate-task training to exploit related information between intermediate tasks.

Acknowledgements

The authors would like to thank the anonymous reviewers for their insightful comments and suggestions. This work is supported by JST SPRING, Grant Number JPMJSP2133, Kajima Foundation's Support Program, and JSPS KAKENHI (No. 22K12146).

References

Iz Beltagy, Kyle Lo, and Arman Cohan. 2019. SciBERT: A pretrained language model for scientific text. In *Proceedings of the 2019 Conference on Empirical Methods in Natural Language Processing and the 9th International Joint Conference on Natural Language Processing (EMNLP-IJCNLP)*, pages 3615–3620, Hong Kong, China. Association for Computational Linguistics.

Laurent Charlin and Richard S. Zemel. 2013. The toronto paper matching system: An automated paper-reviewer assignment system.

Arman Cohan, Waleed Ammar, Madeleine van Zuylen, and Field Cady. 2019. Structural scaffolds for citation intent classification in scientific publications. In *Proceedings of the 2019 Conference of the North American Chapter of the Association for Computational Linguistics: Human Language Technologies, Volume 1 (Long and Short Papers)*, pages 3586–3596, Minneapolis, Minnesota. Association for Computational Linguistics.

Zhongfen Deng, Hao Peng, Congying Xia, Jianxin Li, Lifang He, and Philip Yu. 2020. Hierarchical bi-directional self-attention networks for paper review rating recommendation. In *Proceedings of the 28th International Conference on Computational Linguistics*, pages 6302–6314, Barcelona, Spain (Online). International Committee on Computational Linguistics.

Jacob Devlin, Ming-Wei Chang, Kenton Lee, and Kristina Toutanova. 2019. Bert: Pre-training of deep bidirectional transformers for language understanding.

Panagiotis Fytas, Georgios Rizos, and Lucia Specia. 2021. What makes a scientific paper be accepted for publication? In *Proceedings of the First Workshop on Causal Inference and NLP*, pages 44–60, Punta Cana, Dominican Republic. Association for Computational Linguistics.

Tirthankar Ghosal, Ravi Sonam, Sriparna Saha, Asif Ekbal, and Pushpak Bhattacharyya. 2018a. Investigating domain features for scope detection and classification of scientific articles. In *Proceedings of the Eleventh International Conference on Language Resources and Evaluation (LREC 2018)*, Paris, France. European Language Resources Association (ELRA).

Tirthankar Ghosal, Rajeev Verma, Asif Ekbal, and Pushpak Bhattacharyya. 2019. DeepSentiPeer: Harnessing sentiment in review texts to recommend peer review decisions. In *Proceedings of the 57th Annual Meeting of the Association for Computational Linguistics*, pages 1120–1130, Florence, Italy. Association for Computational Linguistics.

Tirthankar Ghosal, Rajeev Verma, Asif Ekbal, Sriparna Saha, and Pushpak Bhattacharyya. 2018b. Investigating impact features in editorial pre-screening of research papers. In *Proceedings of the 18th ACM/IEEE on Joint Conference on Digital Libraries*, JCDL '18, page 333–334, New York, NY, USA. Association for Computing Machinery.

Chanwoo Jeong, Sion Jang, Hyuna Shin, Eunjeong Park, and Sungchul Choi. 2019. A context-aware citation recommendation model with bert and graph convolutional networks.

David Jurgens, Srijan Kumar, Raine Hoover, Dan McFarland, and Dan Jurafsky. 2018. Measuring the evolution of a scientific field through citation frames. *Transactions of the Association for Computational Linguistics*, 6:391–406.

Dongyeop Kang, Waleed Ammar, Bhavana Dalvi, Madeleine van Zuylen, Sebastian Kohlmeier, Eduard Hovy, and Roy Schwartz. 2018. A dataset of peer reviews (PeerRead): Collection, insights and NLP applications. In *Proceedings of the 2018 Conference of the North American Chapter of the Association for Computational Linguistics: Human Language Technologies, Volume 1 (Long Papers)*, pages 1647–1661, New Orleans, Louisiana. Association for Computational Linguistics.

Jiao Li, Yueping Sun, Robin J. Johnson, Daniela Sciaky, Chih-Hsuan Wei, Robert Leaman, Allan Peter Davis, Carolyn J. Mattingly, Thomas C. Wiegers, and Zhiyong Lu. 2016. BioCreative V CDR task corpus: a resource for chemical disease relation extraction. *Database*, 2016:baw068.

Jiyi Li, Ayaka Sato, Kazuya Shimura, and Fumiyo Fukumoto. 2020. Multi-task peer-review score prediction. In *Proceedings of the First Workshop on Scholarly Document Processing*, pages 121–126, Online. Association for Computational Linguistics.

Xiaodong Liu, Pengcheng He, Weizhu Chen, and Jianfeng Gao. 2019. Multi-task deep neural networks for natural language understanding. In *Proceedings of the 57th Annual Meeting of the Association for Computational Linguistics*, pages 4487–4496, Florence, Italy. Association for Computational Linguistics.

Ilya Loshchilov and Frank Hutter. 2019. Decoupled weight decay regularization.

Yi Luan, Luheng He, Mari Ostendorf, and Hannaneh Hajishirzi. 2018. Multi-task identification of entities, relations, and coreference for scientific knowledge graph construction. In *Proceedings of the 2018 Conference on Empirical Methods in Natural Language*

Processing, pages 3219–3232, Brussels, Belgium. Association for Computational Linguistics.

Gideon Maillette de Buy Wenniger, Thomas van Dongen, Eleri Aedmaa, Herbert Teun Kruitbosch, Edwin A. Valentijn, and Lambert Schomaker. 2020. Structure-tags improve text classification for scholarly document quality prediction. In *Proceedings of the First Workshop on Scholarly Document Processing*, pages 158–167, Online. Association for Computational Linguistics.

Maciej J. Mrowinski, Piotr Fronczak, Agata Fronczak, Marcel Ausloos, and Olgica Nedic. 2017. Artificial intelligence in peer review: How can evolutionary computation support journal editors? *PLOS ONE*, 12(9):1–11.

Panitan Muangkammuen, Fumiyo Fukumoto, Jiyi Li, and Yoshimi Suzuki. 2022. Exploiting labeled and unlabeled data via transformer fine-tuning for peer-review score prediction. In *Findings of the Association for Computational Linguistics: EMNLP 2022*, pages 2233–2240, Abu Dhabi, United Arab Emirates. Association for Computational Linguistics.

Benjamin Nye, Junyi Jessy Li, Roma Patel, Yinfei Yang, Iain Marshall, Ani Nenkova, and Byron Wallace. 2018. A corpus with multi-level annotations of patients, interventions and outcomes to support language processing for medical literature. In *Proceedings of the 56th Annual Meeting of the Association for Computational Linguistics (Volume 1: Long Papers)*, pages 197–207, Melbourne, Australia. Association for Computational Linguistics.

Jeffrey Pennington, Richard Socher, and Christopher Manning. 2014. GloVe: Global vectors for word representation. In *Proceedings of the 2014 Conference on Empirical Methods in Natural Language Processing (EMNLP)*, pages 1532–1543, Doha, Qatar. Association for Computational Linguistics.

Jason Phang, Thibault Févry, and Samuel R. Bowman. 2019. Sentence encoders on stilts: Supplementary training on intermediate labeled-data tasks.

Simon Price and Peter A. Flach. 2017. Computational support for academic peer review: A perspective from artificial intelligence. *Commun. ACM*, 60(3):70–79.

Yada Pruksachatkun, Jason Phang, Haokun Liu, Phu Mon Htut, Xiaoyi Zhang, Richard Yuanzhe Pang, Clara Vania, Katharina Kann, and Samuel R. Bowman. 2020. Intermediate-task transfer learning with pretrained language models: When and why does it work? In *Proceedings of the 58th Annual Meeting of the Association for Computational Linguistics*, pages 5231–5247, Online. Association for Computational Linguistics.

Thomas van Dongen, Gideon Maillette de Buy Wenniger, and Lambert Schomaker. 2020. SChuBERT: Scholarly document chunks with BERT-encoding boost citation count prediction. In *Proceedings of the First Workshop on Scholarly Document Processing*, pages 148–157, Online. Association for Computational Linguistics.

Ke Wang and Xiaojun Wan. 2018. Sentiment analysis of peer review texts for scholarly papers. In *The 41st International ACM SIGIR Conference on Research & Development in Information Retrieval*, SIGIR '18, page 175–184, New York, NY, USA. Association for Computing Machinery.

Qingyun Wang, Qi Zeng, Lifu Huang, Kevin Knight, Heng Ji, and Nazneen Fatema Rajani. 2020. ReviewRobot: Explainable paper review generation based on knowledge synthesis. In *Proceedings of the 13th International Conference on Natural Language Generation*, pages 384–397, Dublin, Ireland. Association for Computational Linguistics.

Weizhe Yuan, Pengfei Liu, and Graham Neubig. 2022. Can we automate scientific reviewing? *J. Artif. Int. Res.*, 75.

Speech Synthesis Model Based on Face Landmarks

Chenji Jin
Hangzhou Dianzi University
epsiotapi@hdu.edu.cn

Yoshimi Suzuki
The university of Yamanashi
ysuzuki@yamanashi.ac.jp

Fei Lin
Hangzhou Dianzi University
linfei@hdu.edu.cn

Abstract

Lip reading recognition aims to predict what people are saying based on the movements of their lips. Most previous works used continuous images to represent lip movements and predict the corresponding textual contents, which does not achieve good performance. In this work, we explore a new approach to synthesizing audio through lip movements by introducing face landmarks for representing the motion features of the face in 3D space and synthesizing the corresponding audio results directly. We propose the FaceLandmarks2Wav model for a preliminary implementation of the above idea. The experimental results confirm that face landmarks can adequately represent facial movement features, and the structure of FaceLandmarks2Wav could synthesize speech results close to natural human voices, only using the face landmarks sequence.

1 Introduction

The relationship between human speech lip movements and pronunciation has been confirmed in many previous studies (Cappelletta and Harte, 2012; Shaikh et al., 2010). Trained professionals can predict what others say by observing their lip shape. People with hearing impairment use a similar method to understand what others say when communicating. Visual speech recognition uses the relationship between lip movements and pronunciation to predict what a speaker says by capturing videos of their lip position. Related research has many practical applications, such as assisting people with acquired aphasia to communicate with others.

Research related to computer lip recognition generally extracts lip gesture features from continuous images of videos (Ma et al., 2022; Huang et al., 2022; Wang et al., 2022). Early studies mainly used image transformation methods to reduce the dimensionality of feature vectors. (Min and Zuo, 2011) performed lip visual feature extraction based on 3D-DCT and 3D-HMM models, which focused on the primary information of images in the low-frequency band. With the development of research in computer vision, the extraction of lip movement features in images using deep learning networks such as CNN (Iezzoni et al., 2004; Fung and Mak, 2018; NadeemHashmi et al., 2018; Chung and Zisserman, 2016) has also received increasing attention. Noda et al. (2014) used a CNN-based multilayer network to extract feature sequences from lip images and modeled them by GMM-HMM. Garg et al. (2016) used LSTM networks to extract lip movement in the temporal dimension information.

Current research has primarily used continuous images of the speaker's face to illustrate lip movements. However, video is not the most intuitive way to represent lip movements. The video samples contain much redundant information, requiring a large-scale network to locate the speaker's lips and extract movement features accurately. Even then, redundant information can also interfere with model predictions. For example, the model relies on the facial details of the speaker in the video and may not make accurate estimations when encountering an unseen speaker, which is more common when training the model with person-specific video datasets. In addition, the possible facial rotation of people while speaking can cause the camera to not continuously capture the face of the picture, which limits the application scenarios of lip recognition research. To solve the problems in video lip recognition, we introduce face landmarks to represent facial movement states in lip recognition. Face landmarks are a series of coordinate points annotated on the human face, often used to track the positional states of facial features.

In this study, we combine face landmarks in the temporal dimension into a sequence to represent the movement features of the face in three-dimensional space. Extract facial movement features from fa-

Proceedings of the 13th International Joint Conference on Natural Language Processing and the 3rd Conference of the Asia-Pacific Chapter of the Association for Computational Linguistics: Student Research Workshop, pages 48–54
November 1–4, 2023.

cial landmarks sequence by an encoder consisting of multilayer convolutional neural networks and LSTM, and use an autoregressive decoder to synthesize the audio close to the speaker's pronunciation.

2 Methods

We refer to the method used by Shen et al. (2018) in the text-to-speech task. Our model does not directly synthesize the audio waveform from the lip movement sequence. Instead, it predicts the mel spectrogram of the corresponding audio segment and uses a vocoder to convert the mel spectrogram to audio results. Assume that the lip movement sequence are represented as $L = (L_1, L_2, \cdots, L_T)$ and the mel spectrogram are represented as $M = (M_1, M_2, \cdots, M_{T'})$, and the mel spectrogram are represented as follows:

$$S = (S_1, S_2, \cdots, S_T),\ S_i = (s_1, \cdots, s_N) \quad (1)$$

$$L = (L_1, L_2, \cdots, L_{T'}),\ L_i = (P_1, \cdots, P_F) \quad (2)$$

Where T and T' are the frame numbers of the lip movement sequence and the mel spectrogram in the same video clip, F is the number of 3D landmarks in the facial feature part selected in the experiment. N is the number of mel filters.

We can assume that the representation of the target mel spectrogram in the t' frame is highly correlated with the lip movements of the speaker at the exact moment. However, since there are possibilities where different phonemes share the same viseme, to determine the mel spectrogram of the t' frame, the model should also reference the context of the lip movement feature. We model the relationship between the mel spectrogram and lip movements using Eq. (3).

$$M_{t'} = f\left(L_{k\in(t\pm\delta)}, M_{<t'}\right) \quad (3)$$

The encoder refers to context information to extract lip movement features. The decoder uses an autoregressive method to synthesize the corresponding mel spectrogram frame by frame. The model structure is shown in Fig. 1.

2.1 Input/Output Representation

2.1.1 Input Representation

FaceLandmarks2Wav model accepts face landmarks as input. Each landmark contains three-dimensional coordinate information. Therefore, the tensor size of the model input is $T \times F \times 3$, where F is the number of landmarks used in the experiment, and T is the number of time steps of the landmarks sequence, each training sample uses 90 continuous frames of image content.

2.1.2 Output Representation

The target synthesized by our model is the audio content corresponding to the given video segment. FaceLandmarks2Wav does not directly synthesize audio results but predicts the corresponding mel spectrogram. We sample the audio at a sampling rate 16kHz, set the window size to 50ms, shift distance per frame to 12.5ms, and set the number of mel filters to 80. As the model obtained the corresponding mel spectrogram, we use the Griffin-Lim algorithm (Griffin and Lim, 1984) to transform it into the corresponding audio wave.

2.2 Spatio-temporal Face Encoder

Previous studies (Bai et al., 2018; Xu et al., 2019) have demonstrated the effectiveness of CNN for feature extraction in the time domain. Therefore, we stacked convolutional blocks to extract movement features from face landmarks input. The input dimension of the encoder is $T \times F \times 3$. Unlike processing images, the number of face landmarks F corresponds to different convolution channels, which helps the convolution kernel respond to all facial landmarks.

We set multiple convolution blocks in the encoder, and each convolution block increases the number of channels used to represent facial features. The number of channels of each convolution block is set according to the face landmarks used in the experiment. Residual connections and batch normalization are used between CNN blocks. The last layer of convolutional blocks will sample the three-dimensional coordinate information into one dimension, and the encoder will permanently preserve the time dimension. The convolutional network's final output size is $T \times F'$, and F' is the number of features modeled by the encoder for a single time step.

The encoder uses a bidirectional LSTM network (Hochreiter and Schmidhuber, 1997) to extract short-term contextual features. This method allows the feature modeling of face landmarks to contain more contextual information after the convolutional network.

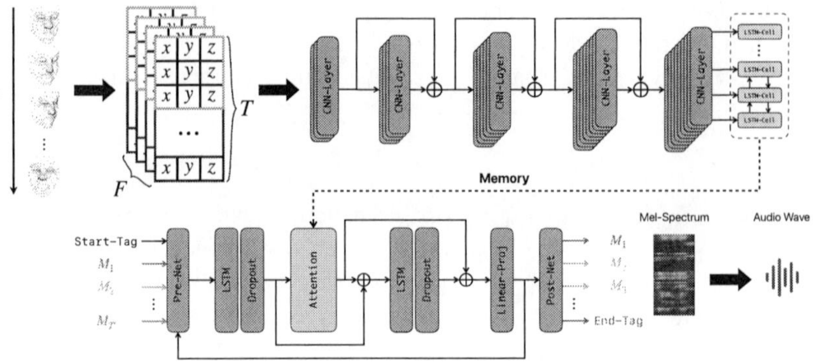

Figure 1: FaceLandmarks2Wav model structure. The encoder uses a 2D convolutional network to extract high-level lip movement features from landmarks. The decoder predicts the mel spectrogram corresponding to the audio result autoregressively.

2.3 Attention-based Speech Decoder

To synthesize smoother and natural speech results, our model refers to the method used in Tacotron2 by Shen et al. (2018). The Tacotron2 is a model for synthesizing audio from text, which uses a sequence-to-sequence network with an attention mechanism to process the text features extracted by the encoder and synthesize a mel spectrogram close to the natural human voice. We use a Tacotron2-like decoder to autoregressively synthesize the mel spectrogram frame by frame from the facial movement features encoded by the encoder. When the decoder synthesizes the mel spectrograms output of the T_k time step, it will refer to the decoder output of T_{k-1} time step and calculates the attention together with the lip movement high-level features extracted by the encoder.

The attention network contains a special location layer (Chorowski et al., 2015), which accepts the accumulated attention weights from previous time steps as an additional condition, which can help the attention network to calculate the attention weights forward and prevent the decoder from falling into repeated patterns. Such a decoder structure contributes to more natural audio results for model synthesis.

2.4 Loss Function

The optimization goal during model training is minimizing the hybrid loss between the synthetic mel spectrogram and the ground truth for end-to-end model training. The hybrid loss function is shown in Eq. 4, and α is the weight used to adjust the loss function and is set to 0.5 in the experiment.

$$\mathcal{L}_{all} = \alpha \cdot \mathcal{L}_1 + \mathcal{L}_{MSE} \tag{4}$$

3 Benchmark Datasets and Training Details

3.1 Datasets

Accurate 3D face landmarks can be annotated on faces using special devices such as the True Depth camera on the iPhone. However, since face landmark is a novel way to describe lip movements, there is no previous research on lip recognition using similar methods. To compare with those studies using video data, we use the face landmarks extractor to extract the face landmarks from the existing video dataset. Build the face landmarks dataset based on the video dataset. We chose the Lip2Wav dataset from Prajwal et al. (2020) as the source of lip recognition video data, which collects about 120 hours of video data from Youtube, including facial images of different speakers when they spoke and divided them into different sub-datasets according to the different speakers in the video. It is very suitable for the model to learn the lip synthesis style of a specific speaker.

We chose the Media Pipe Face Mesh model (MPFM) proposed by Grishchenko et al. (2020) as the face landmarks extractor. The MPFM model could provide 478 3D landmark coordinates of the whole face range. This model also optimizes the face landmarks labeling of continuous images and reduces the jitter of landmarks between frames. Those features make the MPFM model more suitable for labeling face landmarks on video data.

After getting the face landmarks on the video data, we normalize the sequence of time-series face landmarks using Eq.(5). This function will make the coordinates of the face landmarks have appropriate sparsity.

$$\begin{aligned} \boldsymbol{c} &\leftarrow \frac{1}{3n}\sum_{i=1}^{n}\sum_{j=1}^{3}\boldsymbol{p}_{ij} \\ m &\leftarrow \max\left(||\boldsymbol{p}_{ij} - \boldsymbol{c}||\right) \\ \boldsymbol{p}'_{ij} &\leftarrow \frac{1}{m}(\boldsymbol{p}_{ij} - \boldsymbol{c}) \end{aligned} \tag{5}$$

Since the video in the Lip2Wav dataset is captured by fixed camera position, some of the video clips cannot contain the range of the human face, and this part of the samples can not be used in training. To ensure that the encoder can better model the lip-movement contextual features, we set the video window to 90 frames, and this means that only face landmarks extractors can recognize 90 consecutive face frames will be used as samples for model training. The video lip-synthesis model used for comparison was also trained using the same data range, and the number of samples contained in each sub-dataset is shown in Table 1.

Table 1: The number of samples in each sub-dataset when using different face landmarks extractors.

sub-datasets	Media Pipe FaceMesh	Face Alignment
chem	753,834	572,198
chess	787,963	547,220
eh	819,065	739,483

3.2 Details of Training

We use the pre-trained face landmarks extraction model to recognize and mark faces in the video data frame by frame. When using Media Pipe Face Mesh, the video mode will be turned on to reduce the jitter of landmarks. Our model sets a multi-layer convolutional network in the encoder, which finally represents the movement features of each frame as a high-dimensional feature vector as the hidden dimension of the encoder. Taking the experiment with 80 lip landmarks as an example, we sequentially set the number of channels of the convolutional block in the encoder to 120, 240, and 320, and the final hidden dimension is set to 384.

The batch size during model training is set to 32. The learning rate will increase linearly to 0.001 at the beginning of training and gradually decay in subsequent iterations. We used Adam (Kingma and Ba, 2014) as the optimizer and trained the model with about 600,000 iterations. The choice of these parameters was derived from the good results obtained during the experiments.

3.3 Evaluation Metrics

We measure whether the audio synthesized by the model is close to the natural human voice regarding intelligibility and audio quality. We will use the following three metrics to compare our model with previous studies: Short-Term Objective Intelligibility (STOI) (Taal et al., 2010), Extended Short-Term Objective Intelligibility (ESTOI) (Jensen and Taal, 2016), and Perceptual Evaluation of Speech Quality (PESQ) (Rix et al., 2001). In addition to the objective audio quality, we will compare the model's resource consumption and convergence time during the training process and demonstrate the comprehensive advantages of the unique solution of using face landmarks to represent lip movements from many aspects.

4 Results and Disscussion

This section presents a comparative analysis to evaluate the performance differences between FaceLandmarks2Wav and previous deep-learning models that use videos for lip-speech recognition. We choose the Lip2Wav as the baseline model (Prajwal et al., 2020), a lip-speech model that can synthesize audio results close to natural human voice from facial videos. We trained different models on the same dataset using similar settings and compared the differences in the number of parameters, Multiply-Accumulate operations (MACs), and convergence time of the models during training. The results are shown in Table 2. We used a smaller batch size when training Lip2Wav due to the limited video memory capacity of the graphics card used, and even so, the FaceLandmarks2Wav also has more advantages in terms of convergence time and other metrics.

Table 2: Comparison of model details and training time.

Models	Lip2Wav	Ours
Batch Size	16	32
Parameters	39.8 M	31.9 M
MACs	709.3 G	178.4 G
Single Iteration	1.4 sec	0.4 sec
Convergence	$\sim$ 140 hours	$\sim$ 50 hours

During training, we record the attention image generated by the FaceLandmarks2Wav. The horizontal and vertical axes of the image represent the time steps of the decoder and the encoder, respectively. The values represent the degree of attention paid to the encoder's specific time step when the decoder's attention module produces the corresponding time step results. Figure 2 shows how the attentional alignment of the model changes during the training process. The attention image gradually forms a diagonal image as the training progresses, meaning that the decoder refers to the lip features extracted by the encoder at nearby moments when synthesizing the audio results, consistent with the assumption of Eq 3. The attention image at the end of training is shown in Figure 2f, implying that the model could already learn the high-level features of facial motion from the input face landmarks sequence and synthesize the corresponding audio based on these features.

After the training, we compared the synthetic audio quality and intelligibility scores of the two models on the validation set, and the results are shown in Table 3. Compared with Lip2Wav, Our FaceLandmarks2Wav has a significant advantage in STOI and PESQ scores, and the ESTOI scores of Lip2Wav are relatively better. While synthesizing high-quality audio, FaceLandmarks2Wav has shorter training time, inference time, and smaller model sizes than Lip2Wav. Therefore, in scenarios sensitive to video memory usage and requiring high real-time performance, Our approach of synthesizing audio using face landmarks has more advantages.

Discussion. The above experiments prove that using face landmarks can represent the attributes of facial movement well. The experimental results show that using the FaceLandmarks2Wav model can synthesize natural and smooth speech results, and the synthesized audio is not inferior to the model using video data as input in terms of intelligibility and quality. Our proposed model structure can converge faster during the training process, and the requirements for the training environment are further reduced. The small model size allows it to be trained in environments with limited hardware, such as wearable devices. We also implemented corresponding ablation studies to compare the effect of face landmarks extracted differently on model performance.

Table 3: Performance comparison between our model and previous lip speech synthesis studies. The column of total result shows the arithmetic mean of the results of different sub-datasets.

Sub-dataset	Metrics	Models	
		Lip2Wav	Ours
chem	STOI	0.414	**0.478**
	ESTOI	**0.212**	0.193
	PESQ	1.130	**1.149**
chess	STOI	0.168	**0.217**
	ESTOI	**0.101**	0.073
	PESQ	1.143	**1.151**
eh	STOI	0.256	**0.367**
	ESTOI	**0.012**	0.009
	PESQ	1.302	**1.318**
total result	STOI	0.279	**0.354**
	ESTOI	**0.105**	0.092
	PESQ	1.192	**1.201**

5 Ablation Studies

As an initial study of using face landmarks to represent facial movement features, the effect of different ranges of face landmarks on the ability to represent facial motion features is one of our primary concerns, and we designed the corresponding ablation studies to explore this question.

We also try to use the Face Alignment Network (FAN) proposed by Bulat and Tzimiropoulos (2017) as an alternative face landmarks extractor, which can annotate 68 2D-landmarks in the whole face range and provide a way to estimate the depth information.

Table 4: Train the model with different ranges of landmarks. Training is performed on the chem sub-dataset. WF stands for "Whole Face".

Extractor	MPFM	MPFM	FAN
Contents	WF	Lips	WF
Landmarks	478	80	68
Channel	600, 680, 720	120, 240, 320	
Embedding	768	384	384
STOI	0.348	**0.478**	0.372
ESTOI	0.109	**0.193**	0.103
PESQ	1.048	**1.149**	1.034

The results of the ablation studies are shown in Table 4, which also shows the model embedding parameters for different settings of the number of landmarks. Surprisingly, the training results using only the lip landmarks are superior to those

Figure 2: Attention alignment images for FaceLandmarks2Wav

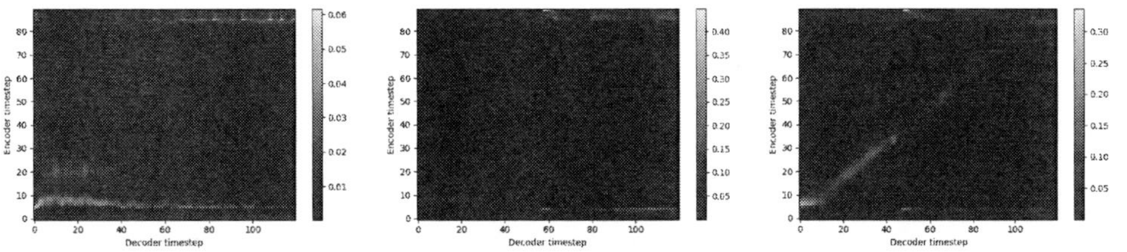

(a) Alignment image at 40K iterations (b) Attention image at 60K iterations (c) Alignment image at 80K iterations

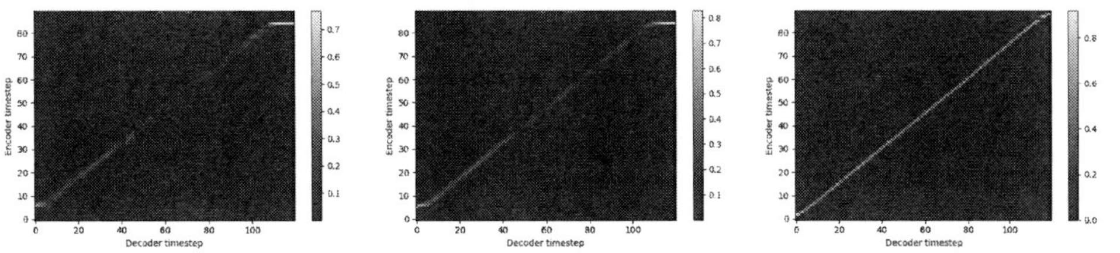

(d) Attention image at 100K iterations (e) Attention image at 120K iterations (f) Alignment image at end of training

using the whole-face range landmarks. This phenomenon is because the target audio synthesized by the model is most closely associated with the lip movements, and the input contains less additional information, making it more advantageous to train directly on the lip content. The experimental results do not show significant differences for different extractors using different numbers of landmarks to represent the full-face range of motion features.

On the other hand, when using the same face landmarks extractor, the performance of 3D landmarks is significantly better than that of 2D landmarks, indicating that even the depth information estimated by the extractor still provides more effective facial motion information to the encoder. This phenomenon is important for our future work, which means that the ability of face landmarks for facial motion representation could be further improved if landmark annotation is performed directly on real faces using a custom device.

6 Conclusion and Future Work

In this study, we initially explored the possibility of an innovative approach to characterize facial motion using face landmarks. We proposed FaceLandmarks2Wav, a model that synthesizes corresponding lip reading audio based on face landmarks and compared it with Lip2Wav, the lip reading model that uses video data to synthesize audio results. Experimental results show that our proposed model structure can synthesize relatively natural and smooth audio structures and be trained in a lower hardware environment. We also performed ablation studies, showing that audio results synthesized only using the lip range are even better than those using the whole face range. In future work, we hope to directly obtain the depth information of lip movement through 3D camera equipment, and more accurate face landmarks information will help further improve the model's performance.

References

Shaojie Bai, J Zico Kolter, and Vladlen Koltun. 2018. An empirical evaluation of generic convolutional and recurrent networks for sequence modeling. *arXiv preprint arXiv:1803.01271*.

Adrian Bulat and Georgios Tzimiropoulos. 2017. How far are we from solving the 2d & 3d face alignment problem?(and a dataset of 230,000 3d facial landmarks). In *Proceedings of the IEEE International Conference on Computer Vision*, pages 1021–1030.

Luca Cappelletta and Naomi Harte. 2012. Phoneme-to-viseme mapping for visual speech recognition. In *ICPRAM (2)*, pages 322–329. Citeseer.

Jan K Chorowski, Dzmitry Bahdanau, Dmitriy Serdyuk, Kyunghyun Cho, and Yoshua Bengio. 2015. Attention-based models for speech recognition. *Advances in neural information processing systems*, 28.

Joon Son Chung and Andrew Zisserman. 2016. Lip reading in the wild. In *Asian conference on computer vision*, pages 87–103. Springer.

Ivan Fung and Brian Mak. 2018. End-to-end low-resource lip-reading with maxout cnn and lstm. In

2018 IEEE International Conference on Acoustics, Speech and Signal Processing (ICASSP), pages 2511–2515. IEEE.

Amit Garg, Jonathan Noyola, and Sameep Bagadia. 2016. Lip reading using cnn and lstm. *Technical report, Stanford University, CS231 n project report.*

Daniel Griffin and Jae Lim. 1984. Signal estimation from modified short-time fourier transform. *IEEE Transactions on acoustics, speech, and signal processing*, 32(2):236–243.

Ivan Grishchenko, Artsiom Ablavatski, Yury Kartynnik, Karthik Raveendran, and Matthias Grundmann. 2020. Attention mesh: High-fidelity face mesh prediction in real-time. *arXiv preprint arXiv:2006.10962*.

Sepp Hochreiter and Jürgen Schmidhuber. 1997. Long short-term memory. *Neural computation*, 9(8):1735–1780.

Hongyang Huang, Chai Song, Jin Ting, Taoling Tian, Chen Hong, Zhang Di, and Danni Gao. 2022. A novel machine lip reading model. *Procedia Computer Science*, 199:1432–1437.

Lisa I Iezzoni, Bonnie L O'Day, Mary Killeen, and Heather Harker. 2004. Communicating about health care: observations from persons who are deaf or hard of hearing. *Annals of internal medicine*, 140(5):356–362.

Jesper Jensen and Cees H Taal. 2016. An algorithm for predicting the intelligibility of speech masked by modulated noise maskers. *IEEE/ACM Transactions on Audio, Speech, and Language Processing*, 24(11):2009–2022.

Diederik P Kingma and Jimmy Ba. 2014. Adam: A method for stochastic optimization. *arXiv preprint arXiv:1412.6980*.

Pingchuan Ma, Stavros Petridis, and Maja Pantic. 2022. Visual speech recognition for multiple languages in the wild. *arXiv preprint arXiv:2202.13084*.

Kim Yong Min and Li Hong Zuo. 2011. A lip reading method based on 3-d dct and 3-d hmm. In *Proceedings of 2011 International Conference on Electronics and Optoelectronics*, volume 1, pages V1–115. IEEE.

Saquib NadeemHashmi, Harsh Gupta, Dhruv Mittal, Kaushtubh Kumar, Aparajita Nanda, and Sarishty Gupta. 2018. A lip reading model using cnn with batch normalization. In *2018 eleventh international conference on contemporary computing (IC3)*, pages 1–6. IEEE.

Kuniaki Noda, Yuki Yamaguchi, Kazuhiro Nakadai, Hiroshi G Okuno, and Tetsuya Ogata. 2014. Lipreading using convolutional neural network. In *fifteenth annual conference of the international speech communication association*.

KR Prajwal, Rudrabha Mukhopadhyay, Vinay P Namboodiri, and CV Jawahar. 2020. Learning individual speaking styles for accurate lip to speech synthesis. In *Proceedings of the IEEE/CVF Conference on Computer Vision and Pattern Recognition*, pages 13796–13805.

Antony W Rix, John G Beerends, Michael P Hollier, and Andries P Hekstra. 2001. Perceptual evaluation of speech quality (pesq)-a new method for speech quality assessment of telephone networks and codecs. In *2001 IEEE international conference on acoustics, speech, and signal processing. Proceedings (Cat. No. 01CH37221)*, volume 2, pages 749–752. IEEE.

Ayaz A Shaikh, Dinesh K Kumar, Wai C Yau, MZ Che Azemin, and Jayavardhana Gubbi. 2010. Lip reading using optical flow and support vector machines. In *2010 3Rd international congress on image and signal processing*, volume 1, pages 327–330. IEEE.

Jonathan Shen, Ruoming Pang, Ron J Weiss, Mike Schuster, Navdeep Jaitly, Zongheng Yang, Zhifeng Chen, Yu Zhang, Yuxuan Wang, Rj Skerrv-Ryan, et al. 2018. Natural tts synthesis by conditioning wavenet on mel spectrogram predictions. In *2018 IEEE international conference on acoustics, speech and signal processing (ICASSP)*, pages 4779–4783. IEEE.

Cees H Taal, Richard C Hendriks, Richard Heusdens, and Jesper Jensen. 2010. A short-time objective intelligibility measure for time-frequency weighted noisy speech. In *2010 IEEE international conference on acoustics, speech and signal processing*, pages 4214–4217. IEEE.

Huijuan Wang, Gangqiang Pu, and Tingyu Chen. 2022. A lip reading method based on 3d convolutional vision transformer. *IEEE Access*, 10:77205–77212.

Kai Xu, Longyin Wen, Guorong Li, Liefeng Bo, and Qingming Huang. 2019. Spatiotemporal cnn for video object segmentation. In *Proceedings of the IEEE/CVF Conference on Computer Vision and Pattern Recognition*, pages 1379–1388.

Rethinking Response Evaluation from Interlocutor's Eye for Open-Domain Dialogue Systems

Yuma Tsuta[1] **Naoki Yoshinaga**[2] **Shoetsu Sato**[2*] **Masashi Toyoda**[2]
[1]The University of Tokyo
[2]Institute of Industrial Science , The University of Tokyo
{tsuta,ynaga,shoetsu,toyoda}@tkl.iis.u-tokyo.ac.jp

Abstract

Open-domain dialogue systems have started to engage in continuous conversations with humans. Those dialogue systems are required to be adjusted to the human interlocutor and evaluated in terms of their perspective. However, it is questionable whether the current automatic evaluation methods can approximate the interlocutor's judgments. In this study, we analyzed and examined what features are needed in an automatic response evaluator from the interlocutor's perspective. The first experiment on the Hazumi dataset revealed that interlocutor awareness plays a critical role in making automatic response evaluation correlate with the interlocutor's judgments. The second experiment using massive conversations on X (formerly Twitter) confirmed that dialogue continuity prediction can train an interlocutor-aware response evaluator without human feedback while revealing the difficulty in evaluating generated responses compared to human responses.

1 Introduction

Along with the growth of open-domain dialogue systems (Xu et al., 2022b,c; Bae et al., 2022; Takasaki et al., 2023), it is crucial to develop automatic methods that efficiently evaluate those systems. The automatic evaluations usually qualify system responses for utterances sampled from human conversation logs (§ 2). Since Liu et al. (2016) showed that automatic evaluation with a single reference response such as BLEU (Papineni et al., 2002; Forgues et al., 2014) did not correlate with human judgments due to the response diversity in open-domain dialogue (Sato et al., 2017; Tsuta et al., 2020), unsupervised reference-free methods and supervised methods that mimic human judgments have become popular (Yeh et al., 2021). However, these studies evaluate their methods in terms of correlation with judges by third-party annotators (*outsiders*), not partaking in the dialogue.

Figure 1: A discrepancy between interlocutor and outsider evaluations for open-domain dialogue systems.

Do the existing methods correctly evaluate the dialogue systems? As illustrated in Figure 1, the interlocutor and evaluators may prefer different yet valid responses. Although Ghazarian et al. (2022) experimentally confirmed a poor correlation with outsider and interlocutor evaluations in terms of appropriateness, they remain focused on outsider evaluations. This study focuses on interlocutor evaluations to enable an automatic evaluation from the interlocutor's perspective. In the experiment, we concentrate on validating our ideas in terms of engagement. Because this metric is more subjective and varies across people.

In this study, for estimating the interlocutor's evaluations, we first analyze the effectiveness of personalizing the evaluation model to the target interlocutor. This is inspired by research on response generation (Li et al., 2016; Xu et al., 2022b), as it has been reported to be important to adjust (personalize) utterances to the interlocutor. For this analysis, we used the Hazumi dataset (Komatani and Okada, 2021), and confirmed that, even when we train a supervised evaluator to mimic interlocutor scores, it cannot accurately predict their scores without making it aware of the target interlocutor.

Motivated by the lessons learned from the above experiments, we then explore automatic response evaluation from the interlocutor's eye (§ 4). To reduce the cost of annotation, we utilize a dialogue continuity prediction (DCP) task to train an

*This affiliation is at the time of the study and differs from at the time of publication.

Proceedings of the 13th International Joint Conference on Natural Language Processing and the 3rd Conference of the Asia-Pacific Chapter of the Association for Computational Linguistics: Student Research Workshop, pages 55–63
November 1–4, 2023.

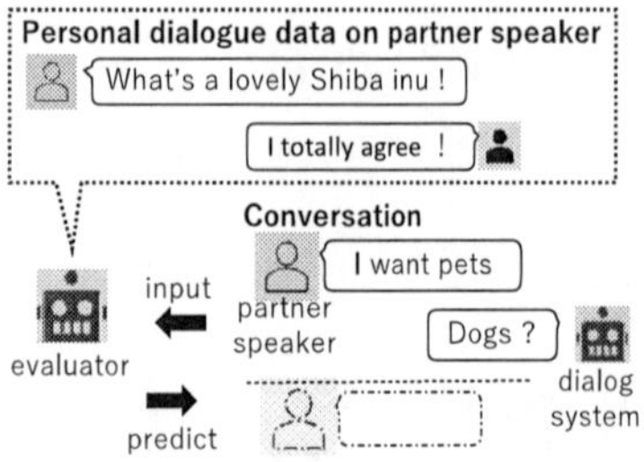

Figure 2: Automatic response evaluation via dialogue continuity prediction from the interlocutor's perspective.

interlocutor-aware evaluator (Figure 2). This task of estimating whether the target speaker will continue speaking or not can take advantage of labels (conversation stop signals) that are naturally annotated by the interlocutor in the conversation log. Experimental results on a conversation log on X (formerly Twitter) confirmed that the interlocutor-aware evaluator can be learned through the DCP task without human feedback while revealing the challenge of evaluating the system responses.

2 Related work

Automatic evaluation of dialogue systems To efficiently develop open-domain dialogue systems, researchers have sought evaluation methods that correlate with human evaluations. Since Liu et al. (2016) showed that reference-based metrics (Papineni et al., 2002; Forgues et al., 2014) using single reference responses do not correlate with human judgments, some studies use multiple reference responses (Galley et al., 2015; Gupta et al., 2019; Tsuta et al., 2020), while others train models by referring to human judgments (Lowe et al., 2017; Ghazarian et al., 2020) or other cues indicating valid responses (Tao et al., 2018; Ghazarian et al., 2019; Gao et al., 2020; Mehri and Eskenazi, 2020b; Xu et al., 2022a; Ghazarian et al., 2022). Recent studies (Mehri and Eskenazi, 2020a; Zhang et al., 2021) rely on language comprehension skills of pre-trained language models such as BERT (Devlin et al., 2019) and GPT-2 (Radford et al., 2019). There are evaluation tasks from the other perspective such as dialogue breakdown detection (Higashinaka et al., 2016). The above studies were, however, developed to follow outsider evaluations and do not assume evaluation from the interlocutor's eye, even though some recent dialogue systems are being adapted to interlocutors in long-term conversations (Xu et al., 2022b,c; Bae et al., 2022; Takasaki et al., 2023).

A few studies have elucidated the relationship between user personality and the performance of dialogue systems from a psychological perspective (Guo et al., 2021; Papangelis et al., 2022). These studies suggest the importance of the interlocutor's traits in evaluating dialogue systems.

User-oriented NLP tasks There are several user-oriented (or personalized) NLP tasks in which users prefer different outputs and hence the systems are expected to be adjusted to match user preferences, including hashtag recommendations on social networking sites (Kywe et al., 2012) and website recommendations (Mishra et al., 2015). Similarly, for text generation tasks in which models have become able to generate decent outputs, researchers are starting to adapt the models to reflect individual preferences; examples of such tasks include summarization (Díaz and Gervás, 2007), machine translation (Mirkin and Meunier, 2015), text simplification (Bingel et al., 2018), and dialogue systems (Liu et al., 2020; Cho et al., 2022). To evaluate these systems, they need human judgments by the system users, which low reproducibility prevents us from efficiently developing the systems.

3 What is important to predict interlocutor evaluations?

To analyze what features are important for predicting interlocutor scores, we train score prediction models with several settings and compare their performances. Specifically, we analyzed the effect of reference scores (*e.g.*, interlocutor or outsider scores) and interlocutor-aware personalization on the evaluation models. Although Ghazarian et al. (2022) confirmed a low correlation between interlocutor and outsider evaluations, we further confirmed that outsider evaluations do not help predict interlocutor scores. For this analysis, we used the Hazumi dataset (Komatani and Okada, 2021), which is an open-domain conversation in the form of the Wizard of Oz experiment.

3.1 Hazumi dialogue datasets

For this analysis, we need a dataset that contains interlocutor and outsider scores to train and test models, and we utilize Hazumi1902 and Hazumi1911 subsets from the Hazumi dataset[1]. This dataset is an open-domain conversation in which "Wizard" behaves like a dialogue system and "Participant"

[1] `https://www.nii.ac.jp/dsc/idr/en/rdata/Hazumi/`

Dataset	Hazumi1902	Hazumi1911
# dialogues (participants)	30	30
Total count of exchanges	2477	2824
Utterance length (Wizard)	22.7	20.8
Utterance length (Participant)	22.2	25.1

Table 1: Statistics of the subsets of the Hazumi datasets after preprocessing (§ 3.1). Utterance length refers to the average number of characters in an utterance.

Training score	Target awareness	Pearson's r
Outsider		0.141
Outsider	✓	0.142
Interlocutor		0.166
Interlocutor	✓	**0.496**

Table 2: Results on interlocutor score prediction with ablation of training score and target speaker awareness.

speaks as the user. These subsets only contain an interlocutor's (*e.g.*, Participant's) and five outsiders' scores for each utterance by the Wizard. The participants and five outsiders rated the Wizard's utterances on a scale of 1 (feeling negative) to 7 (feeling positive) on the basis of user impressions.[2] The direction of the guideline is similar to the engagement metric in Ghazarian et al. (2020) and the annotation on the experiment in § 4.2 in terms of the willingness of dialogue continuity.

In what follows, we preprocess the dataset so that the exchanges, a pair of utterances by a Wizard and the Participant, consist of no empty utterance. After these preprocessing steps, we obtained 5301 exchanges from 60 dialogues. The detailed statistics are shown in Table 1. We split each conversation into 8:1:1 size chunks according to the flow of the conversation (and recombined) to train, validate, and test the prediction models.

3.2 Analyze the effective cues in interlocutor score prediction

We train evaluators using various cues to identify the interlocutor scores and clarify the requisite for automatic interlocutor evaluation. In this task, the models predict the interlocutor score to an utterance by Wizard. We feed Wizard's utterance and the longest contexts possible to the model, adding a special speaker token (`[Wizard]` or `[Participant]`) to distinguish who speaks utterances before the corresponding utterances.

Models We compared four evaluator models based on BERT (Devlin et al., 2019) for ablation. The differences between these models are i) whether to use interlocutor scores or (the averaged) outsider scores as the reference in training and ii) whether to use a speaker token specific to the target participant or the generic participant token preceding each utterance. The distinguished participant token is meant to adjust the evaluator to individual interlocutors, inspired by the speaker token introduced by Li et al. (2016) to model speakers in response generation.

Settings We fine-tuned each model from pretrained Japanese BERT[3] for 10 epochs with the mean squared error loss. Other settings for the model were as follows: learning rate was $3e-5$ and optimized with AdamW (Kingma and Ba, 2015), and batch size was 64. We stored the model after each epoch and adopted the model that achieved the lowest loss for the validation data for testing.

Results Table 2 shows the correlations between model predictions and interlocutor actual scores. When a model is trained to predict the averaged outsider score, the evaluator showed a very low correlation of about 0.14. This confirms that outsider scores are useless in predicting interlocutor scores. Meanwhile, the model exhibits a much higher correlation when trained to predict interlocutor scores only with the awareness of target interlocutors; otherwise, the model shows only a slight improvement over the model learned by the averaged outsider scores. These results suggest that automatic interlocutor evaluation requires us to not only take the interlocutors' view (here, scores) into account but also to be aware of the target interlocutor.

4 Towards Automatic Response Evaluation from Interlocutor's Eye

From the result in § 3, we confirmed that accurate interlocutor score prediction requires personalizing the evaluator to the target interlocutor as well as referring to interlocutor scores. In practice, however, collecting interlocutor scores and creating conversations for the annotation are costly.

Therefore, focusing on evaluating responses in terms of engagement, we propose an alternative

[2]The annotation guidelines for user impressions define keywords and keyphrases such as "wants to keep talking" and "satisfied" as positive impressions, and "doesn't want to keep talking", "frustrated" and "confused" as negative impressions.

[3]`https://huggingface.co/cl-tohoku/bert-base-japanese-v2`

method to train an interlocutor-aware response evaluator via a dialogue continuity prediction task, assuming that utterances replied to by the interlocutors are more engaging than utterances without a response. The task is to predict whether there will be a response to an utterance in dialogue.[4]

4.1 Interlocutor Evaluation via Personalized Dialogue Continuity Prediction (DCP)

We train an automatic response evaluator via the dialogue continuity prediction task (Figure 2). The task settings are as follows. The task input is a conversation containing N utterances $U = \{u_0, u_1, ..., u_{N-1}\}$ made by two speakers s_i and s_j (u_{N-1} is made by s_j). The model output is assumed as the probability of whether the next response u_N is made by s_i, $P(u_N = \textit{exists} \mid U, s_i)$.

How to consider the interlocutor in a model? As we have observed in § 3.2, it is crucial to personalize a response evaluator to the target interlocutor to estimate human judgments given by the interlocutors. Inspired by existing studies on personalizing open-domain dialogue systems (Li et al., 2016; Zhang et al., 2018), we consider two methods for the evaluator to take the interlocutor into account. The first method leverages a speaker token specific to the target interlocutor, which has been used in the experiments in § 3.2, whereas the second method refers to a user profile of the interlocutor. When we train a speaker token specific to the target interlocutor, we follow the procedure described in § 3.2. When using the profile, we input the profile text that accompanies the evaluation datasets (§ 4.2) at the beginning of the model inputs. We also consider the combination of a speaker-specific token and profile. In summary, we use three methods to model the interlocutor: using a speaker-specific token, using the profile, and using both methods simultaneously.

4.2 Experimental Setup

To investigate the effectiveness of our interlocutor-aware evaluators, we conduct experiments focusing on two metrics: 1) **accuracy of the dialogue continuation task** and 2) **correlation with manually-annotated engagement scores**.

[4]Although Ghazarian et al. (2022) has also utilized the dialogue continuity prediction task for evaluating dialogue systems. They requested the interlocutors to explicitly expose to spoken dialogue systems whether or not to stop conversations, whereas we collected this label as an implicit signal from no response in human conversation logs.

Data Type	Train	Dev.	Test
Avg. turns in dialogue	3.4	3.4	3.3
Avg. char. size in turn	31.0	31.1	30.6
Avg. char. size in dialogue	106.5	106.8	101.2
Replied response size	1,779,895	100,899	1,088,970
No replied response size	1,244,530	70,135	832,377

Table 3: Statistics of the X dialogue datasets.

X (formerly Twitter) dialogue dataset We conducted the experiments using conversation logs on X. We can identify the author of a post, and handle a variety of users. We developed a Japanese dialogue dataset between two users using the API[5]. During the construction, we excluded posts that could be noisy, such as repetitive posts by bots, and preprocessed posts referencing studies using dialogues on Twitter (Li et al., 2016; Tsuta et al., 2020). In addition, we used only the conversations where all responses were made within 30 minutes because response rates tend to decrease over time (Gao et al., 2020). We expect these processes to make conversations more engaging, coherent, and less interrupted by others.

We randomly select 10,000 users who have had at least 30 conversations between January 2017 and March 2018. We use up to 400 conversations per user and their profile text to train the evaluator models. The profiles are collected with a field of the API (`user.fields=description`) and the average character size is 75.0. We used conversations of these users between March and December 2018 as test data. Because the intermediate reply is a positive sample and the last reply is a negative sample in the DCP task, several samples are collected from one conversation.

For the second experiment, we need conversations between a human (interlocutor) and a dialogue system, and the interlocutor's engagement score of willingness to reply to the system responses. Thus, we collected personal conversations on X by two members of our research group (a co-author and a graduate student) using the above same process. The dialogue data was added to the above dataset for (19, 6, and 10) and (165, 43, and 27) conversations as training, validation, and test data, respectively. Table 3 shows the statistics of the entire dataset.[6]

[5]`https://developer.twitter.com/en/docs/twitter-api`

[6]The post IDs for datasets other than annotator conversations can be available on `http://www.tkl.iis.u-tokyo.ac.jp/%7Etsuta/aacl-srw`.

Dialog systems To obtain system responses for human annotation, we employed seven dialogue models with two types of base architectures, Transformer encoder-decoder and decoder-only Transformer (GPT-2). As the encoder-decoder model, we used three publicly available dialogue systems that were trained with different datasets (Sugiyama et al., 2021).[7] As GPT-2, We fine-tuned a pre-trained GPT-2[8] (medium) with our dataset (§ 4.2). We prepared four variations of fine-tuned GPT-2 to obtain dialogue systems with diverse conversation abilities. The two options are i) whether to re-initialize the model's parameters before fine-tuning and ii) whether to personalize the system to the interlocutor using a speaker token (Li et al., 2016).

Annotation with interlocutor judgments To obtain manually annotated scores to responses for the second experiment, we asked the two annotators (same as the two interlocutors) to score seven responses generated by the above dialogue systems and one ground-truth response in the test data on a scale of 0 to 100, referring to Ji et al. (2022). 0 means that the annotator never responds to the last utterance of the conversation, and 100 means the opposite. We compensated the annotators at the rate of 1,050 JPY per hour.

Evaluator and baselines We compare the following evaluation models. Because we also evaluate actual human responses, we use reference-free evaluation models that are easily available in our Japanese corpus as baseline models: BERT-NSP (Devlin et al., 2019)[9], BERT-RUBER (Ghazarian et al., 2019), FED (Mehri and Eskenazi, 2020a)[10] and Deep-AM-FM (Zhang et al., 2021). We also adopt the simple baseline model that always outputs the majority class label (i.e., whether or not to reply) based on the training data. We prepared two types of majorities: all users' majority (**Global majority**) and each interlocutor's majority (**Private majority**).[11]

For the baseline models, we adopted a pre-trained BERT[3] for BERT-* and Deep-AM, and GPT-2[8] (small) for FED and Deep-FM. We trained models again for domain adaptation for FED and Deep-AM-FM, and additionally fine-tuned them for BERT-* using training data.[12] For our evaluator models, we trained BERT through the DCP task without the target user awareness (BERT-DCP) and with the personalization using user-specific token (+ user token), profile text (+ profile), or both of them (+ both). The hyperparameters of all models were as follows: learning rate as $3e-5$, batch size as 64, and number of epochs as 5. We used AdamW (Kingma and Ba, 2015) as the optimizer and cross-entropy loss as the loss function. All model parameters trained on our dataset, including the annotator's conversation for the second experiment, are shared across all experiments.

Evaluator	Accuracy	Macro-F_1
Global majority	0.564	0.361
Private majority	0.683	0.659
BERT-NSP	0.548	0.444
BERT-RUBER	0.541	0.488
Deep-AM	0.507	0.495
Deep-FM	0.543	0.533
Deep-AM-FM	0.541	0.531
FED	0.460	0.446
BERT-DCP	0.668	0.653
+ user token	**0.751**	**0.744**
+ profile	0.746	0.738
+ both	**0.751**	**0.744**

Table 4: Binary classification result of dialogue continuity prediction task on X dialogue dataset.

4.3 Results

Table 4 lists the results of binary classification on the dialogue continuity prediction task in terms of accuracy and macro-F_1 to correct label bias. To compare the baseline model which does not output probabilities (Deep-AM-FM, FED), the model output is binarized using a threshold based on the whole user response ratio in the validation data. Unsurprisingly, BERT-DCP fine-tuned through DCP task performed better than the baselines. The evaluator can work with the DCP task by considering the interlocutor and get better results than **Private majority**. We also observed that using a unique speaker token for each interlocutor was a more effective way of taking interlocutors into account.

Table 5 lists the results of Pearson's r correla-

[7]https://github.com/nttcslab/japanese-dialog-transformers

[8]https://huggingface.co/rinna

[9]We employed the next sequence prediction task as an automatic evaluation model as in other studies (Mehri and Eskenazi, 2020b; Phy et al., 2020).

[10]We translated the follow-up utterances to evaluate system responses in terms of engagement.

[11]Note that we use this model only in the first experiment because the second experiment evaluates models by Pearson correlation, but this model can output either 0 or 1.

[12]We created their negative samples with the same amount of positive samples in the training data by randomly combining a dialogue context utterances and a reply.

Evaluator	Annotator 1		Annotator 2	
	Human	System	Human	System
BERT-NSP	0.477	**0.416**	−0.028	**0.337**
BERT-RUBER	0.285	0.243	−0.134	0.210
Deep-AM	0.564	0.293	0.015	0.242
Deep-FM	0.499	0.031	−0.011	−0.070
Deep-AM-FM	0.528	0.074	−0.010	−0.055
FED	0.210	0.051	0.040	−0.070
BERT-DCP	0.646	0.401	0.578	0.156
+ user token	0.720	0.364	**0.582**	0.072
+ profile	**0.754**	0.369	0.543	0.077
+ both	0.727	0.367	0.527	0.078

Table 5: Correlation with human judgment for responses by humans (Human) and dialogue systems (System).

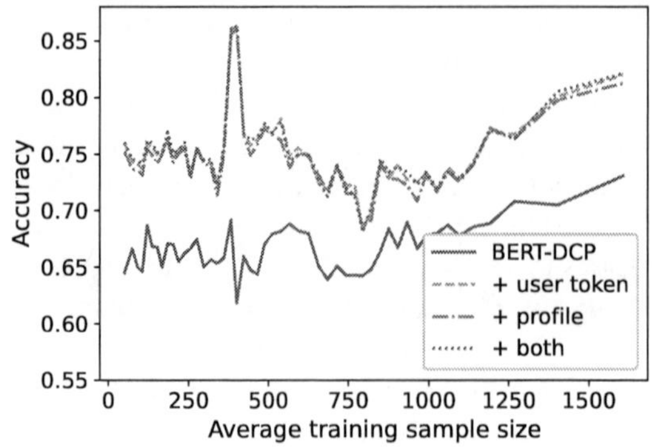

Figure 3: Result of dialogue continuity prediction task per user group split according to training sample size.

tion between each evaluator's outputs (probabilities) and interlocutor scores. Our evaluators, BERT-DCP, have higher correlations with fluent human responses than baseline evaluators, and the improvement of performance by considering personality can be confirmed. This result confirms the usefulness of the DCP task for predicting interlocutor evaluations. In contrast, the BERT-NSP has the highest correlation in the system response, and all BERT-NSPs are worse than the performance in the human response. This may be because the DCP task is trained based on real conversations and is therefore vulnerable to non-fluent and inappropriate responses by the system. A similar tendency of lower correlation with human judgments for system responses than those for human responses has been reported for the other evaluation models on engatement (Ghazarian et al., 2020; Gao et al., 2020).

Because our interlocutor-aware evaluators correlate well with interlocutors' judgments of human responses, our method will be more useful as dialogue systems converse more naturally like humans. However, we still need to improve the evaluator so that it is capable of evaluating dialogue systems in the future.

4.4 Discussion

The performance of our interlocutor-aware evaluator will be affected by the size of the conversation logs given by the target interlocutor. For example, the performance could be poor for users who have a few conversations in the training data. To investigate the relationship between the training sample size for the target interlocutor and the performance of our models, we divide the test dataset into three user groups so that the training sample size for each group is as equal as possible. As a result, the average sample size for each group was approximately 60,000, and the smallest group had an average of 51.1 samples. Table 3 shows the result on each user group in the test dataset. We confirmed that, with the exception of a peak around 400 samples, the accuracy changed only slightly below 1200 samples, improved above 1200 samples, and overall, the personalized models outperformed the BERT-DCP.

5 Conclusions

This study first explored the effect of interlocutor awareness on predicting interlocutor evaluations and then examined an automatic response evaluation method grounded in the perspective of the interlocutor. In the first experiment using the Hazumi dataset, we confirmed interlocutor score prediction requires personalization for interlocutor awareness as well as interlocutor scores. In the second experiment using conversations on X (formerly Twitter), we confirmed that dialogue continuity prediction is effective in training our interlocutor-aware automatic evaluator and the evaluator correlates with the actual interlocutor evaluations on human responses, while the improvement of the evaluation for the system responses is future work.

We plan to leverage recent response generation methods in long-term conversations (Xu et al., 2022b,c; Bae et al., 2022; Takasaki et al., 2023) to personalize our evaluator.

Acknowledgment

This work was partially supported by the special fund of Institute of Industrial Science, The University of Tokyo, by JSPS KAKENHI Grant Number JP21H03494, and by JST, CREST Grant Number JPMJCR19A4, Japan.

Limitations

Although this study illuminates the demand for evaluation from the perspective of the interlocutor, we only confirmed evaluation in terms of engagement. As existing studies on evaluation for open-domain dialogue systems are conducted in a variety of metrics such as understandability and informativeness, etc, (Finch et al., 2023), interlocutor-aware evaluation in the other evaluation metrics needs to be investigated.

To realize the study for a variety of metrics, a dataset with sufficient size of conversations and annotations is needed. In this study, we conducted experiments with two annotators to compare the automatic evaluators, but it is desirable to be annotated by a variety of people. Therefore, it is necessary to overcome the difficulties of the cost of constructing a dataset that includes conversations with multiple dialogue systems and annotations by the speakers, as well as the privacy issues related to dataset publication to reproduce experiments.

References

Sanghwan Bae, Donghyun Kwak, Soyoung Kang, Min Young Lee, Sungdong Kim, Yuin Jeong, Hyeri Kim, Sang-Woo Lee, Woomyoung Park, and Nako Sung. 2022. Keep me updated! memory management in long-term conversations. In *Findings of the Association for Computational Linguistics: EMNLP 2022*, pages 3769–3787, Abu Dhabi, United Arab Emirates. Association for Computational Linguistics.

Joachim Bingel, Gustavo Paetzold, and Anders Søgaard. 2018. Lexi: A tool for adaptive, personalized text simplification. In *Proceedings of the 27th International Conference on Computational Linguistics*, pages 245–258, Santa Fe, New Mexico, USA. Association for Computational Linguistics.

Itsugun Cho, Dongyang Wang, Ryota Takahashi, and Hiroaki Saito. 2022. A personalized dialogue generator with implicit user persona detection. In *Proceedings of the 29th International Conference on Computational Linguistics*, pages 367–377, Gyeongju, Republic of Korea. International Committee on Computational Linguistics.

Jacob Devlin, Ming-Wei Chang, Kenton Lee, and Kristina Toutanova. 2019. BERT: Pre-training of deep bidirectional transformers for language understanding. In *Proceedings of the 2019 Conference of the North American Chapter of the Association for Computational Linguistics: Human Language Technologies, Volume 1 (Long and Short Papers)*, pages 4171–4186, Minneapolis, Minnesota. Association for Computational Linguistics.

Alberto Díaz and Pablo Gervás. 2007. User-model based personalized summarization. *Information Processing & Management*, 43(6):1715–1734. Text Summarization.

Sarah E. Finch, James D. Finch, and Jinho D. Choi. 2023. Don't forget your ABC's: Evaluating the state-of-the-art in chat-oriented dialogue systems. In *Proceedings of the 61st Annual Meeting of the Association for Computational Linguistics (Volume 1: Long Papers)*, pages 15044–15071, Toronto, Canada. Association for Computational Linguistics.

Gabriel Forgues, Joelle Pineau, Jean-Marie Larchevêque, and Réal Tremblay. 2014. Bootstrapping dialog systems with word embeddings. In *NIPS, modern machine learning and natural language processing workshop*, volume 2.

Michel Galley, Chris Brockett, Alessandro Sordoni, Yangfeng Ji, Michael Auli, Chris Quirk, Margaret Mitchell, Jianfeng Gao, and Bill Dolan. 2015. deltaBLEU: A discriminative metric for generation tasks with intrinsically diverse targets. In *Proceedings of the 53rd Annual Meeting of the Association for Computational Linguistics and the 7th International Joint Conference on Natural Language Processing (Volume 2: Short Papers)*, pages 445–450, Beijing, China. Association for Computational Linguistics.

Xiang Gao, Yizhe Zhang, Michel Galley, Chris Brockett, and Bill Dolan. 2020. Dialogue response ranking training with large-scale human feedback data. In *Proceedings of the 2020 Conference on Empirical Methods in Natural Language Processing (EMNLP)*, pages 386–395, Online. Association for Computational Linguistics.

Sarik Ghazarian, Behnam Hedayatnia, Alexandros Papangelis, Yang Liu, and Dilek Hakkani-Tur. 2022. What is wrong with you?: Leveraging user sentiment for automatic dialog evaluation. In *Findings of the Association for Computational Linguistics: ACL 2022*, pages 4194–4204, Dublin, Ireland. Association for Computational Linguistics.

Sarik Ghazarian, Johnny Wei, Aram Galstyan, and Nanyun Peng. 2019. Better Automatic Evaluation of Open-Domain Dialogue Systems with Contextualized Embeddings. In *Proceedings of the Workshop on Methods for Optimizing and Evaluating Neural Language Generation*, pages 82–89, Minneapolis, Minnesota. Association for Computational Linguistics.

Sarik Ghazarian, Ralph Weischedel, Aram Galstyan, and Nanyun Peng. 2020. Predictive engagement: An efficient metric for automatic evaluation of open-domain dialogue systems. *Proceedings of the AAAI Conference on Artificial Intelligence*, 34(05):7789–7796.

Ao Guo, Atsumoto Ohashi, Ryu Hirai, Yuya Chiba, Yuiko Tsunomori, and Ryuichiro Higashinaka. 2021.

Influence of user personality on dialogue task performance: A case study using a rule-based dialogue system. In *Proceedings of the 3rd Workshop on Natural Language Processing for Conversational AI*, pages 263–270, Online. Association for Computational Linguistics.

Prakhar Gupta, Shikib Mehri, Tiancheng Zhao, Amy Pavel, Maxine Eskenazi, and Jeffrey Bigham. 2019. Investigating Evaluation of Open-Domain Dialogue Systems With Human Generated Multiple References. In *Proceedings of the 20th Annual SIGdial Meeting on Discourse and Dialogue*, pages 379–391, Stockholm, Sweden. Association for Computational Linguistics.

Ryuichiro Higashinaka, Kotaro Funakoshi, Yuka Kobayashi, and Michimasa Inaba. 2016. The dialogue breakdown detection challenge: Task description, datasets, and evaluation metrics. In *Proceedings of the Tenth International Conference on Language Resources and Evaluation (LREC'16)*, pages 3146–3150, Portorož, Slovenia. European Language Resources Association (ELRA).

Tianbo Ji, Yvette Graham, Gareth Jones, Chenyang Lyu, and Qun Liu. 2022. Achieving reliable human assessment of open-domain dialogue systems. In *Proceedings of the 60th Annual Meeting of the Association for Computational Linguistics (Volume 1: Long Papers)*, pages 6416–6437, Dublin, Ireland. Association for Computational Linguistics.

Diederik P. Kingma and Jimmy Ba. 2015. Adam: A Method for Stochastic Optimization. In *International Conference for Learning Representations*.

Kazunori Komatani and Shogo Okada. 2021. Multimodal human-agent dialogue corpus with annotations at utterance and dialogue levels. In *2021 9th International Conference on Affective Computing and Intelligent Interaction (ACII)*, pages 1–8.

Su Mon Kywe, Tuan-Anh Hoang, Ee-Peng Lim, and Feida Zhu. 2012. On recommending hashtags in twitter networks. In *Social Informatics*, pages 337–350, Berlin, Heidelberg. Springer Berlin Heidelberg.

Jiwei Li, Michel Galley, Chris Brockett, Georgios Spithourakis, Jianfeng Gao, and Bill Dolan. 2016. A persona-based neural conversation model. In *Proceedings of the 54th Annual Meeting of the Association for Computational Linguistics (Volume 1: Long Papers)*, pages 994–1003, Berlin, Germany. Association for Computational Linguistics.

Chia-Wei Liu, Ryan Lowe, Iulian Serban, Mike Noseworthy, Laurent Charlin, and Joelle Pineau. 2016. How NOT To Evaluate Your Dialogue System: An Empirical Study of Unsupervised Evaluation Metrics for Dialogue Response Generation. In *Proceedings of the 2016 Conference on Empirical Methods in Natural Language Processing*, pages 2122–2132, Austin, Texas. Association for Computational Linguistics.

Qian Liu, Yihong Chen, Bei Chen, Jian-Guang Lou, Zixuan Chen, Bin Zhou, and Dongmei Zhang. 2020. You impress me: Dialogue generation via mutual persona perception. In *Proceedings of the 58th Annual Meeting of the Association for Computational Linguistics*, pages 1417–1427, Online. Association for Computational Linguistics.

Ryan Lowe, Michael Noseworthy, Iulian Vlad Serban, Nicolas Angelard-Gontier, Yoshua Bengio, and Joelle Pineau. 2017. Towards an automatic Turing test: Learning to evaluate dialogue responses. In *Proceedings of the 55th Annual Meeting of the Association for Computational Linguistics (Volume 1: Long Papers)*, pages 1116–1126, Vancouver, Canada. Association for Computational Linguistics.

Shikib Mehri and Maxine Eskenazi. 2020a. Unsupervised evaluation of interactive dialog with DialoGPT. In *Proceedings of the 21th Annual Meeting of the Special Interest Group on Discourse and Dialogue*, pages 225–235, 1st virtual meeting. Association for Computational Linguistics.

Shikib Mehri and Maxine Eskenazi. 2020b. USR: An unsupervised and reference free evaluation metric for dialog generation. In *Proceedings of the 58th Annual Meeting of the Association for Computational Linguistics*, pages 681–707, Online. Association for Computational Linguistics.

Shachar Mirkin and Jean-Luc Meunier. 2015. Personalized machine translation: Predicting translational preferences. In *Proceedings of the 2015 Conference on Empirical Methods in Natural Language Processing*, pages 2019–2025, Lisbon, Portugal. Association for Computational Linguistics.

Rajhans Mishra, Pradeep Kumar, and Bharat Bhasker. 2015. A web recommendation system considering sequential information. *Decision Support Systems*, 75:1–10.

Alexandros Papangelis, Nicole Chartier, Pankaj Rajan, Julia Hirschberg, and Dilek Hakkani-Tur. 2022. Understanding how people rate their conversations. In *Conversational AI for Natural Human-Centric Interaction, the 12th International Workshop on Spoken Dialogue System Technology*, IWSDS 2021,, pages 179–189, Singapore. Springer Singapore.

Kishore Papineni, Salim Roukos, Todd Ward, and Wei-Jing Zhu. 2002. Bleu: A Method for Automatic Evaluation of Machine Translation. In *Proceedings of 40th Annual Meeting of the Association for Computational Linguistics*, pages 311–318, Philadelphia, Pennsylvania, USA. Association for Computational Linguistics.

Vitou Phy, Yang Zhao, and Akiko Aizawa. 2020. Deconstruct to reconstruct a configurable evaluation metric for open-domain dialogue systems. In *Proceedings of the 28th International Conference on Computational Linguistics*, pages 4164–4178, Barcelona, Spain (Online). International Committee on Computational Linguistics.

Alec Radford, Jeffrey Wu, Rewon Child, David Luan, Dario Amodei, and Ilya Sutskever. 2019. Language Models Are Unsupervised Multitask Learners. volume 1, page 9.

Shoetsu Sato, Naoki Yoshinaga, Masashi Toyoda, and Masaru Kitsuregawa. 2017. Modeling situations in neural chat bots. In *Proceedings of ACL 2017, Student Research Workshop*, pages 120–127, Vancouver, Canada. Association for Computational Linguistics.

Hiroaki Sugiyama, Masahiro Mizukami, Tsunehiro Arimoto, Hiromi Narimatsu, Yuya Chiba, Hideharu Nakajima, and Toyomi Meguro. 2021. Empirical analysis of training strategies of transformer-based japanese chit-chat systems.

Meguru Takasaki, Naoki Yoshinaga, and Masashi Toyoda. 2023. Effective dialogue-context retriever for long-term open-domain conversation. In *The 13th International Workshop on Spoken Dialogue Systems Technology*, Los Angeles.

Chongyang Tao, Lili Mou, Dongyan Zhao, and Rui Yan. 2018. RUBER: An Unsupervised Method for Automatic Evaluation of Open-Domain Dialog Systems. In *AAAI Conference on Artificial Intelligence*, pages 722–729.

Yuma Tsuta, Naoki Yoshinaga, and Masashi Toyoda. 2020. uBLEU: Uncertainty-aware automatic evaluation method for open-domain dialogue systems. In *Proceedings of the 58th Annual Meeting of the Association for Computational Linguistics: Student Research Workshop*, pages 199–206, Online. Association for Computational Linguistics.

Guangxuan Xu, Ruibo Liu, Fabrice Harel-Canada, Nischal Reddy Chandra, and Nanyun Peng. 2022a. EnDex: Evaluation of dialogue engagingness at scale. In *Findings of the Association for Computational Linguistics: EMNLP 2022*, pages 4884–4893, Abu Dhabi, United Arab Emirates. Association for Computational Linguistics.

Jing Xu, Arthur Szlam, and Jason Weston. 2022b. Beyond goldfish memory: Long-term open-domain conversation. In *Proceedings of the 60th Annual Meeting of the Association for Computational Linguistics (Volume 1: Long Papers)*, pages 5180–5197, Dublin, Ireland. Association for Computational Linguistics.

Xinchao Xu, Zhibin Gou, Wenquan Wu, Zheng-Yu Niu, Hua Wu, Haifeng Wang, and Shihang Wang. 2022c. Long time no see! open-domain conversation with long-term persona memory. In *Findings of the Association for Computational Linguistics: ACL 2022*, pages 2639–2650, Dublin, Ireland. Association for Computational Linguistics.

Yi-Ting Yeh, Maxine Eskenazi, and Shikib Mehri. 2021. A comprehensive assessment of dialog evaluation metrics. In *The First Workshop on Evaluations and Assessments of Neural Conversation Systems*, pages 15–33, Online. Association for Computational Linguistics.

Chen Zhang, Luis Fernando D'Haro, Rafael E. Banchs, Thomas Friedrichs, and Haizhou Li. 2021. Deep am-fm: Toolkit for automatic dialogue evaluation. In Luis Fernando D'Haro, Zoraida Callejas, and Satoshi Nakamura, editors, *Conversational Dialogue Systems for the Next Decade*, pages 53–69. Springer Singapore, Singapore.

Saizheng Zhang, Emily Dinan, Jack Urbanek, Arthur Szlam, Douwe Kiela, and Jason Weston. 2018. Personalizing dialogue agents: I have a dog, do you have pets too? In *Proceedings of the 56th Annual Meeting of the Association for Computational Linguistics (Volume 1: Long Papers)*, pages 2204–2213, Melbourne, Australia. Association for Computational Linguistics.

Long-form Simultaneous Speech Translation*
Thesis Proposal

Peter Polák
Charles University
Faculty of Mathematics and Physics
Institute of Formal and Applied Linguistics
polak@ufal.mff.cuni.cz

Abstract

Simultaneous speech translation (SST) aims to provide real-time translation of spoken language, even before the speaker finishes their sentence. Traditionally, SST has been addressed primarily by cascaded systems that decompose the task into subtasks, including speech recognition, segmentation, and machine translation. However, the advent of deep learning has sparked significant interest in end-to-end (E2E) systems. Nevertheless, a major limitation of most approaches to E2E SST reported in the current literature is that they assume that the source speech is pre-segmented into sentences, which is a significant obstacle for practical, real-world applications. This thesis proposal addresses end-to-end simultaneous speech translation, particularly in the long-form setting, i.e., without pre-segmentation. We present a survey of the latest advancements in E2E SST, assess the primary obstacles in SST and its relevance to long-form scenarios, and suggest approaches to tackle these challenges.

1 Introduction

In today's highly globalized world, communication among individuals speaking different languages is gaining importance. International conferences and multinational organizations like the European Parliament often rely on human interpreters. However, in many scenarios, employing human interpreters can be impractical and costly. In such cases, simultaneous speech translation[1] (SST) offers a viable solution by enabling real-time translation before the speaker completes their sentence.

Traditionally, both offline speech translation (ST) and simultaneous speech translation (SST) have relied predominantly on cascaded systems that decompose the task into multiple subtasks, including speech recognition, speech segmentation, and machine translation (Osterholtz et al., 1992; Fügen et al., 2007; Bojar et al., 2021). However, recent advancements in deep learning and the availability of abundant data (Tan and Lim, 2018; Sperber and Paulik, 2020) have led to a significant paradigm shift towards end-to-end (E2E) models. While the cascaded approach continues to dominate offline ST, the opposite is true for SST (Anastasopoulos et al., 2022; Agarwal et al., 2023).

Despite the recent popularity of end-to-end SST, the vast majority of research focuses on the "short-form" setting, which assumes that the speech input is already pre-segmented into sentences. Critically, this assumption poses an obstacle to deployment in the wild. Therefore, we aim to achieve a "true" long-form simultaneous speech translation in our thesis. We break down our efforts into three steps:

Quality-latency tradeoff in SST The first step of our research concentrates on enhancing the quality-latency tradeoff, mainly in the traditional "short-form" regime. We will evaluate different approaches and architectures.

Towards the long-form SST In the next step, we will explore the feasibility of long-form simultaneous speech translation by adopting segmented inference.

True long-form SST The final goal of our work is to explore the potential of end-to-end modeling for true long-form SST. We will focus on identifying an appropriate model architecture and effective training procedures to achieve seamless and reliable long-form simultaneous speech translation.

The next section introduces some important aspects of simultaneous speech translation.

*The literature on simultaneous speech translation often uses the word "streaming" as an equivalent of "simultaneous" to refer to the translation of an unfinished utterance. In other literature, however, the term "streaming" refers to input spanning several sentences. To avoid confusion, we use "simultaneous" to refer to the translation of an unfinished utterance and "long-form" to refer to input spanning several sentences.

[1]We consider only the speech-to-text variant in this work.

Proceedings of the 13th International Joint Conference on Natural Language Processing and the 3rd Conference of the Asia-Pacific Chapter of the Association for Computational Linguistics: Student Research Workshop, pages 64–74
November 1–4, 2023.

2 Simultaneous Speech Translation

The ultimate goal of SST is to enable *real-time* communication between people speaking different languages. To achieve this goal, SST systems must meet two important criteria. First, they must be *computationally efficient* to ensure timely translation during ongoing speech. Second, SST systems must be capable of *handling unfinished sentences*. Working with unfinished sentences allows for more timely translations, particularly when waiting for sentences to be completed is impractical, such as matching slides or presenters' gestures. However, translating unfinished sentences increases the risk of translation errors since translation usually requires re-ordering that benefits from a more complete sentence context. Thus, there exists a *quality-latency tradeoff*. This means that given a certain latency constraint, we want the model to produce as good translations as possible. Ideally, we want the model to "predict" the future context without the risk of an incorrect translation. The quality-latency tradeoff is one of the main topics of our research.

2.1 Re-Translation vs. Incremental SST

SST can be classified as either re-translation or incremental. Re-translation SST (Niehues et al., 2016, 2018) can revise the hypothesis or re-rank the set of hypotheses as more speech input is read. Revising the translation allows the re-translation SST to have comparable final translation quality with the offline speech translation (Arivazhagan et al., 2020). This design approach arguably introduces challenges for the user in processing the translation and makes it impossible to use in real-time speech-to-speech translation. Additionally, it also complicates the latency evaluation.

In fact, several SST latency metrics (Ma et al., 2020) were originally developed specifically for incremental translation scenarios.[2] Incremental SST (Cho and Esipova, 2016; Dalvi et al., 2018) differs from the re-translation system in that it prunes all hypotheses to a common prefix, which is then shown to the user. For the user, the translation changes only by incrementally getting longer; none of the previously displayed outputs are ever modified. In our work, we focus on incremental SST.

[2]IWSLT shared tasks (Ansari et al., 2020; Anastasopoulos et al., 2021, 2022) also follow this evaluation standard.

2.2 Cascaded vs. End-to-End

Traditionally, offline speech translation and SST were achieved as a *cascade* of multiple systems: automatic speech recognition (ASR), inverse transcript normalization, which includes punctuation prediction and true casing, and machine translation (MT, Osterholtz et al., 1992; Fügen et al., 2007; Bojar et al., 2021). The advantage of the cascade approach is that we can optimize models for each subtask independently. Also, ASR and MT tasks typically have access to larger and more diverse corpora than direct speech translation.

However, using a cascade system introduces several challenges (Sperber and Paulik, 2020). The most important among them is *error propagation* (Ruiz and Federico, 2014). Further, MT models might suffer from *mismatched domains* when trained on written language. Furthermore, as the source is transformed into a textual form, it *loses crucial information about prosody*, i.e., the rhythm, intonation, and emphasis in speech (Bentivogli et al., 2021). Finally, many languages, especially endangered ones, have no written form, which makes the cascade approach impractical or impossible for such languages (Harrison, 2007; Duong et al., 2016).

As of the latest findings, the current state-of-the-art for offline speech translation continues to be based on a cascaded approach (Anastasopoulos et al., 2022; Agarwal et al., 2023). In simultaneous speech translation, however, both approaches yield competitive performance. The advantage of the end-to-end models in SST may be that they avoid the extra delay caused by ASR-MT collaboration in the cascade (Wang et al., 2022).

In our work, we focus on end-to-end models.

3 Long-form Simultaneous Speech Translation

Most of the contemporary research on SST assumes speech pre-segmented into short utterances with segmentation following the sentence boundaries. However, in any real application, there is no such segmentation available. This section places long-form SST within the broader context of long-form ASR, MT, and offline ST. Subsequently, we explore the current literature on long-form SST.

3.1 Long-Form ASR

In terms of input and output modalities, long-form ASR and ST face similar issues. There are two types of strategies for long-form processing: (1) the *segmented approach*, which divides the input into smaller chunks, and (2) the *true long-form approach*, which handles the entire long-form input as a single unit.

Most of the literature focuses on the *segmented approach*. A typical solution involves pre-segmenting the audio using voice activity detection (VAD). However, VAD segmentation may not be optimal for real-world speech since it might fail to handle hesitations or pauses in sentences that must be treated as undivided units. More sophisticated approaches leverage latent alignments obtained from CTC (Graves et al., 2006) and RNN-T (Graves, 2012) for better segmentation (Yoshimura et al., 2020; Huang et al., 2022). Alternatively, segmentation into *fixed segments* is also popular (Chiu et al., 2019, 2021). To reduce low-quality transcripts close to the segment boundaries, they typically perform overlapped inference and use latent alignments to merge the transcripts correctly. The chunking approach is also adopted by the attentional model Whisper in the offline (Radford et al., 2023) and simultaneous regime (Macháček et al., 2023).

Another line of work focused on *long-form modeling* directly. For example, Chiu et al. (2019) conducted a comprehensive study comparing different architectures, including RNN-T and attention-based models. The findings indicate that only RNN-T and CTC architectures can generalize to unseen lengths. To further improve the true long-form ASR, Narayanan et al. (2019) suggest simulation of long-form training by LSTM state passing.

While the previously mentioned research was predominantly based on RNNs, more recent work has transitioned to utilizing Transformer models. Zhang et al. (2023) compared a chunk-wise attention encoder, which involves an encoder with a limited attention span, in combination with the attention-based decoder (AD) and CTC. We note that while the encoder has a limited attention span, the attention-based decoder sees the entire encoder representation. The model employing AD could not function without chunking, whereas the CTC model processed the entire speech at once and still outperformed the AD model.

3.2 Long-Form MT

The primary objective of long-form MT is to enhance textual coherence, as conventional MT systems assume sentence independence. Early work explored a concatenation of previous (Tiedemann and Scherrer, 2017; Donato et al., 2021) and future sentences (Agrawal et al., 2018). These works showed that MT models benefit from the extra context and better handle the inter-sentential discourse phenomena. However, the benefits diminish if the context grows beyond a few sentences (Agrawal et al., 2018; Kim et al., 2019; Fernandes et al., 2021). This can be attributed to the limitations of attention mechanisms, where an extensive volume of irrelevant information can lead to confusion.

Other body of work tries to model very long sequences directly. Dai et al. (2019) introduced a recurrence mechanism and improved positional encoding scheme in the Transformer. Later work proposed an explicit compressed memory realized by a few dense vectors (Feng et al., 2022).

3.3 Long-Form Offline ST

Unlike written input text in long-form MT, speech input in the ST task lacks explicit information about segmentation. Therefore, the research in the area of long-form offline speech translation concentrates on two separate issues: (1) improving *segmentation* into sentences, and (2) enhancing robustness through the use of larger *context*.

In the traditional cascaded approach with separate speech recognition and machine translation models, the work focused on segmentation strategies for the ASR transcripts.[3] The methods are usually based on re-introducing punctuation to the transcript (Lu and Ng, 2010; Rangarajan Sridhar et al., 2013; Cho et al., 2015, 2017). However, these approaches suffer from ASR error propagation and disregard the source audio's acoustic information. This was addressed by Iranzo-Sánchez et al. (2020a), however, the approach still requires an intermediate ASR transcript that is unavailable in E2E models.

An alternative approach involves source-speech-based segmentation. The early work focused on VAD segmentation. This is usually sub-optimal as speakers place pauses inside sentences, not necessarily between them (e.g., hesitations before words with high information content, Goldman-Eisler, 1958). To this end, researchers tried considering not only the presence of speech but also its length (Potapczyk and Przybysz, 2020; Inaguma et al.,

[3]ASR transcripts are traditionally normalized, i.e., they consist of lowercase words without punctuation.

2021; Gaido et al., 2021). Later studies tried to avoid VAD and focused on more linguistically-motivated approaches, e.g., ASR CTC to predict voiced regions Gállego et al. (2021) or directly modeling the sentence segmentation (Tsiamas et al., 2022b; Fukuda et al., 2022).

To address the problem of inadequate segmentation, Gaido et al. (2020) showed that context-aware ST is less prone to segmentation errors. In an extensive study of context-aware ST, Zhang et al. (2021) observed that context improves quality, but this holds only for a limited number of utterances.

3.4 Long-Form Simultaneous ST

Research focusing on direct long-form simultaneous speech translation remains relatively scarce. The closest works are in long-form simultaneous MT. Schneider and Waibel (2020) proposed a streaming MT model capable of translating unsegmented text input. This model could be theoretically adapted for speech input. However, it was later shown that this model exhibits huge latency (Iranzo Sanchez et al., 2022). Another work (Iranzo Sanchez et al., 2022) explored the extended context and confirmed the findings from long-form MT and offline ST, demonstrating that using the previous context significantly enhances performance. They also confirmed that a too-long context leads to decreased translation quality.

Finally, the only direct SST model that claims to work on a possibly unbounded input is Ma et al. (2021). The model utilizes a Transformer encoder with a restriction on self-attention, allowing it to attend solely to a memory bank and a small segment. Unfortunately, based on the reported experiments, whether the model was specifically evaluated in the long-form setting remains unclear.

3.5 Evaluation

Evaluation of SST is a complex problem as we have to consider not only the translation quality but also the latency. Additionally, in the long-form regime, segmentation becomes another obstacle.

The most commonly used metric for translation quality in speech translation is BLEU (Papineni et al., 2002; Post, 2018). Other metrics such as chrF++ (Popović, 2017) and a neural-based metric COMET (Rei et al., 2020) can be applied, too.

The other important property of an SST system is latency. There are two main types of latencies: computation-unaware (CU) and computation-aware (CA) latency. The computation-unaware latency measures the delay in emitting a translation token relative to the source, regardless of the actual computation time. Hence, CU latency allows for a fair comparison regardless of the hardware infrastructure. However, CU latency cannot penalize the evaluated system for extensive computation; hence, CA latency can offer a more realistic assessment.

Measuring latency relative to the source or reference in SST is quite difficult because of the reordering present in translation. Historically, latency metrics were first developed for simultaneous machine translation (i.e., the source is text rather than speech). The most common are average lagging (AL; Ma et al., 2019) and differentiable average lagging (DAL; Cherry and Foster, 2019). Broadly speaking, they measure "how much of the source was read by the system to translate a word". The latency unit is typically a word. The speech community quickly adopted these metrics. Unfortunately, these metrics assume a uniform distribution of words and uniform length of these words in the speech source. Alternatively, Ansari et al. (2021) proposed to use a statistical word alignment of the candidate translation with the corresponding source transcript. This theoretically allows for more precise latency evaluation, but it is unclear how the alignment errors impact the reliability.

In the unsegmented long-form setting, additional issues arise. In a typical "short-form" segmented setup, the SST model does inference on a pre-segmented input. However, the candidate and reference segmentation into sentences might differ in the long-form unsegmented regime. Traditionally, this issue was addressed by re-segmenting the hypothesis based on the reference (Matusov et al., 2005). After the re-segmentation, a standard sentence-level evaluation of translation quality and latency is done. It should be noted that the commonly used latency metrics (AL, DAL) cannot be used in the long-form regime (Iranzo-Sánchez et al., 2021) without the re-segmentation. Yet, recent work observed that the re-segmentation introduces errors (Amrhein and Haddow, 2022). This poses a risk of incorrect translation and quality assessment and remains an open research question.

4 Thesis Goals

The goal of our thesis is to achieve a "true" long-form simultaneous speech translation. This section outlines the steps we will take to accomplish this goal.

4.1 Data and Evaluation

In our future research, we will mainly use the setup similar to the IWSLT shared tasks (Ansari et al., 2020; Anastasopoulos et al., 2021, 2022), i.e., mostly single speaker data. Identical to the IWSLT, we will treat the TED data as an in-domain setting. We will consider domains such as parliamentary speeches (e.g., Europarl-ST Iranzo-Sánchez et al., 2020b) for the out-of-domain setting. As for the languages, we will include a diverse set of language pairs. A good inspiration might be again the IWSLT, i.e., English-to-{German, Japanese, Chinese}. Challenging will be the long-form setting, as to the best of our knowledge, none of the available data is strictly long-form. Our preliminary review found that the original TED talks can be reconstructed from the MuST-C (Cattoni et al., 2021) development and test set available for English-to-{German, Japanese, Chinese} language pairs.

As highlighted in the literature review in Section 3.5, evaluating the long-form SST remains an open problem. The quality and latency evaluation metrics currently used are designed for sentence-level evaluation. We must re-segment the long hypotheses into sentences based on their word alignment with provided references to use these metrics in the long-form regime. Unfortunately, the re-segmentation introduces errors, which poses a risk to the evaluation reliability. To tackle this, we will investigate alternative evaluation strategies. One potential approach for reducing the alignment error could be to move the alignment to the sentence level rather than the word level and allow an m-to-n mapping between the reference and proposed sentences, similar to the Gale–Church alignment algorithm (Gale et al., 1994), with a reasonably small m and n (e.g., $0 \leq m, n \leq 2$). To verify the effectiveness of this method, we need to compare its correlation with human evaluations.

4.2 Quality-latency tradeoff in SST

The first step of our research concentrates on enhancing the quality-latency tradeoff, mainly in the traditional "short-form" simultaneous speech translation. We hope the insights and improvements from the short-form regime will translate into the long-form regime.

In the research done so far, we already successfully reviewed the possibility of "onlinizing" state-of-the-art offline speech translation models in Polák et al. (2022). Our observations indicated that the attention-based encoder-decoder (AED) models tend to over-generate. This not only affects the resulting quality but also negatively impacts the AL latency evaluation reliability. Therefore, we proposed an improved version of the AL metric, which was later independently proposed under name length-adaptive average lagging (LAAL; Papi et al., 2022). To remedy the over-generation problem, we proposed an improved version of the beam search algorithm in Polák et al. (2023b). While this led to significant improvements in the quality-latency tradeoff, the decoding still relied on label-synchronous decoding. In Polák et al. (2023a), we proposed a novel SST policy dubbed "CTC policy" that uses the output of an auxiliary CTC layer to guide the decoding. The proposed CTC policy led to even greater improvements in quality and reduced the real-time factor to 50 %.

Thus far, our research has focused primarily on the AED architecture. Nonetheless, recent findings (Anastasopoulos et al., 2022; Agarwal et al., 2023) suggest that other approaches, such as transducers (Graves, 2012), yield competitive results. Nevertheless, it remains unclear which approach is the most advantageous for SST. Our goal will be to compare these architectures for SST. We will put a particular emphasis on architectures with latent alignments (e.g., transducers). Generally, the latent alignment models make a strong monotonic assumption on the mapping between the source and the target, which might be problematic for the translation, typically involving word reordering. Therefore, we will assess the alignment quality and potential applications (such as segmentation).

4.3 Towards the Long-Form SST via On-the-Fly Segmentation

In the second stage, we will concentrate on the long-form SST by utilizing on-the-fly segmentation and short-form models from the previous stage.

Drawing inspiration from offline long-form ST, which primarily emphasizes segmentation, we consider direct segmentation modeling the most promising approach (Tsiamas et al., 2022a; Fukuda et al., 2022). The limitation of these approaches is that they do not allow out-of-the-box simultaneous inference. However, we believe their adaptation to the simultaneous regime should be relatively straightforward (e.g., using a unidirectional encoder) and a custom decoding strategy. The main challenge here will be integrating this segmentation with existing models, especially considering the quality-latency tradeoff.

Our hopes go even further: Can we train a model to translate and predict the segmentation at the same time? The translation already contains punctuation marks (full stop, exclamation, and question marks), so if we knew the alignment between the translation and the source speech, we could use this information to segment the utterances directly. Therefore, we will experiment with various alignment approaches and asses their applicability to the segmentation. The results of our initial investigation on on-the-fly separation with CTC outputs are available in Polák and Bojar (2023).

However, we see another valuable use of direct speech-to-translation alignments — dataset creation. Today, ST datasets are created using the cascaded approach (Iranzo-Sánchez et al., 2020b; Cattoni et al., 2021; Salesky et al., 2021). The source transcript is first forced-aligned to the speech, then the transcript is word-aligned to the translations, and finally, these two alignments are used to segment the source speech into sentences based on the punctuation in the translation. In fact, this approach has a critical drawback: it virtually eliminates all data without a source transcript, preventing the research community from utilizing potentially valuable data sources. It is also worth noting that some languages do not have a writing system, which makes the direct speech-to-translation alignment even more attractive. Therefore, if the alignments show promising results, we will explore the feasibility of E2E speech-to-translation dataset creation.

An additional question is how to accommodate long context in the simultaneous regime. As pointed out in Sections 3.2 to 3.4, the performance usually drops with a context longer than a few sentences. Some solutions have been suggested (Kim et al., 2019; Feng et al., 2022), but it remains unclear how to adapt these approaches for SST with the specifics of SST in mind (e.g., computational constraints, speech input).

4.4 True Long-Form SST

The ultimate goal of our work is to achieve true long-form simultaneous speech translation. In other words, we aim to develop an architecture capable of processing a potentially infinite stream of speech input without any segmentation or special inference algorithm, translating the speech directly into the target language in real time. Admittedly, this is a very ambitious goal. However, there is plenty of evidence that it is feasible. For example, in long-form ASR, related work has already observed that the RNN-T and CTC architectures are capable of long-form regime (Chiu et al., 2019; Narayanan et al., 2019; Lu et al., 2021; Zhang et al., 2023; Rekesh et al., 2023). Arguably, speech recognition is simpler than speech translation because it monotonically transcribes speech without reordering. However, the literature also shows that an architecture like RNN-T can be used in the "short-form" offline and simultaneous ST (Yan et al., 2023).

Therefore, based on the previous work in speech recognition and translation, we will propose a novel architecture that will allow simultaneous speech translation of a possibly infinite stream of speech. We will take inspiration from the existing architectures but revise them for the specific needs of simultaneous ST. This will require a particular focus on speech-to-translation alignment so that the source speech and target translation do not get out of sync. This architecture will also contain a "forgetting" mechanism that will allow the storage of essential bits of context while preventing memory issues. Finally, we will address the train-test mismatch because current hardware and training methods do not permit models to fit long inputs.

5 Conclusion

In conclusion, this thesis proposal presents an overview of the challenges involved in simultaneous speech translation (SST). The literature review highlighted the limited research on long-form speech translation. Our research sets out three main goals with an emphasis on long-form speech translation. These include improving the general quality-latency tradeoff in SST, exploring long-form SST through segmented inference, and ultimately achieving true long-form SST modeling. We placed these goals in the context of related work and outlined a clear strategy for achieving them.

Acknowledgments

Peter would like to thank his supervisor, Ondřej Bojar, for his insight and guidance, as well as the anonymous reviewers for their valuable suggestions. This work has received support from GAUK project 244523 of Charles University and partial support from grant 19-26934X (NEUREM3) of the Czech Science Foundation.

References

Milind Agarwal, Sweta Agrawal, Antonios Anastasopoulos, Luisa Bentivogli, Ondřej Bojar, Claudia Borg, Marine Carpuat, Roldano Cattoni, Mauro Cettolo, Mingda Chen, William Chen, Khalid Choukri, Alexandra Chronopoulou, Anna Currey, Thierry Declerck, Qianqian Dong, Kevin Duh, Yannick Estève, Marcello Federico, Souhir Gahbiche, Barry Haddow, Benjamin Hsu, Phu Mon Htut, Hirofumi Inaguma, Dávid Javorský, John Judge, Yasumasa Kano, Tom Ko, Rishu Kumar, Pengwei Li, Xutai Ma, Prashant Mathur, Evgeny Matusov, Paul McNamee, John P. McCrae, Kenton Murray, Maria Nadejde, Satoshi Nakamura, Matteo Negri, Ha Nguyen, Jan Niehues, Xing Niu, Atul Kr. Ojha, John E. Ortega, Proyag Pal, Juan Pino, Lonneke van der Plas, Peter Polák, Elijah Rippeth, Elizabeth Salesky, Jiatong Shi, Matthias Sperber, Sebastian Stüker, Katsuhito Sudoh, Yun Tang, Brian Thompson, Kevin Tran, Marco Turchi, Alex Waibel, Mingxuan Wang, Shinji Watanabe, and Rodolfo Zevallos. 2023. FINDINGS OF THE IWSLT 2023 EVALUATION CAMPAIGN. In *Proceedings of the 20th International Conference on Spoken Language Translation (IWSLT 2023)*, pages 1–61, Toronto, Canada (in-person and online). Association for Computational Linguistics.

Ruchit Agrawal, Marco Turchi, and Matteo Negri. 2018. Contextual handling in neural machine translation: Look behind, ahead and on both sides. In *Proceedings of the 21st Annual Conference of the European Association for Machine Translation*, pages 31–40, Alicante, Spain.

Chantal Amrhein and Barry Haddow. 2022. Don't discard fixed-window audio segmentation in speech-to-text translation. In *Proceedings of the Seventh Conference on Machine Translation (WMT)*, pages 203–219, Abu Dhabi, United Arab Emirates (Hybrid). Association for Computational Linguistics.

Antonios Anastasopoulos, Loïc Barrault, Luisa Bentivogli, Marcely Zanon Boito, Ondřej Bojar, Roldano Cattoni, Anna Currey, Georgiana Dinu, Kevin Duh, Maha Elbayad, Clara Emmanuel, Yannick Estève, Marcello Federico, Christian Federmann, Souhir Gahbiche, Hongyu Gong, Roman Grundkiewicz, Barry Haddow, Benjamin Hsu, Dávid Javorský, Věra Kloudová, Surafel Lakew, Xutai Ma, Prashant Mathur, Paul McNamee, Kenton Murray, Maria Nădejde, Satoshi Nakamura, Matteo Negri, Jan Niehues, Xing Niu, John Ortega, Juan Pino, Elizabeth Salesky, Jiatong Shi, Matthias Sperber, Sebastian Stüker, Katsuhito Sudoh, Marco Turchi, Yogesh Virkar, Alexander Waibel, Changhan Wang, and Shinji Watanabe. 2022. Findings of the IWSLT 2022 evaluation campaign. In *Proceedings of the 19th International Conference on Spoken Language Translation (IWSLT 2022)*, pages 98–157, Dublin, Ireland (in-person and online). Association for Computational Linguistics.

Antonios Anastasopoulos, Ondřej Bojar, Jacob Bremerman, Roldano Cattoni, Maha Elbayad, Marcello Federico, Xutai Ma, Satoshi Nakamura, Matteo Negri, Jan Niehues, Juan Pino, Elizabeth Salesky, Sebastian Stüker, Katsuhito Sudoh, Marco Turchi, Alexander Waibel, Changhan Wang, and Matthew Wiesner. 2021. FINDINGS OF THE IWSLT 2021 EVALUATION CAMPAIGN. In *Proceedings of the 18th International Conference on Spoken Language Translation (IWSLT 2021)*, pages 1–29, Bangkok, Thailand (online). Association for Computational Linguistics.

Ebrahim Ansari, Amittai Axelrod, Nguyen Bach, Ondřej Bojar, Roldano Cattoni, Fahim Dalvi, Nadir Durrani, Marcello Federico, Christian Federmann, Jiatao Gu, Fei Huang, Kevin Knight, Xutai Ma, Ajay Nagesh, Matteo Negri, Jan Niehues, Juan Pino, Elizabeth Salesky, Xing Shi, Sebastian Stüker, Marco Turchi, Alexander Waibel, and Changhan Wang. 2020. FINDINGS OF THE IWSLT 2020 EVALUATION CAMPAIGN. In *Proceedings of the 17th International Conference on Spoken Language Translation*, pages 1–34, Online. Association for Computational Linguistics.

Ebrahim Ansari, Ondřej Bojar, Barry Haddow, and Mohammad Mahmoudi. 2021. SLTEV: Comprehensive evaluation of spoken language translation. In *Proceedings of the 16th Conference of the European Chapter of the Association for Computational Linguistics: System Demonstrations*, pages 71–79, Online. Association for Computational Linguistics.

Naveen Arivazhagan, Colin Cherry, Wolfgang Macherey, and George Foster. 2020. Re-translation versus streaming for simultaneous translation. In *Proceedings of the 17th International Conference on Spoken Language Translation*, pages 220–227, Online. Association for Computational Linguistics.

Luisa Bentivogli, Mauro Cettolo, Marco Gaido, Alina Karakanta, Alberto Martinelli, Matteo Negri, and Marco Turchi. 2021. Cascade versus direct speech translation: Do the differences still make a difference? In *Proceedings of the 59th Annual Meeting of the Association for Computational Linguistics and the 11th International Joint Conference on Natural Language Processing (Volume 1: Long Papers)*, pages 2873–2887, Online. Association for Computational Linguistics.

Ondřej Bojar, Dominik Macháček, Sangeet Sagar, Otakar Smrž, Jonáš Kratochvíl, Peter Polák, Ebrahim Ansari, Mohammad Mahmoudi, Rishu Kumar, Dario Franceschini, Chiara Canton, Ivan Simonini, Thai-Son Nguyen, Felix Schneider, Sebastian Stüker, Alex Waibel, Barry Haddow, Rico Sennrich, and Philip Williams. 2021. ELITR multilingual live subtitling: Demo and strategy. In *Proceedings of the 16th Conference of the European Chapter of the Association for Computational Linguistics: System Demonstrations*, pages 271–277, Online. Association for Computational Linguistics.

Roldano Cattoni, Mattia Antonino Di Gangi, Luisa Bentivogli, Matteo Negri, and Marco Turchi. 2021. Must-c: A multilingual corpus for end-to-end speech translation. *Computer Speech & Language*, 66:101155.

Colin Cherry and George Foster. 2019. Thinking slow about latency evaluation for simultaneous machine translation. *arXiv preprint arXiv:1906.00048*.

Chung-Cheng Chiu, Wei Han, Yu Zhang, Ruoming Pang, Sergey Kishchenko, Patrick Nguyen, Arun Narayanan, Hank Liao, Shuyuan Zhang, Anjuli Kannan, et al. 2019. A comparison of end-to-end models for long-form speech recognition. In *2019 IEEE automatic speech recognition and understanding workshop (ASRU)*, pages 889–896. IEEE.

Chung-Cheng Chiu, Arun Narayanan, Wei Han, Rohit Prabhavalkar, Yu Zhang, Navdeep Jaitly, Ruoming Pang, Tara N Sainath, Patrick Nguyen, Liangliang Cao, et al. 2021. Rnn-t models fail to generalize to out-of-domain audio: Causes and solutions. In *2021 IEEE Spoken Language Technology Workshop (SLT)*, pages 873–880. IEEE.

Eunah Cho, Jan Niehues, Kevin Kilgour, and Alex Waibel. 2015. Punctuation insertion for real-time spoken language translation. In *Proceedings of the 12th International Workshop on Spoken Language Translation: Papers*, pages 173–179.

Eunah Cho, Jan Niehues, and Alex Waibel. 2017. Nmt-based segmentation and punctuation insertion for real-time spoken language translation. In *Interspeech*, pages 2645–2649.

Kyunghyun Cho and Masha Esipova. 2016. Can neural machine translation do simultaneous translation? *arXiv preprint arXiv:1606.02012*.

Zihang Dai, Zhilin Yang, Yiming Yang, Jaime Carbonell, Quoc Le, and Ruslan Salakhutdinov. 2019. Transformer-XL: Attentive language models beyond a fixed-length context. In *Proceedings of the 57th Annual Meeting of the Association for Computational Linguistics*, pages 2978–2988, Florence, Italy. Association for Computational Linguistics.

Fahim Dalvi, Nadir Durrani, Hassan Sajjad, and Stephan Vogel. 2018. Incremental decoding and training methods for simultaneous translation in neural machine translation. In *Proceedings of the 2018 Conference of the North American Chapter of the Association for Computational Linguistics: Human Language Technologies, Volume 2 (Short Papers)*, pages 493–499, New Orleans, Louisiana. Association for Computational Linguistics.

Domenic Donato, Lei Yu, and Chris Dyer. 2021. Diverse pretrained context encodings improve document translation. In *Proceedings of the 59th Annual Meeting of the Association for Computational Linguistics and the 11th International Joint Conference on Natural Language Processing (Volume 1: Long Papers)*, pages 1299–1311, Online. Association for Computational Linguistics.

Long Duong, Antonios Anastasopoulos, David Chiang, Steven Bird, and Trevor Cohn. 2016. An attentional model for speech translation without transcription. In *Proceedings of the 2016 Conference of the North American Chapter of the Association for Computational Linguistics: Human Language Technologies*, pages 949–959, San Diego, California. Association for Computational Linguistics.

Yukun Feng, Feng Li, Ziang Song, Boyuan Zheng, and Philipp Koehn. 2022. Learn to remember: Transformer with recurrent memory for document-level machine translation. In *Findings of the Association for Computational Linguistics: NAACL 2022*, pages 1409–1420, Seattle, United States. Association for Computational Linguistics.

Patrick Fernandes, Kayo Yin, Graham Neubig, and André F. T. Martins. 2021. Measuring and increasing context usage in context-aware machine translation. In *Proceedings of the 59th Annual Meeting of the Association for Computational Linguistics and the 11th International Joint Conference on Natural Language Processing (Volume 1: Long Papers)*, pages 6467–6478, Online. Association for Computational Linguistics.

Christian Fügen, Alex Waibel, and Muntsin Kolss. 2007. Simultaneous translation of lectures and speeches. *Machine translation*, 21:209–252.

Ryo Fukuda, Katsuhito Sudoh, and Satoshi Nakamura. 2022. Speech segmentation optimization using segmented bilingual speech corpus for end-to-end speech translation. *arXiv preprint arXiv:2203.15479*.

Marco Gaido, Mattia A. Di Gangi, Matteo Negri, Mauro Cettolo, and Marco Turchi. 2020. Contextualized Translation of Automatically Segmented Speech. In *Proc. Interspeech 2020*, pages 1471–1475.

Marco Gaido, Matteo Negri, Mauro Cettolo, and Marco Turchi. 2021. Beyond voice activity detection: Hybrid audio segmentation for direct speech translation. In *Proceedings of the 4th International Conference on Natural Language and Speech Processing (ICNLSP 2021)*, pages 55–62.

William A. Gale, Kenneth Ward Church, et al. 1994. A program for aligning sentences in bilingual corpora. *Computational linguistics*, 19(1):75–102.

Gerard I. Gállego, Ioannis Tsiamas, Carlos Escolano, José A. R. Fonollosa, and Marta R. Costa-jussà. 2021. End-to-end speech translation with pre-trained models and adapters: UPC at IWSLT 2021. In *Proceedings of the 18th International Conference on Spoken Language Translation (IWSLT 2021)*, pages 110–119, Bangkok, Thailand (online). Association for Computational Linguistics.

Frieda Goldman-Eisler. 1958. Speech production and the predictability of words in context. *Quarterly Journal of Experimental Psychology*, 10(2):96–106.

Alex Graves. 2012. Sequence transduction with recurrent neural networks. *arXiv preprint arXiv:1211.3711*.

Alex Graves, Santiago Fernández, Faustino Gomez, and Jürgen Schmidhuber. 2006. Connectionist temporal classification: labelling unsegmented sequence data with recurrent neural networks. In *Proceedings of the 23rd international conference on Machine learning*, pages 369–376.

K David Harrison. 2007. *When languages die: The extinction of the world's languages and the erosion of human knowledge*. Oxford University Press.

W Ronny Huang, Shuo-yiin Chang, David Rybach, Rohit Prabhavalkar, Tara N Sainath, Cyril Allauzen, Cal Peyser, and Zhiyun Lu. 2022. E2e segmenter: Joint segmenting and decoding for long-form asr. *arXiv preprint arXiv:2204.10749*.

Hirofumi Inaguma, Brian Yan, Siddharth Dalmia, Pengcheng Guo, Jiatong Shi, Kevin Duh, and Shinji Watanabe. 2021. ESPnet-ST IWSLT 2021 offline speech translation system. In *Proceedings of the 18th International Conference on Spoken Language Translation (IWSLT 2021)*, pages 100–109, Bangkok, Thailand (online). Association for Computational Linguistics.

Javier Iranzo Sanchez, Jorge Civera, and Alfons Juan-Císcar. 2022. From simultaneous to streaming machine translation by leveraging streaming history. In *Proceedings of the 60th Annual Meeting of the Association for Computational Linguistics (Volume 1: Long Papers)*, pages 6972–6985, Dublin, Ireland. Association for Computational Linguistics.

Javier Iranzo-Sánchez, Jorge Civera Saiz, and Alfons Juan. 2021. Stream-level latency evaluation for simultaneous machine translation. In *Findings of the Association for Computational Linguistics: EMNLP 2021*, pages 664–670, Punta Cana, Dominican Republic. Association for Computational Linguistics.

Javier Iranzo-Sánchez, Adrià Giménez Pastor, Joan Albert Silvestre-Cerdà, Pau Baquero-Arnal, Jorge Civera Saiz, and Alfons Juan. 2020a. Direct segmentation models for streaming speech translation. In *Proceedings of the 2020 Conference on Empirical Methods in Natural Language Processing (EMNLP)*, pages 2599–2611, Online. Association for Computational Linguistics.

Javier Iranzo-Sánchez, Joan Albert Silvestre-Cerda, Javier Jorge, Nahuel Roselló, Adria Giménez, Albert Sanchis, Jorge Civera, and Alfons Juan. 2020b. Europarl-st: A multilingual corpus for speech translation of parliamentary debates. In *ICASSP 2020-2020 IEEE International Conference on Acoustics, Speech and Signal Processing (ICASSP)*, pages 8229–8233. IEEE.

Yunsu Kim, Duc Thanh Tran, and Hermann Ney. 2019. When and why is document-level context useful in neural machine translation? In *Proceedings of the Fourth Workshop on Discourse in Machine Translation (DiscoMT 2019)*, page 24–34, Hong Kong, China. Association for Computational Linguistics.

Wei Lu and Hwee Tou Ng. 2010. Better punctuation prediction with dynamic conditional random fields. In *Proceedings of the 2010 conference on empirical methods in natural language processing*, pages 177–186.

Zhiyun Lu, Yanwei Pan, Thibault Doutre, Parisa Haghani, Liangliang Cao, Rohit Prabhavalkar, Chao Zhang, and Trevor Strohman. 2021. Input length matters: Improving rnn-t and mwer training for long-form telephony speech recognition. *arXiv preprint arXiv:2110.03841*.

Mingbo Ma, Liang Huang, Hao Xiong, Renjie Zheng, Kaibo Liu, Baigong Zheng, Chuanqiang Zhang, Zhongjun He, Hairong Liu, Xing Li, Hua Wu, and Haifeng Wang. 2019. STACL: Simultaneous translation with implicit anticipation and controllable latency using prefix-to-prefix framework. In *Proceedings of the 57th Annual Meeting of the Association for Computational Linguistics*, pages 3025–3036, Florence, Italy. Association for Computational Linguistics.

Xutai Ma, Mohammad Javad Dousti, Changhan Wang, Jiatao Gu, and Juan Pino. 2020. SIMULEVAL: An evaluation toolkit for simultaneous translation. In *Proceedings of the 2020 Conference on Empirical Methods in Natural Language Processing: System Demonstrations*, pages 144–150, Online. Association for Computational Linguistics.

Xutai Ma, Yongqiang Wang, Mohammad Javad Dousti, Philipp Koehn, and Juan Pino. 2021. Streaming simultaneous speech translation with augmented memory transformer. In *ICASSP 2021-2021 IEEE International Conference on Acoustics, Speech and Signal Processing (ICASSP)*, pages 7523–7527. IEEE.

Dominik Macháček, Raj Dabre, and Ondřej Bojar. 2023. Turning whisper into real-time transcription system. In *Proceedings of the 3rd Conference of the Asia-Pacific Chapter of the Association for Computational Linguistics and the 13th International Joint Conference on Natural Language Processing: System Demonstrations*, Bali, Indonesia. Association for Computational Linguistics.

Evgeny Matusov, Gregor Leusch, Oliver Bender, and Hermann Ney. 2005. Evaluating machine translation output with automatic sentence segmentation. In *Proceedings of the Second International Workshop on Spoken Language Translation*, Pittsburgh, Pennsylvania, USA.

Arun Narayanan, Rohit Prabhavalkar, Chung-Cheng Chiu, David Rybach, Tara N Sainath, and Trevor Strohman. 2019. Recognizing long-form speech using streaming end-to-end models. In *2019 IEEE automatic speech recognition and understanding workshop (ASRU)*, pages 920–927. IEEE.

J. Niehues, T. S. Nguyen, E. Cho, T.-L. Ha, K. Kilgour, M. Müller, M. Sperber, S. Stüker, and A. Waibel. 2016. Dynamic transcription for low-latency speech translation. In *17th Annual Conference of the International Speech Communication Association, INTERSPEECH 2016; Hyatt Regency San FranciscoSan Francisco; United States; 8 September 2016 through 16 September 2016*, volume 08-12-September-2016 of *Proceedings of the Annual Conference of the International Speech Communication Association. Ed. : N. Morgan*, pages 2513–2517. International Speech Communication Association.

J. Niehues, N.-Q. Pham, T.-L. Ha, M. Sperber, and A. Waibel. 2018. Low-latency neural speech translation. In *19th Annual Conference of the International Speech Communication, INTERSPEECH 2018; Hyderabad International Convention Centre (HICC)Hyderabad; India; 2 September 2018 through 6 September 2018. Ed.: C.C. Sekhar*, volume 2018-September of *Proceedings of the Annual Conference of the International Speech Communication Association, INTERSPEECH*, pages 1293–1297. ISCA.

L. Osterholtz, C. Augustine, A. McNair, I. Rogina, H. Saito, T. Sloboda, J. Tebelskis, and A. Waibel. 1992. Testing generality in janus: a multi-lingual speech translation system. In *[Proceedings] ICASSP-92: 1992 IEEE International Conference on Acoustics, Speech, and Signal Processing*, volume 1, pages 209–212 vol.1.

Sara Papi, Marco Gaido, Matteo Negri, and Marco Turchi. 2022. Over-generation cannot be rewarded: Length-adaptive average lagging for simultaneous speech translation. In *Proceedings of the Third Workshop on Automatic Simultaneous Translation*, pages 12–17, Online. Association for Computational Linguistics.

Kishore Papineni, Salim Roukos, Todd Ward, and Wei-Jing Zhu. 2002. Bleu: a method for automatic evaluation of machine translation. In *Proceedings of the 40th annual meeting of the Association for Computational Linguistics*, pages 311–318.

Peter Polák and Ondřej Bojar. 2023. Long-form end-to-end speech translation via latent alignment segmentation. *arXiv preprint arXiv:2309.11384*.

Peter Polák, Danni Liu, Ngoc-Quan Pham, Jan Niehues, Alexander Waibel, and Ondřej Bojar. 2023a. Towards efficient simultaneous speech translation: CUNI-KIT system for simultaneous track at IWSLT 2023. In *Proceedings of the 20th International Conference on Spoken Language Translation (IWSLT 2023)*, pages 389–396, Toronto, Canada (in-person and online). Association for Computational Linguistics.

Peter Polák, Ngoc-Quan Pham, Tuan Nam Nguyen, Danni Liu, Carlos Mullov, Jan Niehues, Ondřej Bojar, and Alexander Waibel. 2022. CUNI-KIT system for simultaneous speech translation task at IWSLT 2022. In *Proceedings of the 19th International Conference on Spoken Language Translation (IWSLT 2022)*, pages 277–285, Dublin, Ireland (in-person and online). Association for Computational Linguistics.

Peter Polák, Brian Yan, Shinji Watanabe, Alexander Waibel, and Ondrej Bojar. 2023b. Incremental Blockwise Beam Search for Simultaneous Speech Translation with Controllable Quality-Latency Tradeoff. In *Proc. Interspeech 2023*.

Maja Popović. 2017. chrF++: words helping character n-grams. In *Proceedings of the Second Conference on Machine Translation*, pages 612–618, Copenhagen, Denmark. Association for Computational Linguistics.

Matt Post. 2018. A call for clarity in reporting BLEU scores. In *Proceedings of the Third Conference on Machine Translation: Research Papers*, pages 186–191, Brussels, Belgium. Association for Computational Linguistics.

Tomasz Potapczyk and Pawel Przybysz. 2020. SRPOL's system for the IWSLT 2020 end-to-end speech translation task. In *Proceedings of the 17th International Conference on Spoken Language Translation*, pages 89–94, Online. Association for Computational Linguistics.

Alec Radford, Jong Wook Kim, Tao Xu, Greg Brockman, Christine McLeavey, and Ilya Sutskever. 2023. Robust speech recognition via large-scale weak supervision. In *International Conference on Machine Learning*, pages 28492–28518. PMLR.

Vivek Kumar Rangarajan Sridhar, John Chen, Srinivas Bangalore, Andrej Ljolje, and Rathinavelu Chengalvarayan. 2013. Segmentation strategies for streaming speech translation. In *Proceedings of the 2013 Conference of the North American Chapter of the Association for Computational Linguistics: Human Language Technologies*, pages 230–238, Atlanta, Georgia. Association for Computational Linguistics.

Ricardo Rei, Craig Stewart, Ana C Farinha, and Alon Lavie. 2020. Unbabel's participation in the WMT20 metrics shared task. In *Proceedings of the Fifth Conference on Machine Translation*, pages 911–920, Online. Association for Computational Linguistics.

Dima Rekesh, Samuel Kriman, Somshubra Majumdar, Vahid Noroozi, He Juang, Oleksii Hrinchuk, Ankur Kumar, and Boris Ginsburg. 2023. Fast conformer with linearly scalable attention for efficient speech recognition. *arXiv preprint arXiv:2305.05084*.

Nicholas Ruiz and Marcello Federico. 2014. Assessing the impact of speech recognition errors on machine translation quality. In *Proceedings of the 11th Conference of the Association for Machine Translation in the Americas: MT Researchers Track*, pages 261–274.

Elizabeth Salesky, Matthew Wiesner, Jacob Bremerman, Roldano Cattoni, Matteo Negri, Marco Turchi, Douglas W Oard, and Matt Post. 2021. The multilingual tedx corpus for speech recognition and translation. *arXiv preprint arXiv:2102.01757*.

Felix Schneider and Alexander Waibel. 2020. Towards stream translation: Adaptive computation time for simultaneous machine translation. In *Proceedings of the 17th International Conference on Spoken Language Translation*, pages 228–236, Online. Association for Computational Linguistics.

Matthias Sperber and Matthias Paulik. 2020. Speech translation and the end-to-end promise: Taking stock of where we are. In *Proceedings of the 58th Annual Meeting of the Association for Computational Linguistics*, pages 7409–7421, Online. Association for Computational Linguistics.

Kar-Han Tan and Boon Pang Lim. 2018. The artificial intelligence renaissance: deep learning and the road to human-level machine intelligence. *APSIPA Transactions on Signal and Information Processing*, 7:e6.

Jörg Tiedemann and Yves Scherrer. 2017. Neural machine translation with extended context. In *Proceedings of the Third Workshop on Discourse in Machine Translation*, pages 82–92, Copenhagen, Denmark. Association for Computational Linguistics.

Ioannis Tsiamas, Gerard I. Gállego, Carlos Escolano, José Fonollosa, and Marta R. Costa-jussà. 2022a. Pretrained speech encoders and efficient fine-tuning methods for speech translation: UPC at IWSLT 2022. In *Proceedings of the 19th International Conference on Spoken Language Translation (IWSLT 2022)*, pages 265–276, Dublin, Ireland (in-person and online). Association for Computational Linguistics.

Ioannis Tsiamas, Gerard I Gállego, José AR Fonollosa, and Marta R Costa-jussà. 2022b. Shas: Approaching optimal segmentation for end-to-end speech translation. *arXiv preprint arXiv:2202.04774*.

Minghan Wang, Jiaxin Guo, Yinglu Li, Xiaosong Qiao, Yuxia Wang, Zongyao Li, Chang Su, Yimeng Chen, Min Zhang, Shimin Tao, Hao Yang, and Ying Qin. 2022. The HW-TSC's simultaneous speech translation system for IWSLT 2022 evaluation. In *Proceedings of the 19th International Conference on Spoken Language Translation (IWSLT 2022)*, pages 247–254, Dublin, Ireland (in-person and online). Association for Computational Linguistics.

Brian Yan, Jiatong Shi, Yun Tang, Hirofumi Inaguma, Yifan Peng, Siddharth Dalmia, Peter Polak, Patrick Fernandes, Dan Berrebbi, Tomoki Hayashi, Xiaohui Zhang, Zhaoheng Ni, Moto Hira, Soumi Maiti, Juan Pino, and Shinji Watanabe. 2023. ESPnet-ST-v2: Multipurpose spoken language translation toolkit. In *Proceedings of the 61st Annual Meeting of the Association for Computational Linguistics (Volume 3: System Demonstrations)*, pages 400–411, Toronto, Canada. Association for Computational Linguistics.

Takenori Yoshimura, Tomoki Hayashi, Kazuya Takeda, and Shinji Watanabe. 2020. End-to-end automatic speech recognition integrated with ctc-based voice activity detection. In *ICASSP 2020-2020 IEEE International Conference on Acoustics, Speech and Signal Processing (ICASSP)*, pages 6999–7003. IEEE.

Biao Zhang, Ivan Titov, Barry Haddow, and Rico Sennrich. 2021. Beyond sentence-level end-to-end speech translation: Context helps. In *Proceedings of the 59th Annual Meeting of the Association for Computational Linguistics and the 11th International Joint Conference on Natural Language Processing (Volume 1: Long Papers)*, pages 2566–2578.

Yu Zhang, Wei Han, James Qin, Yongqiang Wang, Ankur Bapna, Zhehuai Chen, Nanxin Chen, Bo Li, Vera Axelrod, Gary Wang, et al. 2023. Google usm: Scaling automatic speech recognition beyond 100 languages. *arXiv preprint arXiv:2303.01037*.

Modeling Collaborative Dialogue in Minecraft with Action-Utterance Model

Takuma Ichikawa and **Ryuichiro Higashinaka**
Graduate School of Informatics, Nagoya University, Japan
{ichikawa.takuma.w0@s.mail,higashinaka@i}.nagoya-u.ac.jp

Abstract

With the advancement of dialogue systems propelled by neural-based methods, researchers have been working on developing dialogue systems that can collaborate with humans to complete tasks in the real world and virtual environments. In such collaborative work, the system needs to either perform an action or make an utterance appropriate for the context. However, previous literature has treated action and utterance generation separately. In this study, with the aim of enabling the system to autonomously determine whether to act or utter, we create a model that can handle both action and utterance generation in a unified model. We conducted experiments on a dataset related to collaborative work in Minecraft and show that the proposed model can autonomously determine whether to act or utter and generate better actions and utterances than the baselines.

1 Introduction

With the advancement of dialogue systems by neural-based methods (Bang et al., 2023; Shuster et al., 2022), towards more advanced dialogue systems, researchers have been working on developing dialogue systems that can collaborate with humans to complete tasks (Meena et al., 2013; He et al., 2017). Many studies have focused on collaborative work in virtual environments, such as Minecraft (Narayan-Chen et al., 2019; Ogawa et al., 2020; Bara et al., 2021), and competitions such as the Interactive Grounded Language Understanding (IGLU) challenge[1] have been organized. In such collaborative work, systems need to handle not only dialogue but also actions in their environment. However, studies in previous literature treat action and utterance generation as separate tasks (Narayan-Chen et al., 2019; Jayannavar et al., 2020; Mohanty et al., 2023), making systems incapable of executing both, which is required in realistic settings.

In this study, with the aim of enabling a system to autonomously determine whether to act or utter and execute on the basis of context, we create a unified model, the Action-Utterance Model, that can handle both action and utterance generation. Specifically, the model is trained simultaneously on three tasks: action type classification, action generation, and utterance generation.

We conducted experiments using the Collaborative Garden Task Corpus (Ichikawa and Higashinaka, 2022), which is a dataset related to collaborative work in Minecraft, and the results showed that the proposed model can autonomously determine whether to act or utter and generate better actions and utterances than the baselines. Furthermore, we analyzed the inference results and revealed the difficulty of generating actions unrelated to last actions.

2 Related Work

Studies have been emerging on performing complex collaborative work involving both actions and utterances in virtual worlds such as Minecraft (Kim et al., 2019; Ichikawa and Higashinaka, 2022) with some implemented systems.

For example, Gray et al. (2019) constructed a system that creates simple structures on the basis of user instructions through text chat. Narayan-Chen et al. (2019) and Jayannavar et al. (2020) modelled an instructor and builder for the Collaborative Building Task (Narayan-Chen et al., 2019), which involves two interlocutors working together to create a target structure. Recent research has focused on the IGLU task, which is based on the Collaborative Building Task (Kiseleva et al., 2022; Mohanty et al., 2023; Shi et al., 2023; Mehta et al., 2023). However, while there have been efforts to classify whether to act or utter, these tasks are treated as

[1] https://www.iglu-contest.net/

Proceedings of the 13th International Joint Conference on Natural Language Processing and the 3rd Conference of the Asia-Pacific Chapter of the Association for Computational Linguistics: Student Research Workshop, pages 75–81
November 1–4, 2023.

ID	S	Action or Utterance
1	A	なにか作りたいものありますか？ *(Do you want to make something?)*
2	B	藤？みたいな屋根みたいなのつくってみたいです *(I want to make a roof like a wisteria trellis.)*
	B	{(place, oak_fence, 4, -1, 4), (place, oak_fence, 4, -1, 5)}
3	A	いいですね！ *(Sounds good!)*
	B	{(place, oak_leaves, 4, -1, 6)}
4	A	真ん中にどーんと作ってみてください！ *(Try making it in the middle!)*
5	B	道を真ん中に作ってみます *(I will make a path down the middle.)*
	B	{(place, oak_leaves, 3, -1, 6), {(place, oak_leaves, 2, -1, 6), {(place, oak_leaves, 1, -1, 6), {(place, oak_leaves, 0, -1, 6), ...}

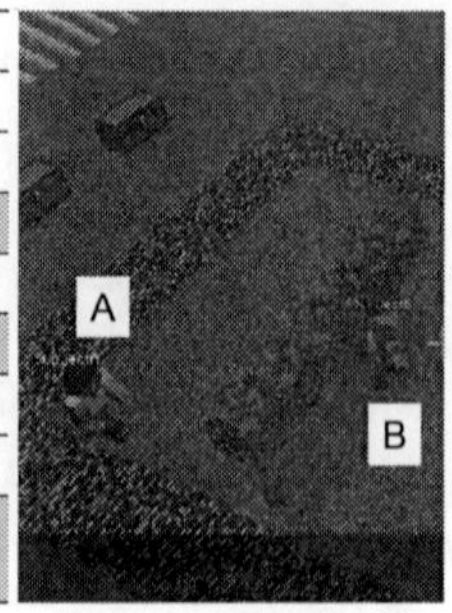

Figure 1: Dialogue in Collaborative Garden Task Corpus. ID represents utterance number, and S represents interlocutor. Utterances were originally in Japanese and have been translated into English by authors. Shaded rows indicate actions. Figure on right shows situation immediately after last action.

independent. Since actions and utterances are interrelated at the intent level and should not be treated separately, in this study, we focus on a model that can handle both action and utterance generation.

In fields outside of collaborative work, there are studies that aim to develop systems that can handle both actions and utterances. For example, Chen et al. (2021) constructed a task-oriented dialogue dataset that incorporates both actions, such as search and purchase, and utterances. Reed et al. (2022) proposed a model called Gato, which utilizes a single Transformer architecture to perform various tasks, including text generation tasks, such as utterance generation and caption generation, as well as action generation tasks. However, these studies do not use a model that can handle both actions and utterances. In this paper, we investigate the effectiveness of a unified model in collaborative work tasks.

3 Dataset and Task

3.1 Collaborative Garden Task Corpus

In this study, we adopt the Collaborative Garden Task Corpus constructed by Ichikawa and Higashinaka (2022) as a collaborative work dataset. Figure 1 shows an example of a dialogue included in the corpus. In the Collaborative Garden Task, two interlocutors interact via text chat while manipulating blocks in order to cooperatively create a beautiful and unique garden in Minecraft (here, beauty and uniqueness are based on the subjective evaluation of the interlocutors). In the dataset, the interlocutors can freely use 17 different types of blocks within a 10 × 10 × 4 area; they need to decide on the design of the garden through dialogue with their partner. Since the activity combines actions and utterances, we determined it to be a suitable dataset for evaluation. The Collaborative Garden Task Corpus contains 1,092 dialogues, each of which records in-game information such as utterances, block manipulations, and avatar movements. The language used is Japanese, with a total of 31,416 utterances, an average word count of 13.9 per utterance, and a total of 657,693 block manipulations.

3.2 Next Action-Utterance Generation Task

In this study, we address the Next Action-Utterance Generation Task, which aims to predict the next action or utterance to be performed. In this task, the goal is to predict the interlocutor's next actions (which may include making utterances), denoted as a_t, given the dialogue and state history H_t, the world state W_t, and the avatar's position (x_t, y_t, z_t) and orientation $(yaw_t, pitch_t)$ at turn t.

An action a_t is composed of one of four action types [utterance (UTT), block manipulation (BLOCK), SKIP, FINISH], along with its subsidiary information. In the case of UTT, we additionally predict utterance u_t. In the case of BLOCK, we additionally predict the set of block operations $b_t = \{(block\_action, [block\_name], x, y, z), ...\}$; $block\_action$ represents whether to place or break and (x, y, z) represents the block coordinates. In the case of placement, the block type $block\_name$ is also to be output. SKIP represents the interlocutors' non-operation at turn t. SKIP is introduced to model complex mixed-initiative interactions into a simple turn-by-turn dialogue. FINISH represents the end of the dialogue; the dialogue ends when one of the interlocutors outputs FINISH.

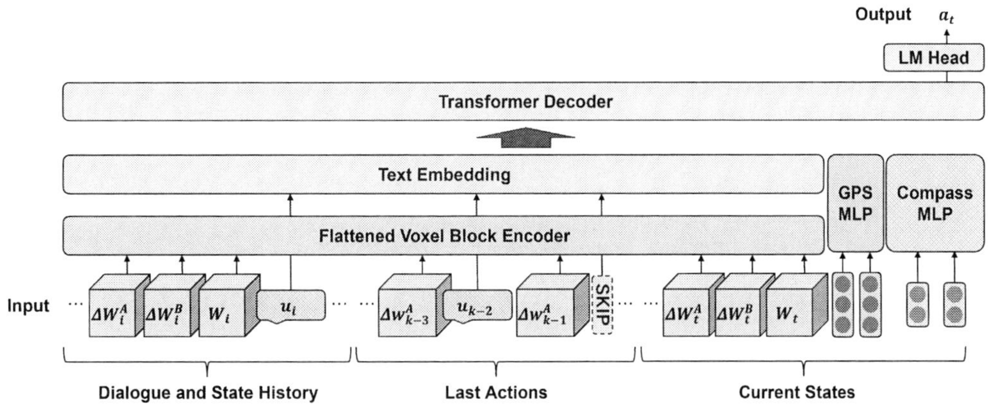

Figure 2: Overall architecture of proposed model. Model takes as input dialogue and state history $H_t = \{(\Delta W_{i_0}, W_{i_0}, u_{i_0}), ..., (\Delta W_i, W_i, u_i), ...\}$, actions (which may include making utterances) performed in last N turns, change in world state between previous utterance and current time, ΔW_t, current world state W_t, and avatar's positions and orientations. Model outputs next action type along with its content.

4 Model

4.1 Model Architecture

Figure 2 shows the overall architecture of the proposed model, the Action-Utterance Model. We use a pretrained Transformer decoder model as the underlying Large Language Model (LLM). Additionally, to embed non-verbal information, such as the world state and the avatar's position and orientation, into the same dimension as text, various encoders are prepared, including the Flattened Voxel Block Encoder, GPS multi-layer perceptron (MLP), and Compass MLP. These encoders were inspired by the implementation in MineDojo (Fan et al., 2022).

The Flattened Voxel Block Encoder consists of an embedding layer and a 3-layer MLP. It converts voxel data representing the world state into a vector equivalent to one token. The GPS MLP and Compass MLP consist of 2-layer MLPs, each transforming the avatar's positional and orientation information into a vector equivalent to one token. Each MLP is composed of linear and ReLU layers. Non-verbal information such as the world state embedded in the same vector space as the text is concatenated with the text embedding and input into the decoder. The LM Head receives the information processed by the decoder and outputs the next action.

4.2 Model Input

The model receives input at turn t, which includes the dialogue and state history, H_t, actions taken in the most recent N turns (we use $N = 10$ in this paper), the change in the world state between the previous utterance and the current time, ΔW_t, the current world state W_t, and the avatar's position (x_t, y_t, z_t) and orientation $(yaw_t, pitch_t)$.

The dialogue and state history consist of a set of tuples, ΔW_i, W_i, and the utterance u_i, formulated as follows.

$$H_t = \{(\Delta W_{i_0}, W_{i_0}, u_{i_0}), ..., (\Delta W_i, W_i, u_i), ...\} \quad (1)$$

ΔW_i represents changes in the world state between the previous utterance and the current utterance, while W_i represents the world state at the time of the utterance. Note that due to the increase in processing time when considering all actions up to the current time, we use the world state and its differences instead of all actions. ΔW_i is further divided into those representing interlocutor A's changes ΔW_i^A and interlocutor B's changes ΔW_i^B. The world state W and changes in the world state ΔW are represented in 10 × 10 × 4 voxels. W contains the block IDs at each coordinate, while ΔW stores the block IDs after the changes (if there is no change, it is 0).

For the actions taken in the most recent N turns, we include action types (UTT, BLOCK, SKIP, and FINISH) and, in the case of UTT or BLOCK, we also include the content of these actions. Each action type corresponds to a single token. In the case of UTT, we include the utterance text u_k. In the case of BLOCK, we include the change in the world state, denoted as Δw_k, occurring between the previous action a_{k-1} and the next action a_k. Δw is a compressed representation of block operations and is in the same format as ΔW.

The avatar's position (x_t, y_t, z_t) and orientation $(yaw_t, pitch_t)$ represent the coordinates and facial orientations in the environment.

4.3 Model Output

The model's output is action a_t at turn t. The model first outputs a token representing each action type, followed by, for UTT, the utterance text u_t, and for BLOCK, the set of block operations b_t. In this paper, to reduce complexity, the block operations are handled by dividing them into groups with up to L block operations, and we set L as the average size of b in the corpus, which is four. Therefore, the maximum length of b_t is four. All processing is performed by the LM Head. To facilitate this, tokens related to action types and block operations are added to the tokenizer in advance.

5 Experiment

5.1 Settings

In this study, we investigated the performance of the proposed model (Action-Utterance Model; AU) and baselines for the Next Action-Utterance Generation Task using the Collaborative Garden Task Corpus (Ichikawa and Higashinaka, 2022). Out of the 1,092 dialogues in the corpus, we randomly split the data and used 980 dialogues for training, 56 for validation, and 56 for testing.

To examine whether the proposed model can determine the appropriate action type to take next in a given context and perform suitable actions and utterances, we prepared baselines for action type classification, action generation, and utterance generation.

For action type classification, we used the following two baselines:

Random Selects one of the four action types at random.

Majority Always predicts the action type that is most frequently observed in the training data.

For action generation, we used the following baseline:

Random On the basis of the current world state, one to four feasible block operations are randomly selected.

Additionally, we established a human upper bound. For this, one of the authors predicted the set of next block operations to be performed for 20 samples randomly extracted from the test data.

For utterance generation, we used the following baseline:

Utterance Generation Only (UG) Transformer decoder model trained only for the utterance generation task. The model predicts the next utterance on the basis of all preceding utterances.

We used OpenCALM-Large[2], a Japanese LLM that contains 830 million parameters, and conducted LoRA tuning using the PEFT library (Mangrulkar et al., 2022). We optimized the model using Maximum Likelihood Estimation (MLE). During the evaluation, we used a checkpoint with the smallest loss calculated using the validation data.

5.2 Evaluation

We prepared the following evaluation metrics for each task: action type classification, action generation, and utterance generation. All metrics were computed by comparing the ground truth data with the inference results and yield values between 0 and 1, with higher values indicating better performance.

Accuracy Accuracy based on the classification results for action types and ground truth data.

Macro-F1 Macro-average of F1 scores calculated from the classification results and ground truth data for each action type.

BLEU-1, BLEU-2 Average BLEU-1 and BLEU-2 (Papineni et al., 2002) scores calculated by using generated utterances and gold response. If the system fails to generate an utterance due to the system predicting a value other than UTT, the value will be 0.

Distinct-1 Distinct-1 (Li et al., 2016) calculated on the basis of uni-grams of words present in generated utterances.

Jaccard Jaccard index calculated for the generated set of block operations $\bar{b}$ and the ground truth data b using the following formula.

$$Jaccard = \frac{1}{N}\sum_{i=1}^{N}\frac{|\bar{b_i} \cap b_i|}{|\bar{b_i} \cup b_i|} \quad (2)$$

To allow for a more lenient evaluation, two other metric values were also computed by considering only the set of block operation types (**Jacc-type**) and only the set of block

[2]https://huggingface.co/cyberagent/open-calm-large

Model	Accuracy	Macro-F1
Random	0.24	0.19
Majority	0.61	0.19
AU (ours)	**0.81***	0.67

Table 1: Evaluation results for action type classification. Bold indicates best value. * indicates **Accuracy** was significantly better than Random and Majority at $p < 0.05$ in McNemar test with Bonferroni correction.

Model	Jaccard	Jacc-type	Jacc-loc
Random	0.00	0.04	0.00
AU (ours)	**0.17***	**0.38***	**0.27***
Human	0.30	0.55	0.32

Table 2: Evaluation results for action generation. Bold values indicate best value except for Human. * indicates metrics were significantly better than Random at $p < 0.05$ in Wilcoxon signed-rank test with Bonferroni correction.

positions (**Jacc-loc**). If the system fails to generate an action due to the system predicting a value other than BLOCK, the value will be 0.

5.3 Results

Table 1 shows the results for action type classification, Table 2 shows those for action generation, and Table 3 shows those for utterance generation. The proposed model significantly outperformed the baselines in action type classification and action generation. Furthermore, it achieved a higher score in utterance generation compared with the baseline, especially in terms of Distinct-1. These results show that the proposed model can effectively determine the appropriate next action types and generate better actions and utterances by handling both action and utterance generation in a unified model.

Figure 3 shows a sample from the test data and actions generated by the proposed model and the baseline. The proposed model, while selecting to utter, generated utterances relevant to the flow of the dialogue and the current world state.

6 Analysis

To understand the current challenges with the proposed model, we conducted a detailed analysis of the inference results. When categorizing action generation on the basis of the characteristics of ground truth block operations, we found that the Jaccard index was high at 0.20 when the same types of blocks as the previous actions were included, while it dropped significantly to 0.07 when they were not. Similarly, when adjacent blocks were included as previous actions, the Jaccard index was high at 0.21, but it was low at 0.10 when they were not. These results show that predicting cases unrelated to the last actions is a challenge. They also suggest that there is insufficient grounding between dialogue and the world state and a lack of understanding of symmetries and regularities that humans comprehend.

Model	BLEU-1	BLEU-2	Distinct-1
UG	0.148	0.096	0.136
AU (ours)	**0.153**	**0.098**	**0.155**

Table 3: Evaluation results for utterance generation. Bold indicates best value.

7 Conclusion

In this study, we proposed a novel model for simultaneously generating actions and utterances during collaborative work in Minecraft. The experimental results showed that the proposed model can autonomously determine whether to act or utter and generate better actions and utterances than the baselines. Furthermore, we analyzed the inference results and revealed the difficulty in generating actions unrelated to the last actions.

There are limitations in our study. We compared our proposed model to simple baselines for action type classification and action generation; we need to perform comparisons with models introduced in previous work such as (Mohanty et al., 2023) and (Mehta et al., 2023). In addition, we only conducted turn-level evaluations; we need to consider dialogue-level evaluations in order to more accurately measure the model's performance. While we utilized the Jaccard index as the evaluation metric for action generation in this paper, the similarity of block operations may not be sufficient; therefore, we would like to conduct human evaluations and explore more appropriate evaluation metrics.

Additionally, we will also work towards building systems capable of actual collaborative dialogue. Due to the high flexibility of the next action and collaborative work themselves, rather than optimizing by MLE, we will aim to acquire higher-performing dialogue agents by incorporating reinforcement learning.

Last Actions	B: {(place, dandelion, -2, 4, 4)} A: 素晴らしい今までで一番出来栄えがいいです *(It's the best I've ever done, fantastic!)* B: そうですか *(Yes.)* A: SKIP B: よかった *(I'm glad to hear that!)*
Worldstate	[12, 12, 7, 12, 14, 12, 7, 12, 12, 12, … , 1, 1, 1, 1, 1, 1, 1, 1, 1, 1] (Corresponding to the state as in the right figure)
Gold Response	A: なんというか、別荘でのんびりしてる感じがします *(I feel like I'm relaxing at a vacation home.)*
UG	A: ありがとうございました *(Thank you.)*
AU (ours)	A: 木もいい味出してますね *(The wood also adds a nice touch, doesn't it?)*

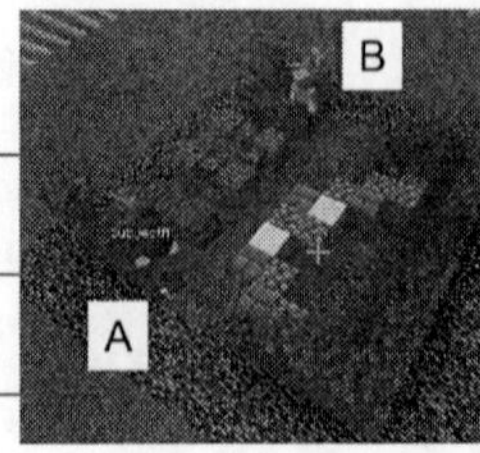

Figure 3: Samples from test dataset and generation example for proposed model (translated to English by authors)

Acknowledgments

This work was supported by JSPS KAKENHI Grant Number 19H05692.

References

Namo Bang, Jeehyun Lee, and Myoung-Wan Koo. 2023. Task-Optimized Adapters for an End-to-End Task-Oriented Dialogue System. In *Findings of the Association for Computational Linguistics: ACL 2023*, pages 7355–7369.

Cristian-Paul Bara, Sky CH-Wang, and Joyce Chai. 2021. MindCraft: Theory of Mind Modeling for Situated Dialogue in Collaborative Tasks. In *Proceedings of the 2021 Conference on Empirical Methods in Natural Language Processing*, pages 1112–1125.

Derek Chen, Howard Chen, Yi Yang, Alexander Lin, and Zhou Yu. 2021. Action-Based Conversations Dataset: A Corpus for Building More In-Depth Task-Oriented Dialogue Systems. In *Proceedings of the 2021 Conference of the North American Chapter of the Association for Computational Linguistics: Human Language Technologies*, pages 3002–3017.

Linxi Fan, Guanzhi Wang, Yunfan Jiang, Ajay Mandlekar, Yuncong Yang, Haoyi Zhu, Andrew Tang, De-An Huang, Yuke Zhu, and Anima Anandkumar. 2022. MineDojo: Building Open-Ended Embodied Agents with Internet-Scale Knowledge. In *Proceedings of the Thirty-sixth Conference on Neural Information Processing Systems Datasets and Benchmarks Track*, pages 18343–18362.

Jonathan Gray, Kavya Srinet, Yacine Jernite, Haonan Yu, Zhuoyuan Chen, Demi Guo, Siddharth Goyal, C. Lawrence Zitnick, and Arthur Szlam. 2019. Craftassist: A Framework for Dialogue-enabled Interactive Agents. *arXiv preprint arXiv:1907.08584*.

He He, Anusha Balakrishnan, Mihail Eric, and Percy Liang. 2017. Learning Symmetric Collaborative Dialogue Agents with Dynamic Knowledge Graph Embeddings. In *Proceedings of the 55th Annual Meeting of the Association for Computational Linguistics (Volume 1: Long Papers)*, pages 1766–1776.

Takuma Ichikawa and Ryuichiro Higashinaka. 2022. Analysis of Dialogue in Human-Human Collaboration in Minecraft. In *Proceedings of the Thirteenth Language Resources and Evaluation Conference*, pages 4051–4059.

Prashant Jayannavar, Anjali Narayan-Chen, and Julia Hockenmaier. 2020. Learning to execute instructions in a Minecraft dialogue. In *Proceedings of the 58th Annual Meeting of the Association for Computational Linguistics*, pages 2589–2602.

Jin-Hwa Kim, Nikita Kitaev, Xinlei Chen, Marcus Rohrbach, Byoung-Tak Zhang, Yuandong Tian, Dhruv Batra, and Devi Parikh. 2019. CoDraw: Collaborative Drawing as a Testbed for Grounded Goal-driven Communication. In *Proceedings of the 57th Annual Meeting of the Association for Computational Linguistics*, pages 6495–6513.

Julia Kiseleva, Alexey Skrynnik, Artem Zholus, Shrestha Mohanty, Negar Arabzadeh, Marc-Alexandre Côté, Mohammad Aliannejadi, Milagro Teruel, Ziming Li, Mikhail Burtsev, Maartje ter Hoeve, Zoya Volovikova, Aleksandr Panov, Yuxuan Sun, Kavya Srinet, Arthur Szlam, and Ahmed Awadallah. 2022. IGLU 2022: Interactive Grounded Language Understanding in a Collaborative Environment at NeurIPS 2022. *arXiv preprint arXiv:2205.13771*.

Jiwei Li, Michel Galley, Chris Brockett, Jianfeng Gao, and Bill Dolan. 2016. A Diversity-Promoting Objective Function for Neural Conversation Models. In *Proceedings of the 2016 Conference of the North American Chapter of the Association for Computational Linguistics: Human Language Technologies*, pages 110–119.

Sourab Mangrulkar, Sylvain Gugger, Lysandre Debut, Younes Belkada, and Sayak Paul. 2022. PEFT: State-of-the-art Parameter-Efficient Fine-Tuning methods. `https://github.com/huggingface/peft`.

Raveesh Meena, Gabriel Skantze, and Joakim Gustafson. 2013. A Data-driven Model for Timing Feedback in a Map Task Dialogue System. In *Proceedings of the 14th Annual Meeting of the Special*

Interest Group on Discourse and Dialogue-SIGdial, pages 375–383.

Nikhil Mehta, Milagro Teruel, Patricio Figueroa Sanz, Xin Deng, Ahmed Hassan Awadallah, and Julia Kiseleva. 2023. Improving Grounded Language Understanding in a Collaborative Environment by Interacting with Agents Through Help Feedback. *arXiv preprint arXiv:2304.10750*.

Shrestha Mohanty, Negar Arabzadeh, Julia Kiseleva, Artem Zholus, Milagro Teruel, Ahmed Awadallah, Yuxuan Sun, Kavya Srinet, and Arthur Szlam. 2023. Transforming Human-Centered AI Collaboration: Redefining Embodied Agents Capabilities through Interactive Grounded Language Instructions. *arXiv preprint arXiv:2305.10783*.

Anjali Narayan-Chen, Prashant Jayannavar, and Julia Hockenmaier. 2019. Collaborative Dialogue in Minecraft. In *Proceedings of the 57th Annual Meeting of the Association for Computational Linguistics*, pages 5405–5415.

Haruna Ogawa, Hitoshi Nishikawa, Takenobu Tokunaga, and Hikaru Yokono. 2020. Gamification Platform for Collecting Task-oriented Dialogue Data. In *Proceedings of the Twelfth Language Resources and Evaluation Conference*, pages 7084–7093.

Kishore Papineni, Salim Roukos, Todd Ward, and Wei-Jing Zhu. 2002. BLEU: a Method for Automatic Evaluation of Machine Translation. In *Proceedings of the 40th Annual Meeting of the Association for Computational Linguistics*, pages 311–318.

Scott E. Reed, Konrad Zolna, Emilio Parisotto, Sergio Gómez Colmenarejo, Alexander Novikov, Gabriel Barth-Maron, Mai Gimenez, Yury Sulsky, Jackie Kay, Jost Tobias Springenberg, Tom Eccles, Jake Bruce, Ali Razavi, Ashley Edwards, Nicolas Heess, Yutian Chen, Raia Hadsell, Oriol Vinyals, Mahyar Bordbar, and Nando de Freitas. 2022. A Generalist Agent. *arXiv preprint arXiv:2205.06175*.

Zhengxiang Shi, Jerome Ramos, To Eun Kim, Xi Wang, Hossein A. Rahmani, and Aldo Lipani. 2023. When and What to Ask Through World States and Text Instructions: IGLU NLP Challenge Solution. *arXiv preprint arXiv:2305.05754*.

Kurt Shuster, Jing Xu, Mojtaba Komeili, Da Ju, Eric Michael Smith, Stephen Roller, Megan Ung, Moya Chen, Kushal Arora, Joshua Lane, Morteza Behrooz, William Ngan, Spencer Poff, Naman Goyal, Arthur Szlam, Y-Lan Boureau, Melanie Kambadur, and Jason Weston. 2022. BlenderBot 3: a deployed conversational agent that continually learns to responsibly engage. *arXiv preprint arXiv:2208.03188*.

Graph-Enriched Biomedical Language Models: A Research Proposal

Andrey Sakhovskiy[1,2,3], Alexander Panchenko[3,4], and Elena Tutubalina[1,2]
[1]Sber AI, [2]Kazan Federal University, [3]Skolkovo Institute of Science and Technology,
[4]Artificial Intelligence Research Institute
{andrey.sakhovskiy, panchenko.alexander, tutubalinaev}@gmail.com

Abstract

Recent advancements in biomedical NLP have been driven by domain-specific pre-trained language models (LMs), yet the challenge of effectively storing extensive biomedical factual knowledge remains. Despite the superior performance of fine-tuned LMs in downstream NLP tasks, these models exhibit limitations in ontology memorization, reasoning abilities, and capturing complex specialized domain terminology. To address these issues, we present four research questions that explore the integration of LMs with large knowledge graphs (KGs) like the Unified Medical Language System (UMLS). Our proposal introduces novel alignment methods to bridge LMs with the UMLS KG, with the aim of leveraging structured background knowledge to enhance the reasoning and generalization capabilities of biomedical LMs. The research proposal discusses multilingual specifics of KBs and evaluation metrics across various datasets.

1 Introduction

Recent years have witnessed significant progress in various biomedical Natural Language Processing (NLP) caused by domain-specific pre-trained Language Models (LMs) (Lee et al., 2020; Peng et al., 2019; Alsentzer et al., 2019; Beltagy et al., 2019; Michalopoulos et al., 2021; Gu et al., 2022; Yasunaga et al., 2022b). Although, these models demonstrate superior performance on Biomedical Language Understanding and Reasoning Benchmark (BLURB) (Gu et al., 2022) and BigBio benchmark (Fries et al., 2022), their ability to store extensive biomedical factual knowledge remains an open question. In the general domain, Large LMs (LLMs) were shown to have limited ontology memorization and reasoning abilities (Wu et al., 2023). Existing research on biomedical knowledge probing task indicate that the biomedical LMs struggle to capture complex specialized domain terminology (Meng et al., 2022), are highly biased towards certain prompts, and are unaware of synonyms (Sung et al., 2021). Making LM well-informed about in-domain facts could assist various NLP applications including drug discovery (Wu et al., 2018; Khrabrov et al., 2022; Zitnik et al., 2018), clinical decision making (Sutton et al., 2020; Peiffer-Smadja et al., 2020), and biomedical research (Lee et al., 2016; Fiorini et al., 2018; Soni and Roberts, 2021).

In the biomedical domain, vast multilingual Knowledge Bases (KBs) such as the Unified Medical Language System (UMLS) (Bodenreider, 2004) are available, making the infusion of factual knowledge into LMs possible. Over 166 lexicons/thesauri with over 4M concepts and 15M concept names from 27 languages are present in the UMLS. However, as seen from Tab. 1, severe language imbalance is a great challenge for processing texts in low-resource languages.

In KBs, factual information is usually stored in the form of knowledge triples (h, r, t). Each triple reflects the fact that concept h is in relation to type r with concept t. The combination of concept set V and relation triples $E \in \{V \times R \times V\}$ can be seen as a knowledge graph (KG) $G = G(V, E, R)$ where R is a set of possible relation types. Although plenty of research focused on developing effective knowledge-augmented general-purpose pre-training methods for LMs, this topic remains challenging. One approach is to apply an LM on textual sequences augmented by KB triples (Wang et al., 2019a; Mannion et al., 2023; Xu et al., 2023; Liu et al., 2020). These approaches share two major limitations (Ke et al., 2021). First, the fully connected nature of the attention mechanism present in modern LMs contradicts the sparse structure of the existing KB graphs. Second, the linearization of a KB graph prevents a direct alignment between the textual and the KB modalities. Wang et al. (2021) obtained representations for Wikipedia en-

Proceedings of the 13th International Joint Conference on Natural Language Processing and the 3rd Conference of the Asia-Pacific Chapter of the Association for Computational Linguistics: Student Research Workshop, pages 82–92
November 1–4, 2023.

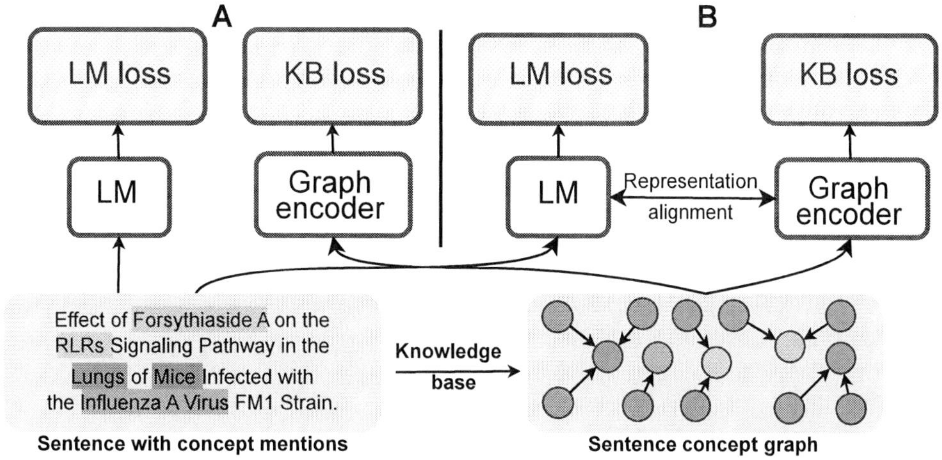

Figure 1: Visualization of different approaches towards knowledge-enhanced LM training. **A**: During KB-enhanced LM pre-training or fine-tuning, a text encoder and a graph encoder independently minimize a textual loss (i.e., masked language modeling) and a graph-related task (i.e., link prediction) with an implicit interaction between the two encoders. An implicit interaction may be in the form of LM embeddings being initial node representations for the graph model. **B**: A less common approach is to add an explicit alignment loss to stimulate an information exchange between two modalities. Named entities can serve as anchor points for this kind of intermodal interaction.

tities by encoding short textual entity and relation descriptions with an LM, which is not feasible in the biomedical domain since most biomedical concepts lack a textual description.

As LM pre-training from scratch requires extensive computational resources, a cheaper alternative is a task-specific KB-aware fine-tuning. Recently, a series of studies focused on the utilization of the UMLS concept names and inter-concept relations for improved Biomedical Concept Normalization (BCN) (Liu et al., 2021a,b; Yuan et al., 2022b; Sakhovskiy et al., 2023). While GEBERT proposed by Sakhovskiy et al. (2023) explicitly learns the identity between synonymous concept names and concept node representations, the model is extremely tied to BCN and leaves no room for its generalization to other biomedical tasks. Recently proposed Question Answering (QA) (Yasunaga et al., 2022a, 2021a; Zhang et al., 2022b) systems adopt Message Passing (MP) (Gilmer et al., 2017) graph neural networks to perform well-grounded reasoning over KB which results in an improved quality in both general and biomedical domains. These models rely on implicit interaction between an LM and a graph encoder and do not explicitly learn an alignment between two modalities, thus limiting LM's ability to memorize KB facts.

2 Related work

An extensive comparison of various biomedical knowledge representation learning approaches was conducted by Chang et al. (2020). They compared semantic matching methods, such as TransE (Bordes et al., 2013), DistMult (Yang et al., 2015), ComplEx (Trouillon et al., 2016), SimplE (Kazemi and Poole, 2018), and RotatE (Sun et al., 2019), for link prediction quality on SNOMED-CT dataset. Although these methods outperform simpler Snomed2Vec (Agarwal et al., 2019) and Cui2Vec (Beam et al., 2020) baselines, they fall short of LM-based approaches (Wang et al., 2019a).

Several attempts to integrate a pre-trained biomedical LM with an external KB have increased performance in various downstream tasks. Sakhovskiy et al. (2021); Sakhovskiy and Tutubalina (2022) employed DrugBank (Wishart et al., 2008, 2017), a drug-oriented chemical database, to combine LM embeddings with drug chemical features in a classification layer to detect texts that mention an adverse drug reaction. SapBERT (Liu et al., 2021a,b) achieved state-of-the-art Medical Concept Normalization (MCN) performance by applying a contrastive objective to learn from synonymous biomedical concept names from the Unified Medical Language System

(UMLS) ontology. CODER (Yuan et al., 2022b) and GEBERT (Sakhovskiy et al., 2023) extended the idea by introducing additional graph-based contrastive objectives to capture inter-concept relations from the UMLS graph. CODER (Yuan et al., 2022b) and multilingual SapBERT (Liu et al., 2021b) achieve a normalization improvement in both monolingual English and multilingual setups.

In both general and biomedical domains, numerous state-of-the-art QA solutions retrieve a relevant subgraph from a KB (Lin et al., 2019; Feng et al., 2020; Yasunaga et al., 2021a; Zhang et al., 2022b,a; Yasunaga et al., 2022a) to perform a knowledge-aware reasoning. Yasunaga et al. (2022a) proposed a language-knowledge DRAGON model that benefits from joint language modeling and graph completion objectives and bidirectional interaction between text and graph encoders in both general and biomedical domains.

Thus, the existing knowledge-enhanced text processing models possess at least one of the following key limitations. First, they are too tied to a specific downstream task, such as MCN or QA. Second, they provide no explicit alignment between a biomedical concept and its mention in a text but instead rely on implicit interaction between textual and graph encoders. Third, except for multilingual BCN methods, they mostly focus on English, which has the most extensive KBs, ignoring a low-resource case.

Language	# concept names	percentage
English	11,280,428	70.78%
Spanish	1,589,581	9.97%
French	431,527	2.71%
Portuguese	423,826	2.66%
Japanese	332,099	2.08%
Dutch	293,817	1.84%
Russian	293,031	1.84%
Italian	251,912	1.58%
German	235,736	1.48%
Czech	198,115	1.24%
Korean	147,217	0.92%
Hungarian	109,271	0.69%
Chinese	81,916	0.51%
Norwegian	63,797	0.4%
Polish	51,778	0.32%
Turkish	51,597	0.32%
Estonian	31,183	0.2%
Swedish	30,439	0.19%
Finnish	25,489	0.16%
Croatian	10,035	0.06%
Greek	2,286	0.01%
Latvian	1405	0.01%
Danish	723	0.1%
Basque	695	<0.1%
Hebrew	485	<0.1%

Table 1: UMLS statistics on the number of concept names.

3 Research plan

3.1 Research questions

Although a wide range of knowledge-aware Language Modeling techniques have been proposed, several fundamental research questions remain unanswered. In this proposal, we formulate some important questions as well as possible trajectories for answering them. First of all, we see three major knowledge fusion strategies:

1. Knowledge-enhanced LM pre-training from scratch;
2. KB-augmented task-specific fine-tuning;
3. Alignment between pre-trained LM and informative KB representations.

RQ1. What is an optimal knowledge fusion strategy?

While existing knowledge-enhanced general-domain and biomedical LMs benefit from pre-training with external knowledge, they usually share at least one of the following critical limitations. First, they imply a modification of an LM architecture (Peters et al., 2019; Zhang et al., 2022b; Yasunaga et al., 2022a). Second, they require additional pre-training of all model parameters on textual inputs augmented with external knowledge (Wang et al., 2021; Lauscher et al., 2020; El Boukkouri et al., 2022; Yuan et al., 2022a; Mannion et al., 2023). Both limitations lead to a resource-intensive pre-training of all the LM parameters from scratch which might not be feasible. Recently proposed FROMAGe (Koh et al., 2023b) and GILL (Koh et al., 2023a) in text-and-image domain propose to align image representations with their textual captions via contrastive InfoNCE (Oord et al., 2018) objective in a significantly more light-weighted scenario of frozen textual encoder. With far less trainable parameters, these alignment methods manage to even outperform fully trainable bi-modal Transformer (Vaswani et al., 2017) models. Inspired by the success of alignment-based strategy in text and image tasks, we strive to explore its applicability and effectiveness in the biomedical domain in comparison with the remaining two strategies.

RQ2. How to align KB and LM in the biomedical domain?

To the best of our knowledge, no LM and biomedical KB representation alignment method is proposed so far. A direct adaptation of GILL and FROMAGe to biomedical texts and KBs is hindered by two critical issues. First, both models rely on Transformer encoder-decoder architecture and adopt text generation tasks, while the majority of the existing state-of-the-art biomedical LMs are encoder-only BERT models (Alsentzer et al., 2019; Peng et al., 2019; Beltagy et al., 2019; Lee et al., 2020; Gu et al., 2022; Liu et al., 2021a; Mannion et al., 2023). Second, while image-to-text and text-to-image tasks are inherently bi-modal, it is not the case for most biomedical NLP tasks (i.e., only textual sequence is provided during fine-tuning and evaluation).

3.1.1 RQ3. How to enrich an LM with biomedical knowledge?

Current biomedical knowledge probing benchmarks (Sung et al., 2021; Meng et al., 2022) indicate that the existing domain-specific LMs lack factual knowledge. This might be caused by either of two reasons: (i) imperfection of prompting approaches or (ii) an actual absence or incompleteness of knowledge in LMs. We believe, the integration of in-domain knowledge from biomedical KBs (e.g., interaction between biomedical concepts from the UMLS) remains an open challenge and requires a thorough exploration.

RQ4. How to exploit rich English KBs for low-resource languages?

Most existing research in biomedical NLP employ extensive English data leaving low-resource languages out-of-scope. While the alignment of multilingual UMLS concept names was shown to significantly improve the BCN quality in uni-modal setting (Liu et al., 2021b; Yuan et al., 2022b), they still struggle to deal with severe language imbalance of the UMLS concept names (see Table 1). Alternatively, the UMLS KB can be approached from a bi-modal text and graph perspective with graph modality capturing language-independent concept node's features.

3.2 Proposed methodology

3.2.1 Representation alignment

Currently, the alignment of textual and KB representations remains under-expored topic. To answer **RQ1** and **RQ2** we plan to develop novel alignment methods. To align textual representations with KB knowledge, we plan to use biomedical concept representations obtained from their contextualized mention embeddings in texts. We foresee two possible alignment approaches: (i) implicit alignment via an auxiliary KB-guided training objective and (ii) via an explicit alignment of textual and graph representations.

Implicit alignment One of the ways to enable information exchange between two or more modalities is to introduce a multi-modal objective. Prior work on general domain QA (Yasunaga et al., 2022a; Ke et al., 2021) introduced multi-task text and graph restoration objectives to learn from aligned textual sequences and KB subgraphs of entities mention in a text. However, this approaches rely on implicit interaction between text and graph modalities and do not explicitly inform the model that the subgraph is induced by text and is in fact its alternative representation obtained from another modality. In our work, we plan to adopt and extend the idea of graph restoration objective the idea and consider two its following cases:

- **Single modality graph restoration**: Following Yasunaga et al. (2022a) and Ke et al. (2021) we will treat text and graph restoration tasks as separate uni-modal tasks with a single graph encoder to encode both head and tail concepts of a triple;
- **Mixed-modality graph restoration**: As LM- and graph-based representations of a concept are complementary, we propose to initialize a head concept with an embedding of the first modality and a tail concept with an embedding of the second one.

While the first case is conventional, the mixed-modality problem statement is, to the best of our knowledge, under-explored. For both cases, we will employ TransE or ComplEx which model a tail concept as a relation-based transformation of a head concept.

Explicit alignment Another way to combine multiple modalities is to explicitly inform the model that text and graph embeddings are two complementary representations of a single concept.

Early attempts of alignments of graphs with linguistic models were presented by Biemann et al. (2018): sparse representations of graphs were linked with sparse distributional representations of word senses. Nikishina et al. (2022) attempts to align standard text BERT model with graph-based BERT by learning projections of their internal representations. Similarly, projections between static graph and text embeddings can be used for computing similarity search in graphs given text e.g. for question answering (Huang et al., 2019).

In prior work (Sakhovskiy et al., 2023), a contrastive objective was applied to learn from bi-modal positive pairs consisting of a concept name and a concept node. GILL and FROMAGe benefited from aligning in-context LM tokens and images via a contrastive objective and a small alignment model. In our research, we plan to combine these two approaches and perform an in-context alignment of contextualized concept mentions and their graph representations obtained from the UMLS via a graph encoder. We expect to introduce either the Multi-Similarity (Wang et al., 2019b) or the InfoNCE (Oord et al., 2018) loss function, to directly minimize the distance between textual and graph representations of the same biomedical concept.

3.2.2 Knowledge probing

Two possible ways to improve LM capabilities as KB and answer **RQ3** are (i) an improvement of prompting strategies and (ii) a modification of LM and its training pipeline. Although Meng et al. (2022) and Sung et al. (2021) have observed a probing quality improvement after a proper prompt tuning, the task is still far from being solved with about only 10% in terms of accuracy. We will stick to the second option and attempt to improve the knowledge awareness of biomedical LMs through alignment with KB modality: both implicit and explicit. As current biomedical knowledge probing benchmarks require filling masked concepts in a prompt inferred from a knowledge triple, we will investigate the knowledge infusion as a bi-modal problem and focus on the following knowledge probing problem statements:

Uni-modal textual approach involves filling masked concept slot using solely an LM;

Bi-modal text and KB approach reformulates triplet completion baseline as a bi-modal text-to-graph task: given a textual prompt, the goal is to predict the best matching KG node.

While text-only approaches commonly struggle with multi-word concept names, we aim at exploring whether the reformulation of the task will help overcome the issue. Moreover, the second approach enables the incorporation of aforementioned modality alignment strategies: both explicit and implicit.

3.2.3 Cross-lingual alignment

We expect to address the **RQ4** with the cross-lingual cross-modal representation alignment. While a fixed concept name is monolingual, a concept itself is multilingual from the language perspective and is independent of language from the graph perspective. While cross-lingual concept name alignment improved BCN quality (Liu et al., 2021b; Yuan et al., 2022b), our goal is to investigate whether cross-modal alignment could further boost the performance. Unfortunately, application on other biomedical tasks is hindered by the lack of non-English data but the experiments on BCN could serve as a good starting point.

3.3 Experimental setting

Training data As training data for various alignment methods, we will utilize PubMed abstracts. To recognize and align textual concept mentions with UMLS concepts, we will adopt BERN2 (Sung et al., 2022), a recently proposed biomedical entity recognition and normalization tool.

Text and graph encoders To obtain language representations, we will adopt PubMedBERT (Gu et al., 2022), a state-of-the-art biomedical LM pre-trained on PubMed abstracts. To produce graph representations, we will adopt the Message Passing framework (Gilmer et al., 2017) and obtain concept node embeddings with either GraphSAGE (Hamilton et al., 2017) or GAT (Veličković et al., 2018) encoder. Each node will be initialized with a PubMedBERT embedding of its concept name at random.

Computational efficiency Since for alignment strategy, we assume both textual and graph encoder are already well-trained, we strive to explore if we can reduce the computational burden of the alignment procedure. For each encoder, we will consider three cases: (i) fully frozen encoder with a small external alignment model, (ii) partially frozen encoder, (iii) fully trainable encoder.

Concept masking To enforce a KB-aligned LM learns from full context rather than concept mentions only, we will mask concept mentions with a fixed probability. Similarly, to stimulate graph encoder pass more informative messages from concept neighboring concepts in a KG, we will mask a concept name of an anchor. Masking is expected to improve model's compatibility with knowledge probing benchmarks.

3.4 Evaluation

Fries et al. (2022) released BigBio, a large data-centric benchmark that includes 126 biomedical NLP datasets, covering 13 tasks, including QA and BCN in more than 10 languages. To answer the **RQ1** and **RQ2**, we will primarily focus on QA and BCN since these tasks already have knowledge-enhanced task-specific solutions to compare with. To explore the **RQ4**, we will compare against current state-of-the-art cross-lingual models for BCN (Liu et al., 2021b; Yuan et al., 2022b; Sakhovskiy et al., 2023) and additionally adopt two cross-lingual BCN benchmarks for zero-shot ranking-based avaluation: (i) the one (Alekseev et al., 2022) based on Mantra corpus (Kors et al., 2015) and (ii) XL-BEL (Liu et al., 2021b). We will adopt KG-enhanced state-of-the-art QA models: QA-GNN (Yasunaga et al., 2021b), GreaseLM (Zhang et al., 2022b), JointGT (Ke et al., 2021), and DRAGON (Yasunaga et al., 2022a) as knowledge-enhanced QA baselines. For both BCN and QA as well as other tasks, we will adopt strong domain-specific biomedical LMs, e.g., BioBERT (Lee et al., 2020).

For biomedical knowledge probing task and **RQ3**, we will adopt the aforementioned MedLAMA and BioLAMA benchmarks. We will evaluate against the existing biomedical LMs, such as the BioBERT (Lee et al., 2020), Bio-LM (Lewis et al., 2020), and PubMedBERT (Gu et al., 2022).

4 Conclusion

In this paper, we identify critical limitations of the existing domain-specific pre-trained biomedical LMs and current state-of-the-art domain-specific solutions for solving downstream NLP tasks. We raise four important research questions and present a plan for exploring them. Modern LMs are unable to reveal the potential of factual knowledge fully and lack an explicit text-KB alignment procedure in current pre-training pipelines. While the usage of KB has already advanced the quality of biomedical concept normalization and question answering, a method for the fusion of domain knowledge into a general-purpose biomedical LM awaits to be explored. To overcome the existing LM limitations, we propose ideas for explicit alignment of KB concepts and their representatives in texts. The completion of our research plan is expected to deepen the understanding of text-KB interaction and give a better understanding of an optimal strategy for KB utilization in biomedical NLP.

Acknowledgements The work has been supported by the Russian Science Foundation grant # 23-11-00358.

5 Ethics, limitations, and risks

Large domain-specific graphs. We plan to employ a large biomedical knowledge graph, the Unified Medical Language System (UMLS), which contains over 4 million concepts and 15 million concept names. It is important to note that using knowledge graphs for different domains with a smaller number of nodes and edges may affect the performance. The knowledge graph's size and complexity can significantly impact the model's ability to learn and make accurate predictions.

Biases. Consequently, it is important to acknowledge that trained models can inherit biases and toxic behaviors present in the language models and knowledge graphs used for their initialization. Language models, for instance, have been demonstrated to incorporate biases about race, gender, and other demographic attributes. Biomedical research and clinical trials may not adequately represent certain populations. Likewise, a knowledge graph may incorporate stereotypes instead of providing unbiased, commonsense knowledge.

Diversity of biomedical concepts. It is important to highlight that the datasets and knowledge graphs primarily focus on well-documented medical concepts found in the literature. This limits the exposure of models to infrequent or uncommon occurrences. Consequently, adapting trained models to handle rare biomedical events may require additional effort and attention.

References

Khushbu Agarwal, Tome Eftimov, Raghavendra Addanki, Sutanay Choudhury, Suzanne Tamang, and Robert Rallo. 2019. Snomed2vec: Random walk and poincaré embeddings of a clinical knowledge base for healthcare analytics. *CoRR*, abs/1907.08650.

Anton Alekseev, Zulfat Miftahutdinov, Elena Tutubalina, Artem Shelmanov, Vladimir Ivanov, Vladimir Kokh, Alexander Nesterov, Manvel Avetisian, Andrei Chertok, and Sergey Nikolenko. 2022. Medical crossing: a cross-lingual evaluation of clinical entity linking. In *Proceedings of the Thirteenth Language Resources and Evaluation Conference*, pages 4212–4220, Marseille, France. European Language Resources Association.

Emily Alsentzer, John Murphy, William Boag, Wei-Hung Weng, Di Jindi, Tristan Naumann, and Matthew McDermott. 2019. Publicly available clinical BERT embeddings. In *Proceedings of the 2nd Clinical Natural Language Processing Workshop*, pages 72–78, Minneapolis, Minnesota, USA. Association for Computational Linguistics.

Andrew L. Beam, Benjamin Kompa, Allen Schmaltz, Inbar Fried, Griffin M. Weber, Nathan P. Palmer, Xu Shi, Tianxi Cai, and Isaac S. Kohane. 2020. Clinical concept embeddings learned from massive sources of multimodal medical data. In *Pacific Symposium on Biocomputing 2020, Fairmont Orchid, Hawaii, USA, January 3-7, 2020*, pages 295–306.

Iz Beltagy, Kyle Lo, and Arman Cohan. 2019. SciBERT: A pretrained language model for scientific text. In *Proceedings of the 2019 Conference on Empirical Methods in Natural Language Processing and the 9th International Joint Conference on Natural Language Processing (EMNLP-IJCNLP)*, pages 3615–3620, Hong Kong, China. Association for Computational Linguistics.

Chris Biemann, Stefano Faralli, Alexander Panchenko, and Simone Paolo Ponzetto. 2018. A framework for enriching lexical semantic resources with distributional semantics. *Natural Language Engineering*, 24(2):265–312.

Olivier Bodenreider. 2004. The unified medical language system (UMLS): integrating biomedical terminology. *Nucleic Acids Res.*, 32(Database-Issue):267–270.

Antoine Bordes, Nicolas Usunier, Alberto García-Durán, Jason Weston, and Oksana Yakhnenko. 2013. Translating embeddings for modeling multi-relational data. In *Advances in Neural Information Processing Systems 26: 27th Annual Conference on Neural Information Processing Systems 2013. Proceedings of a meeting held December 5-8, 2013, Lake Tahoe, Nevada, United States*, pages 2787–2795.

David Chang, Ivana Balažević, Carl Allen, Daniel Chawla, Cynthia Brandt, and Andrew Taylor. 2020. Benchmark and best practices for biomedical knowledge graph embeddings. In *Proceedings of the 19th SIGBioMed Workshop on Biomedical Language Processing*, pages 167–176, Online. Association for Computational Linguistics.

Hicham El Boukkouri, Olivier Ferret, Thomas Lavergne, and Pierre Zweigenbaum. 2022. Specializing static and contextual embeddings in the medical domain using knowledge graphs: Let's keep it simple. In *Proceedings of the 13th International Workshop on Health Text Mining and Information Analysis (LOUHI)*, pages 69–80, Abu Dhabi, United Arab Emirates (Hybrid). Association for Computational Linguistics.

Yanlin Feng, Xinyue Chen, Bill Yuchen Lin, Peifeng Wang, Jun Yan, and Xiang Ren. 2020. Scalable multi-hop relational reasoning for knowledge-aware question answering. In *Proceedings of the 2020 Conference on Empirical Methods in Natural Language Processing (EMNLP)*, pages 1295–1309, Online. Association for Computational Linguistics.

Nicolas Fiorini, Kathi Canese, Grisha Starchenko, Evgeny Kireev, Won Kim, Vadim Miller, Maxim Osipov, Michael Kholodov, Rafis Ismagilov, Sunil Mohan, et al. 2018. Best match: new relevance search for pubmed. *PLoS biology*, 16(8):e2005343.

Jason A. Fries, Leon Weber, Natasha Seelam, Gabriel Altay, Debajyoti Datta, Samuele Garda, Sunny Kang, Rosaline Su, Wojciech Kusa, Samuel Cahyawijaya, Fabio Barth, Simon Ott, Matthias Samwald, Stephen H. Bach, Stella Biderman, Mario Sänger, Bo Wang, Alison Callahan, Daniel León Periñán, Théo Gigant, Patrick Haller, Jenny Chim, José D. Posada, John M. Giorgi, Karthik Rangasai Sivaraman, Marc Pàmies, Marianna Nezhurina, Robert Martin, Michael Cullan, Moritz Freidank, Nathan Dahlberg, Shubhanshu Mishra, Shamik Bose, Nicholas Broad, Yanis Labrak, Shlok Deshmukh, Sid Kiblawi, Ayush Singh, Minh Chien Vu, Trishala Neeraj, Jonas Golde, Albert Villanova del Moral, and Benjamin Beilharz. 2022. Bigbio: A framework for data-centric biomedical natural language processing. In *NeurIPS*.

Justin Gilmer, Samuel S. Schoenholz, Patrick F. Riley, Oriol Vinyals, and George E. Dahl. 2017. Neural message passing for quantum chemistry. In *Proceedings of the 34th International Conference on Machine Learning, ICML 2017, Sydney, NSW, Australia, 6-11 August 2017*, volume 70 of *Proceedings of Machine Learning Research*, pages 1263–1272. PMLR.

Yu Gu, Robert Tinn, Hao Cheng, Michael Lucas, Naoto Usuyama, Xiaodong Liu, Tristan Naumann, Jianfeng Gao, and Hoifung Poon. 2022. Domain-specific language model pretraining for biomedical natural language processing. *ACM Trans. Comput. Heal.*, 3(1):2:1–2:23.

William L. Hamilton, Zhitao Ying, and Jure Leskovec. 2017. Inductive representation learning on large graphs. In *Advances in Neural Information Processing Systems 30: Annual Conference on Neural Information Processing Systems 2017, December 4-9, 2017, Long Beach, CA, USA*, pages 1024–1034.

Xiao Huang, Jingyuan Zhang, Dingcheng Li, and Ping Li. 2019. Knowledge graph embedding based question answering. In *Proceedings of the Twelfth ACM International Conference on Web Search and Data Mining, WSDM 2019, Melbourne, VIC, Australia, February 11-15, 2019*, pages 105–113. ACM.

Seyed Mehran Kazemi and David Poole. 2018. Simple embedding for link prediction in knowledge graphs. In *Advances in Neural Information Processing Systems 31: Annual Conference on Neural Information Processing Systems 2018, NeurIPS 2018, December 3-8, 2018, Montréal, Canada*, pages 4289–4300.

Pei Ke, Haozhe Ji, Yu Ran, Xin Cui, Liwei Wang, Linfeng Song, Xiaoyan Zhu, and Minlie Huang. 2021. JointGT: Graph-text joint representation learning for text generation from knowledge graphs. In *Findings of the Association for Computational Linguistics: ACL-IJCNLP 2021*, pages 2526–2538, Online. Association for Computational Linguistics.

Kuzma Khrabrov, Ilya Shenbin, Alexander Ryabov, Artem Tsypin, Alexander Telepov, Anton Alekseev, Alexander Grishin, Pavel Strashnov, Petr Zhilyaev, Sergey Nikolenko, and Artur Kadurin. 2022. nablaDFT: Large-Scale conformational energy and hamiltonian prediction benchmark and dataset. *Phys. Chem. Chem. Phys.*, 24(42):25853–25863.

Jing Yu Koh, Daniel Fried, and Ruslan Salakhutdinov. 2023a. Generating images with multimodal language models. *NeurIPS*.

Jing Yu Koh, Ruslan Salakhutdinov, and Daniel Fried. 2023b. Grounding language models to images for multimodal inputs and outputs. In *International Conference on Machine Learning, ICML 2023, 23-29 July 2023, Honolulu, Hawaii, USA*, volume 202 of *Proceedings of Machine Learning Research*, pages 17283–17300. PMLR.

Jan A. Kors, Simon Clematide, Saber A. Akhondi, Erik M. van Mulligen, and Dietrich Rebholz-Schuhmann. 2015. A multilingual gold-standard corpus for biomedical concept recognition: the mantra GSC. *J. Am. Medical Informatics Assoc.*, 22(5):948–956.

Anne Lauscher, Ivan Vulić, Edoardo Maria Ponti, Anna Korhonen, and Goran Glavaš. 2020. Specializing unsupervised pretraining models for word-level semantic similarity. In *Proceedings of the 28th International Conference on Computational Linguistics*, pages 1371–1383, Barcelona, Spain (Online). International Committee on Computational Linguistics.

Jinhyuk Lee, Wonjin Yoon, Sungdong Kim, Donghyeon Kim, Sunkyu Kim, Chan Ho So, and Jaewoo Kang. 2020. Biobert: a pre-trained biomedical language representation model for biomedical text mining. *Bioinform.*, 36(4):1234–1240.

Sunwon Lee, Donghyeon Kim, Kyubum Lee, Jaehoon Choi, Seongsoon Kim, Minji Jeon, Sangrak Lim, Donghee Choi, Sunkyu Kim, Aik-Choon Tan, et al. 2016. Best: next-generation biomedical entity search tool for knowledge discovery from biomedical literature. *PloS one*, 11(10):e0164680.

Patrick Lewis, Myle Ott, Jingfei Du, and Veselin Stoyanov. 2020. Pretrained language models for biomedical and clinical tasks: Understanding and extending the state-of-the-art. In *Proceedings of the 3rd Clinical Natural Language Processing Workshop*, pages 146–157, Online. Association for Computational Linguistics.

Bill Yuchen Lin, Xinyue Chen, Jamin Chen, and Xiang Ren. 2019. KagNet: Knowledge-aware graph networks for commonsense reasoning. In *Proceedings of the 2019 Conference on Empirical Methods in Natural Language Processing and the 9th International Joint Conference on Natural Language Processing (EMNLP-IJCNLP)*, pages 2829–2839, Hong Kong, China. Association for Computational Linguistics.

Fangyu Liu, Ehsan Shareghi, Zaiqiao Meng, Marco Basaldella, and Nigel Collier. 2021a. Self-alignment pretraining for biomedical entity representations. In *Proceedings of the 2021 Conference of the North American Chapter of the Association for Computational Linguistics: Human Language Technologies*, pages 4228–4238, Online. Association for Computational Linguistics.

Fangyu Liu, Ivan Vulić, Anna Korhonen, and Nigel Collier. 2021b. Learning domain-specialised representations for cross-lingual biomedical entity linking. In *Proceedings of the 59th Annual Meeting of the Association for Computational Linguistics and the 11th International Joint Conference on Natural Language Processing (Volume 2: Short Papers)*, pages 565–574, Online. Association for Computational Linguistics.

Weijie Liu, Peng Zhou, Zhe Zhao, Zhiruo Wang, Qi Ju, Haotang Deng, and Ping Wang. 2020. K-BERT: enabling language representation with knowledge graph. In *The Thirty-Fourth AAAI Conference on Artificial Intelligence, AAAI 2020, The Thirty-Second Innovative Applications of Artificial Intelligence Conference, IAAI 2020, The Tenth AAAI Symposium on Educational Advances in Artificial Intelligence, EAAI 2020, New York, NY, USA, February 7-12, 2020*, pages 2901–2908. AAAI Press.

Aidan Mannion, Didier Schwab, and Lorraine Goeuriot. 2023. UMLS-KGI-BERT: Data-centric knowledge integration in transformers for biomedical entity recognition. In *Proceedings of the 5th Clinical Natural Language Processing Workshop*, pages 312–322, Toronto, Canada. Association for Computational Linguistics.

Zaiqiao Meng, Fangyu Liu, Ehsan Shareghi, Yixuan Su, Charlotte Collins, and Nigel Collier. 2022. Rewire-then-probe: A contrastive recipe for probing biomedical knowledge of pre-trained language models. In *Proceedings of the 60th Annual Meeting of the Association for Computational Linguistics (Volume 1: Long Papers)*, pages 4798–4810, Dublin, Ireland. Association for Computational Linguistics.

George Michalopoulos, Yuanxin Wang, Hussam Kaka, Helen Chen, and Alexander Wong. 2021. Umls-BERT: Clinical domain knowledge augmentation of contextual embeddings using the Unified Medical Language System Metathesaurus. In *Proceedings of the 2021 Conference of the North American Chapter of the Association for Computational Linguistics: Human Language Technologies*, pages 1744–1753, Online. Association for Computational Linguistics.

Irina Nikishina, Alsu Vakhitova, Elena Tutubalina, and Alexander Panchenko. 2022. Cross-modal contextualized hidden state projection method for expanding of taxonomic graphs. In *Proceedings of TextGraphs-16: Graph-based Methods for Natural Language Processing*, pages 11–24, Gyeongju, Republic of Korea. Association for Computational Linguistics.

Aaron van den Oord, Yazhe Li, and Oriol Vinyals. 2018. Representation learning with contrastive predictive coding. *arXiv preprint arXiv:1807.03748*.

Nathan Peiffer-Smadja, Timothy Miles Rawson, Raheelah Ahmad, Albert Buchard, P Georgiou, F-X Lescure, Gabriel Birgand, and Alison Helen Holmes. 2020. Machine learning for clinical decision support in infectious diseases: a narrative review of current applications. *Clinical Microbiology and Infection*, 26(5):584–595.

Yifan Peng, Shankai Yan, and Zhiyong Lu. 2019. Transfer learning in biomedical natural language processing: An evaluation of BERT and ELMo on ten benchmarking datasets. In *Proceedings of the 18th BioNLP Workshop and Shared Task*, pages 58–65, Florence, Italy. Association for Computational Linguistics.

Matthew E. Peters, Mark Neumann, Robert Logan, Roy Schwartz, Vidur Joshi, Sameer Singh, and Noah A. Smith. 2019. Knowledge enhanced contextual word representations. In *Proceedings of the 2019 Conference on Empirical Methods in Natural Language Processing and the 9th International Joint Conference on Natural Language Processing (EMNLP-IJCNLP)*, pages 43–54, Hong Kong, China. Association for Computational Linguistics.

Andrey Sakhovskiy, Zulfat Miftahutdinov, and Elena Tutubalina. 2021. KFU NLP team at SMM4H 2021 tasks: Cross-lingual and cross-modal BERT-based models for adverse drug effects. In *Proceedings of the Sixth Social Media Mining for Health (#SMM4H) Workshop and Shared Task*, pages 39–43, Mexico City, Mexico. Association for Computational Linguistics.

Andrey Sakhovskiy, Natalia Semenova, Artur Kadurin, and Elena Tutubalina. 2023. Graph-enriched biomedical entity representation transformer. In *Experimental IR Meets Multilinguality, Multimodality, and Interaction - 14th International Conference of the CLEF Association, CLEF 2023, Thessaloniki, Greece, September 18-21, 2023, Proceedings*, volume 14163 of *Lecture Notes in Computer Science*, pages 109–120. Springer.

Andrey Sakhovskiy and Elena Tutubalina. 2022. Multimodal model with text and drug embeddings for adverse drug reaction classification. *Journal of Biomedical Informatics*, 135:104182.

Sarvesh Soni and Kirk Roberts. 2021. An evaluation of two commercial deep learning-based information retrieval systems for COVID-19 literature. *Journal of the American Medical Informatics Association*, 28(1):132–137.

Zhiqing Sun, Zhi-Hong Deng, Jian-Yun Nie, and Jian Tang. 2019. Rotate: Knowledge graph embedding by relational rotation in complex space. In *International Conference on Learning Representations*.

Mujeen Sung, Minbyul Jeong, Yonghwa Choi, Donghyeon Kim, Jinhyuk Lee, and Jaewoo Kang. 2022. BERN2: an advanced neural biomedical named entity recognition and normalization tool. *Bioinformatics*, 38(20):4837–4839.

Mujeen Sung, Jinhyuk Lee, Sean Yi, Minji Jeon, Sungdong Kim, and Jaewoo Kang. 2021. Can language models be biomedical knowledge bases? In *Proceedings of the 2021 Conference on Empirical Methods in Natural Language Processing*, pages 4723–4734, Online and Punta Cana, Dominican Republic. Association for Computational Linguistics.

Reed T. Sutton, David Pincock, Daniel C. Baumgart, Daniel C. Sadowski, Richard N. Fedorak, and Karen I. Kroeker. 2020. An overview of clinical decision support systems: benefits, risks, and strategies for success. *NPJ digital medicine*, 3.

Théo Trouillon, Johannes Welbl, Sebastian Riedel, Eric Gaussier, and Guillaume Bouchard. 2016. Complex embeddings for simple link prediction. In *Proceedings of The 33rd International Conference on Machine Learning*, volume 48 of *Proceedings of Machine Learning Research*, pages 2071–2080, New York, New York, USA. PMLR.

Ashish Vaswani, Noam Shazeer, Niki Parmar, Jakob Uszkoreit, Llion Jones, Aidan N. Gomez, Lukasz Kaiser, and Illia Polosukhin. 2017. Attention is all you need. In *Advances in Neural Information Processing Systems 30: Annual Conference on Neural Information Processing Systems 2017, December 4-9, 2017, Long Beach, CA, USA*, pages 5998–6008.

Petar Veličković, Guillem Cucurull, Arantxa Casanova, Adriana Romero, Pietro Liò, and Yoshua Bengio.

2018. Graph Attention Networks. *International Conference on Learning Representations*. Accepted as poster.

Quan Wang, Pingping Huang, Haifeng Wang, Songtai Dai, Wenbin Jiang, Jing Liu, Yajuan Lyu, Yong Zhu, and Hua Wu. 2019a. Coke: Contextualized knowledge graph embedding. *arXiv preprint arXiv:1911.02168*.

Xiaozhi Wang, Tianyu Gao, Zhaocheng Zhu, Zhengyan Zhang, Zhiyuan Liu, Juanzi Li, and Jian Tang. 2021. KEPLER: A unified model for knowledge embedding and pre-trained language representation. *Transactions of the Association for Computational Linguistics*, 9:176–194.

Xun Wang, Xintong Han, Weilin Huang, Dengke Dong, and Matthew R. Scott. 2019b. Multi-similarity loss with general pair weighting for deep metric learning. In *IEEE Conference on Computer Vision and Pattern Recognition, CVPR 2019, Long Beach, CA, USA, June 16-20, 2019*, pages 5022–5030. Computer Vision Foundation / IEEE.

David S Wishart, Yannick D Feunang, An C Guo, Elvis J Lo, Ana Marcu, Jason R Grant, Tanvir Sajed, Daniel Johnson, Carin Li, Zinat Sayeeda, Nazanin Assempour, Ithayavani Iynkkaran, Yifeng Liu, Adam Maciejewski, Nicola Gale, Alex Wilson, Lucy Chin, Ryan Cummings, Diana Le, Allison Pon, Craig Knox, and Michael Wilson. 2017. DrugBank 5.0: a major update to the DrugBank database for 2018. *Nucleic Acids Research*, 46(D1):D1074–D1082.

David S. Wishart, Craig Knox, Anchi Guo, Dean Cheng, Savita Shrivastava, Dan Tzur, Bijaya Gautam, and Murtaza Hassanali. 2008. Drugbank: a knowledgebase for drugs, drug actions and drug targets. *Nucleic Acids Res.*, 36(Database-Issue):901–906.

Weiqi Wu, Chengyue Jiang, Yong Jiang, Pengjun Xie, and Kewei Tu. 2023. Do PLMs know and understand ontological knowledge? In *Proceedings of the 61st Annual Meeting of the Association for Computational Linguistics (Volume 1: Long Papers)*, pages 3080–3101, Toronto, Canada. Association for Computational Linguistics.

Zhenqin Wu, Bharath Ramsundar, Evan N. Feinberg, Joseph Gomes, Caleb Geniesse, Aneesh S. Pappu, Karl Leswing, and Vijay Pande. 2018. Moleculenet: a benchmark for molecular machine learning. *Chem. Sci.*, 9:513–530.

Hanwen Xu, Jiayou Zhang, Zhirui Wang, Shizhuo Zhang, Megh Bhalerao, Yucong Liu, Dawei Zhu, and Sheng Wang. 2023. Graphprompt: Graph-based prompt templates for biomedical synonym prediction. In *Thirty-Seventh AAAI Conference on Artificial Intelligence, AAAI 2023, Thirty-Fifth Conference on Innovative Applications of Artificial Intelligence, IAAI 2023, Thirteenth Symposium on Educational Advances in Artificial Intelligence, EAAI 2023, Washington, DC, USA, February 7-14, 2023*, pages 10576–10584. AAAI Press.

Bishan Yang, Wen-tau Yih, Xiaodong He, Jianfeng Gao, and Li Deng. 2015. Embedding entities and relations for learning and inference in knowledge bases. In *3rd International Conference on Learning Representations, ICLR 2015, San Diego, CA, USA, May 7-9, 2015, Conference Track Proceedings*.

Michihiro Yasunaga, Antoine Bosselut, Hongyu Ren, Xikun Zhang, Christopher D. Manning, Percy Liang, and Jure Leskovec. 2022a. Deep bidirectional language-knowledge graph pretraining. In *NeurIPS*.

Michihiro Yasunaga, Jure Leskovec, and Percy Liang. 2022b. LinkBERT: Pretraining language models with document links. In *Proceedings of the 60th Annual Meeting of the Association for Computational Linguistics (Volume 1: Long Papers)*, pages 8003–8016, Dublin, Ireland. Association for Computational Linguistics.

Michihiro Yasunaga, Hongyu Ren, Antoine Bosselut, Percy Liang, and Jure Leskovec. 2021a. QA-GNN: Reasoning with language models and knowledge graphs for question answering. In *Proceedings of the 2021 Conference of the North American Chapter of the Association for Computational Linguistics: Human Language Technologies*, pages 535–546, Online. Association for Computational Linguistics.

Michihiro Yasunaga, Hongyu Ren, Antoine Bosselut, Percy Liang, and Jure Leskovec. 2021b. QA-GNN: Reasoning with language models and knowledge graphs for question answering. In *Proceedings of the 2021 Conference of the North American Chapter of the Association for Computational Linguistics: Human Language Technologies*, pages 535–546, Online. Association for Computational Linguistics.

Hongyi Yuan, Zheng Yuan, and Sheng Yu. 2022a. Generative biomedical entity linking via knowledge base-guided pre-training and synonyms-aware fine-tuning. In *Proceedings of the 2022 Conference of the North American Chapter of the Association for Computational Linguistics: Human Language Technologies*, pages 4038–4048, Seattle, United States. Association for Computational Linguistics.

Zheng Yuan, Zhengyun Zhao, Haixia Sun, Jiao Li, Fei Wang, and Sheng Yu. 2022b. Coder: Knowledge-infused cross-lingual medical term embedding for term normalization. *Journal of Biomedical Informatics*, 126:103983.

Miao Zhang, Rufeng Dai, Ming Dong, and Tingting He. 2022a. DRLK: Dynamic hierarchical reasoning with language model and knowledge graph for question answering. In *Proceedings of the 2022 Conference on Empirical Methods in Natural Language Processing*, pages 5123–5133, Abu Dhabi, United Arab Emirates. Association for Computational Linguistics.

Xikun Zhang, Antoine Bosselut, Michihiro Yasunaga, Hongyu Ren, Percy Liang, Christopher D. Manning, and Jure Leskovec. 2022b. Greaselm: Graph reasoning enhanced language models. In *The Tenth International Conference on Learning Representations, ICLR 2022, Virtual Event, April 25-29, 2022*.

Marinka Zitnik, Monica Agrawal, and Jure Leskovec. 2018. Modeling polypharmacy side effects with graph convolutional networks. *Bioinformatics*, 34(13):i457–i466.

Evaluating Large Language Models' Understanding of Financial Terminology via Definition Modeling

James Jhirad[1] **Edison Marrese-Taylor**[2,3] **Yutaka Matsuo**[3]
[1] Faculty of Arts & Science, University of Toronto
[2] National Institute of Advanced Industrial Science and Technology
[3] Graduate School of Engineering, The University of Tokyo
james.jhirad@mail.utoronto.ca, {emarrese,matsuo}@weblab.t.u-tokyo.ac.jp

Abstract

As machine learning models grow increasingly sophisticated, the question of their reliability and understanding becomes critical, especially within specialized domains like finance, medicine, and law. Definition modeling, the task of generating a textual definition from a word, has proven a useful technique to help better understand word sense and embeddings, which is at the core of language learning and word acquisition. Drawing upon a repository of financial terminology (Investopedia), we build a dataset of 14,000 terms and definitions. We design a number of tasks to evaluate the capacity of various LLMs to generate accurate and expansive definitions in this domain, and propose to utilize definition modeling to probe the abilities of Large Language Models (LLMs) in the context of the financial domain. Using our dataset, we present an empirical study where we test a broad selection of LLMs on our tasks with zero-shot and k-shot approaches. We show the extent to which these models are able to define financial terms. We observe large performance increases for smaller models with in-context learning, and see that they are almost comparable to GPT-3.5. Our work shows the boons of using definition modeling to evaluate models in more specific fields of study, such as finance.

1 Introduction

Definition modeling is the task of estimating the probability of a textual definition, given a word being defined. Since its conception (Noraset et al., 2017) several approaches have tackled this task, and over the past few years have achieved substantial performance improvements. This task has been shown to give an arguably more transparent view of the extent to which syntax and semantics are captured by a model.

So far, existing approaches for this task have followed the traditional approach, where models are trained on a corpus of word-definition pairs to later be tested on how well they generate definitions for words not seen during training. However, the recent success of Large Language Models (LLMs) has caused a shift in our field, showing that such models can achieve excellent performance on a wide variety of downstream tasks, utilizing zero-shot or few-shot approaches (Brown et al., 2020; Kojima et al., 2022), i.e. without fine-tuning.

Term	Definition (1st Key Takeaway)
Enterprise value (EV)	Enterprise value (EV) measures a company's total value, often used as a more comprehensive alternative to equity market capitalization.
Bonds	Bonds are units of corporate debt issued by companies and securitized as tradeable assets.

Table 1: Examples of Term-Definition pairs taken from dataset built out of Investopedia

Furthermore, while the definition modeling task was originally intended for the study of *general* words, we note that some recent work has focused on extending the task to domain specific terms. These works propose domain specific models trained to define specialized terminology. While these efforts are welcome, and remain an interesting and useful approach, we note that they are still limited in terms of scope, with key domains such as finance or chemistry, being left out so far.

In this paper, we tackle the two aforementioned issues by: (1) Using definition modeling tasks as a probe to test the abilities of LLMs in a zero-shot or few-shot setting, motivated by the original ideas of (Noraset et al., 2017), and (2) Introducing a new dataset with 14,000 term-definition pairs in the financial domain - so far an unexplored direction which we believe is particularly relevant due to the way in which LLMs are trained, while also

Proceedings of the 13th International Joint Conference on Natural Language Processing and the 3rd Conference of the Asia-Pacific Chapter of the Association for Computational Linguistics: Student Research Workshop, pages 93–100
November 1–4, 2023.

presenting relevant use-cases.

To this end, we construct a new dataset of approximately 14,000 terms specific to the financial domain. Table 1 shows examples of how our data looks like. We use this new dataset to assess the quality of financial definitions generated from some of the latest LLMs with a zero-shot and few-shot approach. Our proposals offer a concrete direction for prompting methodology, examining variables such as number of shots, usage of word context, role of domain, and evaluation.

Our experiments show that while some of the larger and most cutting-edge LLMs are able to define financial terms, they outperform classical definition modeling tasks. Our choice of COMET as an evaluation metric also appears like an adequate metric to use for definition modeling tasks. Lastly, we release our code to encourage research in this direction[1].

2 Related Work

Our work is primarily related to the seminal work by Noraset et al. (2017) and Hill et al. (2016), in which a model is tasked with generating a definition for a word given its respective embedding, or with mapping dictionary definitions to lexical representations of words, respectively.

After this, several works have proposed improvements. Many introducing techniques and datasets to address several shortcomings of the initial ideas. For example, Gadetsky et al. (2018) addresses polysemy and presents a dataset from Oxford Dictionaries, where each definition is also supplemented with context sentences, in which each example word is used, allowing models to disambiguate. Ni and Wang (2017) proposed an approach for automatically explaining slang English terms in a sentence, and introduced yet another dataset. Ishiwatari et al. (2019) and Reid et al. (2020) propose to further rely on local and global contexts, with the latter also introducing a dataset based on Cambridge Dictionaries, and a dataset for French.

More recently, Huang et al. (2021) study the problem of definition specificity, and propose a method for tuning a model to account for hyper focused (over-specific) or highly general (under-specific) definitions. Chen and Zhao (2022) propose to unify the seminal ideas of reverse dictionary and definition modeling in a single model, with the goal of helping better understand word sense and embeddings.

Finally, we find several works aiming to generate definitions in specialized fields, whose efforts are well aligned with our work. August et al. (2022) propose to generate definitions of scientific and medical terms with varying complexity, using a dataset constructed from consumer medical questions and science glossaries (MedQuAD and Wikipedia). Liu et al. (2021) introduce Graphine, a dataset for biomedical terminology definition, and Huang et al. (2022) propose to model 'jargon', with a dataset constructed semi-automatically based on Wikipedia and Springer. Though our work is similar, since we also extend definition modeling to a new domain, critically our approach differs as we 'probe' our models' understanding of financial terms through definition modeling.

3 The INVESTOPEDIA Dataset

To construct a dataset of financial terms, we rely on Investopedia, an extensive repository of financial information and terminology. We initiated our data collection by fetching every available link on the website. Out of approximately 25,000 extracted links, half were found to contain articles or news discussing specific events, while the remaining comprised pages focused on delineating specific financial terms or concepts.

The extraction of the main term from the article presented a complex task due to the variety in article title structures. To achieve this, we employed a set of heuristics that guided the selection of the most appropriate string as the main term, which were also combined with manual annotation.

A similar strategy was used for identifying potential acronyms associated with each term, incorporating both heuristic and manual processes.

Investopedia Dataset	
# of Terms	13,609
Definition Length (in tokens)	19.69 ± 7.33
Mean # Key Takeaways	3.66
Oxford Dataset	
# of Terms	122,319
Definition Length (in tokens)	11.03 ± 6.97

Table 2: Statistics on our financial data and the Oxford dataset. The definitions for the financial data is considered to be the first key takeaway.

[1]https://github.com/KobiJames/Financial-DefMod

The second phase of our data scraping involved the extraction of the "Key Takeaways" section found in each article. This section, typically consisting of 3 to 5 bullet points summarizing the article, is a critical part of our dataset. We chose to leverage this section over the first paragraph to generate the definitions for each term. The choice of the "Key Takeaways" section over the first paragraph was primarily due to its structure and ease of extraction. While both sections offered a general description of the term, the former provided something more akin to a set of distinct 'mini definitions'. Each point in the "Key Takeaways" is grammatically independent of the previous, and captures something different about the article than the other points. This encapsulation of the entire article's content in conveniently parsed pieces, made it an ideal source for our definitions.

Our finalized dataset consists of data points, each corresponding to a single article. The primary components of each data point include the processed term name, any associated acronym, and a list of key takeaways serving as the definition. Supplementary data, added for convenience and potential further research, encompasses the article's header, and the full text of the article, separated by HTML tags ('h1','h2','p', etc...) and ordered from top to bottom in an array.

4 Empirical Study

4.1 Experimental Setup

To test the abilities of LLMs in performing definition modeling in the financial domain, we leverage the "Key Takeaways" section in INVESTOPEDIA. Based on the success of previous work in augmenting definition modeling with contextual information (Gadetsky et al., 2018; Ishiwatari et al., 2019; Reid et al., 2020), we additionally leverage sample phrases from the article content, which we present to the models as context in addition to the term, for generating the definition. They are presented to our models by appending them to the prompt, and we refer to them as "examples" in further discussion.

The structure and wording of the prompts presented to the models were established through a systematic testing process. Most notably, we observed that prompting the models with the task to define a "financial term" led to consistently significant performance improvements. A similar improvement was seen when the models were asked to present their responses as points or bullet points, leading us to incorporate these findings into our final prompt, which we used across all the experimental runs in the zero-shot scenario. For our experiments incorporating examples or for the k-shots settings, we append each phrase or shot above the prompt, and add a newline character to separate the base prompt, examples, and shots. For prompts with both examples and shots, shots are put above examples. For prompts with examples, we use two examples, and for prompts with shots, we use two shots. Please see our supplementary material for details.

Regarding model choice, we consider a broad section of LLMs varying widely in terms of the number of parameters and training scheme. Concretely, we work with the following models: OPT-IML 1.3B (Iyer et al., 2023), GPT-J (6B parameters) (Wang and Komatsuzaki, 2021), GPT-JT (6B parameters) (Rel, 2022), MT0-XXL (13B parameters), FLAN-UL2 (20B parameters) (Tay et al., 2023; Muennighoff et al., 2023), and ChatGPT/GPT-3.5 Turbo (175B parameters).

In terms of evaluation, we note that previous work has mainly utilized n-gram overall metrics such as BLEU (Papineni et al., 2002) and METEOR (Banerjee and Lavie, 2005). Reid et al. (2020) showed that by migrating to metrics based on Machine Learning (ML), such as BERTScore (Zhang et al., 2019), it was possible to more adequately capture nuance in the definitions generated by their approach, which led more recent models to adopt this evaluation metric as well. In this paper, we take another step in this direction and experiment with COMET (Rei et al., 2020) as an evaluation metric for our task. Though COMET is intended for evaluation of Machine Translation models, in our early experiments we found that it offered a robust alternative to other ML-based metrics such as BERT-Score and worked well at capturing the ability of the models at generating accurate and expansive definitions.

We also note that the complexity of our terms, evidenced by the length and detail of the "Key Takeaways" section of our dataset, pose a considerable challenge in our evaluation process. We observe that any of the takeaway points can, to a degree, serve as a separate definition of the term. To avoid penalizing the model when it generates such relevant information, we propose a scoring scheme where we compare the output of the model against combinations of "Key Takeaways". Let x_i be our target financial term. For $i \in [1 \dots L]$, we have $j \in [1 \dots N_i]$, where L is the size of our dataset,

Data	Model	Params.	COMET				METEOR				BLEU			
			base	ex.	sh.	sh.+ex.	base	ex.	sh.	sh.+ex.	base	ex.	sh.	sh.+ex.
Investopedia (1st KTAW)	OPT-IML	1.3B	47.82	47.41	59.75	60.01	15.92	17.11	25.96	29.74	4.54	5.26	6.48	6.36
	GPT-J	6.0B	50.77	43.73	57.55	60.80	22.17	16.94	28.32	32.37	3.56	3.30	4.97	6.52
	GPT-JT	6.0B	33.23	44.41	57.18	60.35	6.65	18.60	27.99	31.16	0.96	3.33	4.44	5.85
	MT0-XXL	13B	55.21	64.55	63.06	66.10	24.68	30.18	24.82	28.85	4.90	7.81	6.72	8.95
	FLAN-UL2	20B	66.30	68.49	68.15	68.98	27.30	30.17	30.16	32.31	7.93	10.16	9.73	10.66
	GPT-3.5-Turbo	175B	68.64	69.12	68.51	**69.79**	35.82	37.29	36.63	38.22	5.74	6.36	6.73	7.15
Investopedia	OPT-IML	1.3B	48.45	48.92	61.21	62.95	16.38	18.48	27.33	32.67	2.99	4.28	5.65	7.06
	GPT-J	6.0B	52.11	45.27	59.93	63.77	23.56	18.39	29.86	34.97	3.93	3.81	5.51	7.55
	GPT-JT	6.0B	33.99	45.98	59.61	63.68	7.12	20.49	29.62	34.39	1.01	3.76	4.98	7.01
	MT0-XXL	13B	56.43	67.47	63.69	68.10	26.12	33.28	25.40	31.00	4.38	7.17	3.85	6.46
	FLAN-UL2	20B	66.63	69.74	68.67	70.61	27.71	31.72	30.68	34.19	4.11	6.50	5.82	7.44
	GPT-3.5-Turbo	175B	72.18	72.82	71.98	**73.57**	38.50	40.02	39.38	41.20	6.65	7.38	7.78	8.32
Oxford	OPT-IML	1.3B	32.66	32.88	47.23	49.02	2.78	2.65	7.80	9.09	0.29	0.39	3.29	3.43
	GPT-J	6.0B	39.00	40.61	38.20	42.80	8.14	10.49	10.45	13.21	0.84	1.12	1.26	1.28
	GPT-JT	6.0B	40.88	40.59	39.54	42.64	9.22	10.18	12.10	14.40	0.97	1.24	1.38	1.61
	MT0-XXL	13B	46.08	50.39	33.75	39.45	8.70	9.75	3.32	8.50	2.80	3.35	0.50	1.40
	FLAN-UL2	20B	45.72	50.10	47.52	50.46	6.73	9.83	8.41	10.70	2.63	4.03	3.40	4.40
	GPT-3.5-Turbo	175B	55.93	59.69	57.96	**61.75**	23.90	27.99	25.26	29.93	3.57	4.74	8.63	9.84

Table 3: Scores across COMET, METEOR and BLEU on financial definition modeling tasks and the Oxford dataset on "dictionary" definition modeling, where we use. 'ex.' to indicate use of examples, 'sh.' to indicate use of 2-shot, and KTAW is short for "Key Takeaway". Values which are bold & underlined are the best out of all the models; values that are only underlined are the best results from open-source models

and N_i denotes the number of "Key Takeaways" for term x_i. Let $y_{i,j}$ be the jth "Key Takeaway" for x_i, and the set $\{y_{i,j}|j \in [1 \dots N_i]\}$ is the list of sorted "Key Takeaways" to be used as targets. Finally, let $P(s)$ be the function that generates the power set of a set s. Then, for a given evaluation Metric M, our final score is computed following Equation 1, below, where $a; B$ denotes the sequential string concatenation of every element in B to the end of a in order (i.e. $a + b_1 + b_2 + \ldots$).

$$S_i := \max\{M(\hat{y}, [y_{i,1}; K])|K \in P([y_{i,2}, \ldots y_{i,N_i}])\} \quad (1)$$

The idea of combining "Key Takeaways" in such a way derives from the fact that the first bullet point typically provides the most straightforward definition of the term. By combining this with the rest of the points, we ensured that a wide array of definitions, ranging from simplistic to comprehensive, were accounted for in our evaluation scheme.

While this method of evaluation is holistic, it also makes it difficult to compare results of our evaluations against different datasets that lack this type of information for their gold standard. Evaluation scores could possibly be inflated, which would cause an uneven comparison. Evaluations over our dataset just using the first key takeaway as a gold standard were added as a baseline for the purpose of comparability. Finally, to understand the complexity of defining financial terms, we also test our approach on the dataset constructed from Oxford dictionaries (Gadetsky et al., 2018). To the best of our knowledge, our work is the first one to test the abilities of LLMs on the "dictionary" definition modeling task using zero-shot or few-shot settings. We believe results on this will help contextualize our results in the financial domain, while also giving new insight into the abilities of LLMs.

4.2 Prompts

The following is the prompt structure we used for each term, as well as every variation of the prompt we used for the term "*A-B Trust*".

$$T \in \textbf{Investopedia Terms}$$

$$E_i^T \in \textbf{Examples for term } T|i \in 0, 1$$

$$S_i \in \textbf{Shot List}|i \in 0, 1$$

Prompt Structure

"S_0
S_1
E_0^T
E_1^T
Define, in a financial context, '[T]' with bullet points. Please list up to 2 bullet points.

Definition: "
Prompt without examples or shots
"Define, in a financial context, 'A-B trust' with bullet points. Please list up to 2 bullet points.
Definition: "
Prompt with examples
"06 million will opt for an A-B trust in 2022
While A-B trusts are a great way to minimize estate taxes, they are not used much today
Define, in a financial context, 'A-B trust' with bullet points. Please list up to 2 bullet points.
Definition: "
Prompt with shots
"Define, in a financial context, 'Enterprise Value' with bullet points. Please list up to 2 bullet points.
Definition: Enterprise value (EV) measures a company's total value, often used as a more comprehensive alternative to equity market capitalization. Enterprise value includes in its calculation the market capitalization of a company but also short-term and long-term debt and any cash on the company's balance sheet.
Define, in a financial context, 'Bond' with bullet points. Please list up to 2 bullet points.
Definition: Bonds are units of corporate debt issued by companies and securitized as tradeable assets. A bond is referred to as a fixed-income instrument since bonds traditionally paid a fixed interest rate (coupon) to debtholders.
Define, in a financial context, 'A-B trust' with bullet points. Please list up to 2 bullet points.
Definition: "
Prompt with examples and shots
"Define, in a financial context, 'Enterprise Value' with bullet points. Please list up to 2 bullet points.
Definition: Enterprise value (EV) measures a company's total value, often used as a more comprehensive alternative to equity market capitalization. Enterprise value includes in its calculation the market capitalization of a company but also short-term and long-term debt and any cash on the company's balance sheet.
Define, in a financial context, 'Bond' with bullet points. Please list up to 2 bullet points. Definition: Bonds are units of corporate debt issued by companies and securitized as tradeable assets. A bond is referred to as a fixed-income instrument since bonds traditionally paid a fixed interest rate (coupon) to debtholders.
06 million will opt for an A-B trust in 2022
While A-B trusts are a great way to minimize estate taxes, they are not used much today
Define, in a financial context, 'A-B trust' with bullet points. Please list up to 2 bullet points.
Definition: "

4.3 Results

The performance outcomes for all selected models, based on INVESTOPEDIA are displayed in Table 3. We also show our results on the classic or "dictionary" definition modeling task, for which all models were evaluated under comparable configurations. To assess the performance of the models, three evaluation metrics were employed, namely COMET, METEOR, and BLEU, with focus on the former. We use four different prompting methods, as described in section 4.1; 'base' for no shot, no examples, 'ex.' for no shot, 2 examples, 'shot' for 2 shot, no examples, and 'shot+ex.' for 2 shots, 2 examples.

As shown in Table 3 we observe that the performance of all considered models aligns with respective size — the larger the model, the better the performance. We also note that smaller models seem to be unable to perform well without the help of the additional context presented. Finally, the performance gain of smaller models with in-context learning is substantial relative to the baselines.

In our exploration of the effects of differing prompting styles, an interesting pattern emerged, particularly when contrasting the smaller models with larger ones. The performance of MT0-XXL, Flan-UL2, and GPT-3.5-Turbo increase when augmented with examples in the prompt (i.e. from base to ex., or sh. to sh.+ex.), while OPT-IML, GPT-J, and GPT-JT are unaffected by this change. This discrepancy is also seen in the results on the Oxford dataset, further exemplifying the relevance of this observation. Since, MT0-XXL, Flan-UL2, and GPT-3.5-Turbo are larger models. This raises a compelling hypothesis that, for models without direct knowledge of terms, model size may be correlated with enhanced capabilities of utilizing non-shot context to increase performance. This is seen by the aforementioned model's increase in performance with examples over our other models.

Results on the Oxford dataset exhibit a decrease in performance relative to the financial definition modeling tasks. We ascribe this primarily to the discrepancy in length between the Oxford gold standard and the model outputs, as can be seen in Table 2. The brevity of the Oxford definitions contrasts with the verbose model responses, contributing to the performance gap for GPT-3.5-turbo on a seem-

Model	COMET	METEOR	BLEU
INVESTOPEDIA			
Ours (FLAN-UL2)	68.98	32.31	10.66
Oxford			
Gadetsky et al. (2018)	-	-	23.77
Ishiwatari et al. (2019)	-	-	25.19
Reid et al. (2020)	57.00	35.05	27.38
Huang et al. (2021)	-	-	26.52
Ours (GPT-3.5-Turbo)	61.75	29.93	9.84

Table 4: Comparison of our best performing models against state-of-the-art approaches for the Oxford dataset.

ingly simpler task. While we intend for Oxford to be a type of baseline for our tests, INVESTOPEDIA has more expansive definitions, which make comparisons using COMET difficult. For comparison, our dataset has around three to four key points for each definition, each, at minimum, the length of a definition from the Oxford dataset. This discrepancy exposes a limitation of the COMET evaluation metric, despite its many advantages.

Concerning results of our special evaluation schema which uses multiple gold standards, compared to only using the first key takeaway, we see an across the board improvement of each model by a few comet points. This is expected, as taking a max across multiple gold standards will inevitably boost evaluation scores.

Finally, we compare our best results on INVESTOPEDIA and the Oxford benchmark against state-of-the-art models for the latter, all based on fine-tuning. Specifically, we consider the approaches by Gadetsky et al. (2018) who released the Oxford dataset, Ishiwatari et al. (2019) who proposed a local-and-global context model based on word embeddings, Reid et al. (2020) who leveraged BERT (Devlin et al., 2019) and combined it with a variational inference framework, and Huang et al. (2021) who propose a specificity-sensitive approach with models based on T5 (Raffel et al., 2020).

As Table 4 shows, we see that finetuning-based approaches are able to outperform our k-shot and zero-shot techniques based on prompting by a large margin in terms of BLEU. We also see that the overall best performance of the latter techniques on INVESTOPEDIA remain on pair with Oxford in terms of all metrics, suggesting that fine-tuning could also lead to improved results in our dataset as well. We think this could be interesting for specific applications where generating accurate definitions of financial terms is needed.

5 Conclusions

In summary, this paper advances our understanding of the capabilities and limitations of Large Language Models (LLMs) in specialized domains by using definition modeling tasks as a lens into our models abilities. We have established a framework for testing LLMs in a zero-shot or few-shot setting and demonstrated the utility of this approach with a novel dataset of 14,000 term-definition pairs in the financial domain - an area so far underrepresented in such studies. Our empirical results, derived from an array of LLMs, highlight the degree to which these models can define financial terms accurately and expansively. Notably, we observed considerable performance enhancements when adding in-context learning to smaller models, indicating that they can approach the performance levels of larger counterparts, such as GPT3.5. While our study presents a significant step towards comprehending the nuances of LLMs in specialized areas like finance, it also underscores the challenges that remain. The performance gap witnessed on tasks with shorter definitions, like those in the Oxford dataset, reveals inherent limitations of the evaluated models and evaluation metrics. We hope our work inspires further research into the application of definition modeling as a means to understand and refine LLMs, particularly in critical fields such as finance, law, and medicine.

Limitations

There are a few notable limitations of our work. Firstly, the methods we used were primarily in-context learning. We did not fine-tune any models, although this was by intention. While our goal was to 'probe' the models we chose, it does remain a question whether our dataset can be used for performance gains with training. We leave this to future work.

Ethics Statement

Our main objective is to propose a new task to evaluate the abilities of LLMs, introducing a dataset of financial term definition. One potential use-case is to have a model generate fake definitions that may mislead users that interact with an LLM when deployed. By publicly releasing our data, we hope to minimize such risks.

Acknowledgements

For our experiments, computational resources of AI Bridging Cloud Infrastructure (ABCI) provided by National Institute of Advanced Industrial Science and Technology (AIST) were used. We are also grateful to the NVIDIA Corporation, which donated one of the GPUs used for this research.

References

2022. Releasing GPT-JT powered by open-source AI.

Tal August, Katharina Reinecke, and Noah A. Smith. 2022. Generating Scientific Definitions with Controllable Complexity. In *Proceedings of the 60th Annual Meeting of the Association for Computational Linguistics (Volume 1: Long Papers)*, pages 8298–8317, Dublin, Ireland. Association for Computational Linguistics.

Satanjeev Banerjee and Alon Lavie. 2005. METEOR: An automatic metric for MT evaluation with improved correlation with human judgments. In *Proceedings of the ACL Workshop on Intrinsic and Extrinsic Evaluation Measures for Machine Translation and/or Summarization*, pages 65–72, Ann Arbor, Michigan. Association for Computational Linguistics.

Tom Brown, Benjamin Mann, Nick Ryder, Melanie Subbiah, Jared D Kaplan, Prafulla Dhariwal, Arvind Neelakantan, Pranav Shyam, Girish Sastry, Amanda Askell, Sandhini Agarwal, Ariel Herbert-Voss, Gretchen Krueger, Tom Henighan, Rewon Child, Aditya Ramesh, Daniel Ziegler, Jeffrey Wu, Clemens Winter, Chris Hesse, Mark Chen, Eric Sigler, Mateusz Litwin, Scott Gray, Benjamin Chess, Jack Clark, Christopher Berner, Sam McCandlish, Alec Radford, Ilya Sutskever, and Dario Amodei. 2020. Language Models are Few-Shot Learners. In *Advances in Neural Information Processing Systems*, volume 33, pages 1877–1901. Curran Associates, Inc.

Pinzhen Chen and Zheng Zhao. 2022. A Unified Model for Reverse Dictionary and Definition Modelling. In *Proceedings of the 2nd Conference of the Asia-Pacific Chapter of the Association for Computational Linguistics and the 12th International Joint Conference on Natural Language Processing (Volume 2: Short Papers)*, pages 8–13, Online only. Association for Computational Linguistics.

Jacob Devlin, Ming-Wei Chang, Kenton Lee, and Kristina Toutanova. 2019. BERT: Pre-training of Deep Bidirectional Transformers for Language Understanding. In *Proceedings of the 2019 Conference of the North American Chapter of the Association for Computational Linguistics: Human Language Technologies, Volume 1 (Long and Short Papers)*, pages 4171–4186, Minneapolis, Minnesota. Association for Computational Linguistics.

Artyom Gadetsky, Ilya Yakubovskiy, and Dmitry Vetrov. 2018. Conditional generators of words definitions. In *Proceedings of the 56th Annual Meeting of the Association for Computational Linguistics (Volume 2: Short Papers)*, pages 266–271, Melbourne, Australia. Association for Computational Linguistics.

Felix Hill, Kyunghyun Cho, Anna Korhonen, and Yoshua Bengio. 2016. Learning to understand phrases by embedding the dictionary. *Transactions of the Association for Computational Linguistics*, 4:17–30.

Han Huang, Tomoyuki Kajiwara, and Yuki Arase. 2021. Definition Modelling for Appropriate Specificity. In *Proceedings of the 2021 Conference on Empirical Methods in Natural Language Processing*, pages 2499–2509, Online and Punta Cana, Dominican Republic. Association for Computational Linguistics.

Jie Huang, Hanyin Shao, Kevin Chen-Chuan Chang, Jinjun Xiong, and Wen-mei Hwu. 2022. Understanding Jargon: Combining Extraction and Generation for Definition Modeling. In *Proceedings of the 2022 Conference on Empirical Methods in Natural Language Processing*, pages 3994–4004, Abu Dhabi, United Arab Emirates. Association for Computational Linguistics.

Shonosuke Ishiwatari, Hiroaki Hayashi, Naoki Yoshinaga, Graham Neubig, Shoetsu Sato, Masashi Toyoda, and Masaru Kitsuregawa. 2019. Learning to Describe Unknown Phrases with Local and Global Contexts. In *Proceedings of the 2019 Conference of the North American Chapter of the Association for Computational Linguistics: Human Language Technologies, Volume 1 (Long and Short Papers)*, pages 3467–3476, Minneapolis, Minnesota. Association for Computational Linguistics.

Srinivasan Iyer, Xi Victoria Lin, Ramakanth Pasunuru, Todor Mihaylov, Daniel Simig, Ping Yu, Kurt Shuster, Tianlu Wang, Qing Liu, Punit Singh Koura, Xian Li, Brian O'Horo, Gabriel Pereyra, Jeff Wang, Christopher Dewan, Asli Celikyilmaz, Luke Zettlemoyer, and Ves Stoyanov. 2023. Opt-iml: Scaling language model instruction meta learning through the lens of generalization.

Takeshi Kojima, Shixiang Shane Gu, Machel Reid, Yutaka Matsuo, and Yusuke Iwasawa. 2022. Large Language Models are Zero-Shot Reasoners. In *Advances in Neural Information Processing Systems*.

Zequn Liu, Shukai Wang, Yiyang Gu, Ruiyi Zhang, Ming Zhang, and Sheng Wang. 2021. Graphine: A Dataset for Graph-aware Terminology Definition Generation. In *Proceedings of the 2021 Conference on Empirical Methods in Natural Language Processing*, pages 3453–3463, Online and Punta Cana, Dominican Republic. Association for Computational Linguistics.

Niklas Muennighoff, Thomas Wang, Lintang Sutawika, Adam Roberts, Stella Biderman, Teven Le Scao,

M. Saiful Bari, Sheng Shen, Zheng-Xin Yong, Hailey Schoelkopf, Xiangru Tang, Dragomir Radev, Alham Fikri Aji, Khalid Almubarak, Samuel Albanie, Zaid Alyafeai, Albert Webson, Edward Raff, and Colin Raffel. 2023. Crosslingual Generalization through Multitask Finetuning.

Ke Ni and William Yang Wang. 2017. Learning to Explain Non-Standard English Words and Phrases. In *Proceedings of the Eighth International Joint Conference on Natural Language Processing (Volume 2: Short Papers)*, pages 413–417, Taipei, Taiwan. Asian Federation of Natural Language Processing.

Thanapon Noraset, Chen Liang, Larry Birnbaum, and Doug Downey. 2017. Definition modeling: Learning to define word embeddings in natural language. In *AAAI Conference on Artificial Intelligence*. AAAI Conference on Artificial Intelligence.

Kishore Papineni, Salim Roukos, Todd Ward, and Wei-Jing Zhu. 2002. Bleu: a method for automatic evaluation of machine translation. In *Proceedings of the 40th Annual Meeting of the Association for Computational Linguistics*, pages 311–318, Philadelphia, Pennsylvania, USA. Association for Computational Linguistics.

Colin Raffel, Noam Shazeer, Adam Roberts, Katherine Lee, Sharan Narang, Michael Matena, Yanqi Zhou, Wei Li, and Peter J. Liu. 2020. Exploring the Limits of Transfer Learning with a Unified Text-to-Text Transformer. *Journal of Machine Learning Research*, 21(140):1–67.

Ricardo Rei, Craig Stewart, Ana C Farinha, and Alon Lavie. 2020. COMET: A Neural Framework for MT Evaluation. In *Proceedings of the 2020 Conference on Empirical Methods in Natural Language Processing (EMNLP)*, pages 2685–2702, Online. Association for Computational Linguistics.

Machel Reid, Edison Marrese-Taylor, and Yutaka Matsuo. 2020. VCDM: Leveraging Variational Bi-encoding and Deep Contextualized Word Representations for Improved Definition Modeling. In *Proceedings of the 2020 Conference on Empirical Methods in Natural Language Processing (EMNLP)*, pages 6331–6344, Online. Association for Computational Linguistics.

Yi Tay, Mostafa Dehghani, Vinh Q. Tran, Xavier Garcia, Jason Wei, Xuezhi Wang, Hyung Won Chung, Siamak Shakeri, Dara Bahri, Tal Schuster, Huaixiu Steven Zheng, Denny Zhou, Neil Houlsby, and Donald Metzler. 2023. Ul2: Unifying language learning paradigms.

Ben Wang and Aran Komatsuzaki. 2021. GPT-J-6B: A 6 Billion Parameter Autoregressive Language Model.

Tianyi Zhang, Varsha Kishore, Felix Wu, Kilian Q. Weinberger, and Yoav Artzi. 2019. BERTScore: Evaluating Text Generation with BERT. In *International Conference on Learning Representations*.